A Nation Developing

A Brief History of Canada

A Nation Developing

A BRIEF HISTORY OF CANADA

J. A. LOWER

UNIVERSITY HILL SECONDARY SCHOOL
VANCOUVER

Reading Consultant
Paul Barker
North York Board of Education

RYERSON EDUCATIONAL DIVISION
McGRAW-HILL COMPANY OF CANADA LTD.

Toronto Montreal New York London Sydney
Mexico Johannesburg Panama Düsseldorf Singapore
Rio de Janeiro Kuala Lumpur New Delhi

Maps by Robert Kunz, C. C. J. Bond and Marion Paton

ISBN 0-7700-3208-7
Printed and bound in Canada

9 10 11 EP 5432

Contents

Maps

Charts and Tables

1

Canada: The Natural Background

Geography has been a vital factor in determining the course of Canadian history. Therefore, examining the natural surroundings is necessary in order to have a complete understanding of Canada's development as a nation.

Canada consists of the whole northern part of North America (except Alaska) and stretches from Cape Spear, Newfoundland (52°37'W) to the St. Elias Mountains, the Yukon Territory (141°W). The most southerly mainland point in Canada is Point Pelee (41°41'N) jutting into Lake Erie, while the most northerly point is Cape Columbia on Ellesmere Island (87°07'N). Thus Canada is very much a northern country. In all, Canadian territory covers 3,560,238 square miles, making it, after Russia, the second largest country in the world.

The name Canada is believed to derive from the Huron-Iroquois word for a village or community, *kanata*. Although in use as early as 1534, the term was not officially recognized until The Canada Act of 1791, by which the Crown-in-Council was authorized to divide Quebec into Lower and Upper Canada.

Canada's physiography consists of eight natural regions: the Canadian Shield; the Canadian Appalachians; the St. Lawrence-Great Lakes Lowlands; the Interior Plains; the Western Cordilleras; the Hudson Bay Lowlands; the Innuitias (Arctic Ranges); and the Arctic Coastal Plain.

The Canadian Shield. The Canadian Shield, covering approximately forty-six per cent of the country's total area, is a vast, V-shaped expanse of lake, rock, bush and bog, having Hudson

1

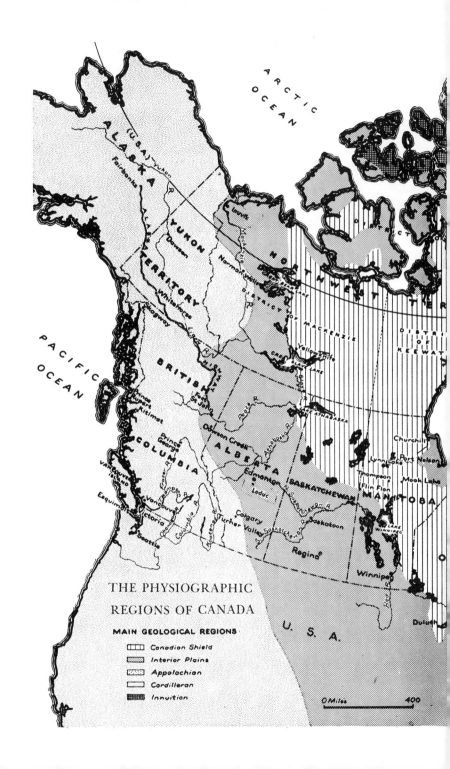

THE PHYSIOGRAPHIC
REGIONS OF CANADA

MAIN GEOLOGICAL REGIONS

- Canadian Shield
- Interior Plains
- Appalachian
- Cordilleran
- Innuitian

0 Miles   400

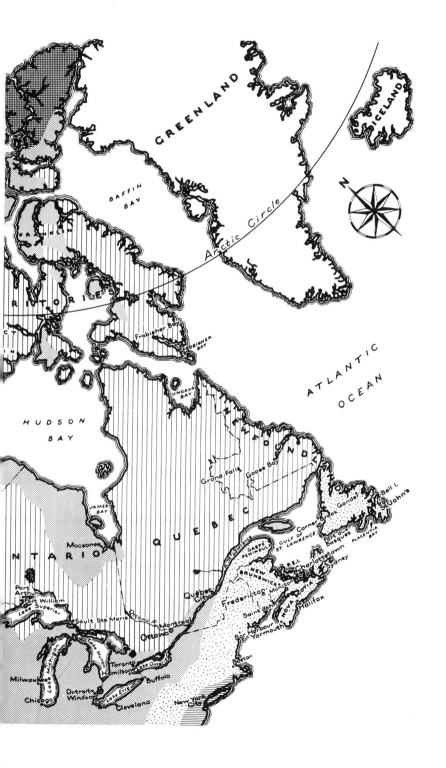

Bay at its approximate centre. Tilted at its edges, the shield sinks at its centre below the waters of the Bay. A large part of the provinces of Ontario, Quebec and Manitoba, the Labrador portion of Newfoundland and much of the North-West Territories lie within this region of Precambrian rock (the oldest in the world). Where once there were many ranges of high mountains, today's Shield, the result of the erosion of great continental ice sheets, is a land of hills, ridges and valleys. The surface of the Shield varies in elevation from 600 feet to 1,200 feet above sea level, although in northern Labrador and on Baffin Island there are mountains rising to 5,500 and 8,500 feet respectively. The most noticeable feature of the Shield is its innumerable lakes and streams. The Shield is Canada's principal source of iron, nickel, copper, lead, zinc, uranium, potash, and many other metals and minerals. It is also extremely valuable because of its vast timber resources and as a mighty source of water power.

The Canadian Appalachians. The Canadian Appalachians are a continuation of a long belt of mountains and ridges in the eastern United States and cover the provinces of New Brunswick, Nova Scotia, Prince Edward Island, Newfoundland and the Gaspé area of the Province of Quebec. The Appalachian region is characterized by low, rolling mountain ranges, none of which is higher than 4,200 feet. This succession of highlands and lowlands in a moist, maritime climate provides conditions suited to mixed farming and the production of vegetables and fruit. In addition, the Appalachians have considerable timber stands and several ore-bearing formations.

The St. Lawrence-Great Lakes Lowlands. Flanking the Canadian Shield to the south and southeast are the St. Lawrence-Great Lakes Lowlands. These large expanses of plains and lowlands occupy a triangular area between Georgian Bay and Lakes Ontario and Erie. Included in this region is the valley of the St. Lawrence River as far east as Quebec City. Fertile soil and a moderate climate make this area one of the richest and most varied agricultural belts in Canada. Although these lowlands comprise Canada's smallest physical region, they now support almost two-thirds of the country's population.

The Interior Plains. Canada's largest lowland area, the Interior Plains are part of the Great Plains of North America, which sweep northwest from the Gulf of Mexico to the Arctic Ocean. They are the immense prairies of Western Canada, occupying the area between the Rocky Mountains and the Canadian Shield and consisting of three levels or steps sloping to the east. Although this region has long been considered best suited to the production of wheat, other grains, beef cattle (and some logging and trapping), it also possesses Canada's largest known fuel resources of oil and gas.

The Western Cordilleras. The Western Cordilleras, lying between the Pacific Ocean and the prairies, are an average 400 miles wide and form the greatest sweep of mountain ranges in Canada. These ranges form three main divisions: the Coast Range, with peaks just under 20,000 feet; the Interior Plateau, a rolling, mountainous country with deep, fertile valleys; and the Monashee, Selkirk and Rocky Mountains to the east, some of whose peaks soar as high as 12,000 feet. Second to the Canadian Shield in wealth of metals and minerals, the Cordilleras also possess extensive forests and a vast hydro-electric potential. Agriculture is limited, except in the delta of the Fraser River, Southern Vancouver Island, and in some interior valleys.

The Hudson Bay Lowlands. The Hudson Bay Lowlands stretch along the southwest shore of Hudson and James Bays between Churchill and Moosonee. These limestone plains, partially buried under marine deposits, lie beneath a swampy region, where the climate is severe and the subsoil is permanently frozen. The only vegetation is moss and lichens. These Lowlands are known to contain deposits of low-grade coal, but so far little else of value has been discovered.

The Innuitias and the Arctic Coastal Plain. The Innuitias or Arctic ranges form one of the most inhospitable regions of Canada, supporting little animal and vegetable life. Extending from northernmost Ellesmere Island south and west to Melville Island, this 300-mile wide belt of mountains is 800 miles long. Some peaks rise as high as 12,000 feet. To the south and southwest of the Innuitias are the islands of the Arctic Coastal Plain. This area slopes gently westward toward the Arctic Ocean. Numerous finds of coal, salt and gypsum have been made and geological surveys have indicated the presence of valuable deposits of oil and gas.

Canada's Place in Continental Geography. It has often been said that the geology of Canada provides north-south alignments that are contrary to the east-west extension of the country. It has also been remarked that Canada's geological structure is directly linked with that of the United States. This is easily observed. The Cana-

dian Shield extends without a break into the northern reaches of
the states of Minnesota, Wisconsin and Michigan; the Canadian
Appalachians reach down unbroken into the eastern states; Canada
and the United States share the Great Lakes basin; the Canadian
prairies become the Great Plains of the American West; the
Western Cordilleras continue down most of the Pacific coast of the
United States.

Canada's Rivers. The physical shape of Canada has sometimes
been regarded as a drawback—if not a barrier—to national development. However, while mountains, plateaus and escarpments
can be barriers, they create rivers (and contain passes) by which
men can overcome these same barriers. Thus, the west-east and
east-west rivers of Canada served the early explorers and settlers
as excellent natural highways. The St. John River offers a route
from the Atlantic shore through the Appalachians to the St.
Lawrence Lowland. The St. Lawrence River and the five Great
Lakes—Ontario, Erie, Huron, Michigan, Superior—combine to
from a natural waterway leading through the Shield all the way
(via several rivers and lakes) to the edge of the prairies. Alternately, the historic Ottawa River—Mattawa River—Lake Nipissing—French River route led, via Georgian Bay, to Lakes Huron
and Superior and thus to the heart of the North American continent. The North and South Saskatchewan Rivers and the Peace
River afford water routes across the prairies to the passes of the
Rockies. The Thompson and Fraser rivers pierce the west coast
mountains and run eventually into the Pacific Ocean.

Thus Canada's rivers have become major forces in the evolution of the country as a nation. Since rivers are used as routes (or
are followed by them), the general east-west alignment of rivers
in Canada has led to a large framework of eastward- and westward-
running canals, roads and railways. In addition, the estuaries of
the rivers face the Atlantic and Pacific Oceans and thus "pull"
Canada eastward to Europe and westward to the Far East. Therefore the rivers of Canada have drawn together regions that are
separated by major geographic features—mountains, high plateaus
and escarpments. The natural "pull to the south" has been more
than offset by another natural "pull to the east" by the great river
systems and by an historic "drive to the west."

The "pull to the south" is also offset by the east-west alignment
of almost all of Canada's climatic, vegetation and soil zones. With
the exception of southern British Columbia, these zones make
broad arcs across the country.

Canada's Climates.   The climates of Canada lie within the Cool Temperate Zone where weather conditions are marked by short summers and long winters, by a high frequency of storms and by late spring and early fall frosts. Generally speaking, the climates of the southern portion of Canada can be compared with those of northwestern Europe and central Asia. The moderate temperatures and heavy rainfall of the British Columbia coastline are conditions similar to those of coastal Norway. The semi-arid climate of the prairies is comparable to that of the central regions of European Russia. The humid weather of southeastern Canada is similar to that of Manchuria. The humid but cooler weather of the Atlantic provinces is characteristic of the northern Japanese islands.

Dry, cold weather conditions prevail over the rest of the country, the northern reaches. Indeed, their effect is such that the term "arctic," originally an astronomical term, has come to be a climatic one. Arctic conditions are not confined to the Arctic Circle. The straits leading into Hudson Bay from the high north bring down very cold streams of water, which contribute to arctic conditions in northern Manitoba, Ontario and Quebec. Although waves of warm weather do invade northern Canada and the Canadian Arctic from time to time, these invasions are infrequent and rarely bring high temperatures. Thus, even the July average is below 50°, and, in parts of the Arctic, below 32°.

Canada's Vegetation.   The physical face of Canada and the climates of the land are largely responsible for the distribution of plants, the chief vegetation types being moss, trees and grass.

The Arctic region, almost a third of the land area of Canada, is an immense, flat, treeless wasteland of snow, ice, and stone, with occasional stretches of thin, tundra soil. This soil bears a vegetation of stunted bushes, mosses and lichens (and, in the brief Arctic summer, some grass and certain varieties of wild flowers).

South of the tundra lies a vast, deep belt of forest land stretching from Newfoundland to Alaska and occupying a little more than a third of Canada's land area. These dense stands of timber include the short trees of the sub-Arctic areas (white and black spruce, white birch, balsam, poplar and tamarack), the somewhat larger trees of the eastern forests (birch, oak, maple, pine, red spruce, hemlock and cedar), and the large often giant trees of the western forests, (lodgepole pine, Englemann spruce, Douglas fir, western hemlock and western red cedar).

Surrounded on three sides by forest land are the grasslands or prairies, too dry for forest growth because they are cut off by mountains (or by sheer distance) from moisture-laden winds. Today, the area under grass is quite small because cultivated crops, wheat in particular, have replaced grass in all but the driest or most hilly areas of the prairies (for example, southern Alberta and southwest Saskatchewan).

Canada's Soils. Because of the mountains, hills, uplands, early frosts and the wintry climates of most of Canada, the soils of the land are difficult to work. Agriculture is limited to the more favoured southern fringes of the country—the valleys of southwest British Columbia, the fertile black and brown earth of the prairies, the lower Great Lakes and St. Lawrence valley and certain areas in New Brunswick, Nova Scotia and Prince Edward Island. There are, of course, pockets of good soil farther north, for example in the Canadian Shield and in the Peace River district of Alberta. However, the variety and quality of soil has made farmers depend on science and technology for help in making the most of the relatively few acres suited to agriculture. As a result, Canadian farming methods are among the most advanced in the world.

The close relationship between geology, climate, vegetation and soil produces the natural environment fundamental to the history of a nation. In spite of the great expanse of Canada, environment is rather limited in variety. It is, on the whole, harsh, wild, and challenging, and is fully reflected in Canada's history.

BIBLIOGRAPHY

ANDERSON, F. W. *Frontier Books: The Frank Slide Story.* Frontiers Unlimited, 1961.

ANDERSON, F. W. *Frontier Books: The Hope Slide Story.* Frontiers Unlimited, 1967.

ANDERSON, F. W. *Frontier Books: The Incredible Rogers Pass.* Frontiers Unlimited, 1965.

CORNELL, P. G., *et al. Canada, Unity in Diversity.* Holt, Rinehart and Winston, 1967.

DE LEEUW, G. *Manitoba Its People and Places.* Holt, Rinehart and Winston.

Exploring Canada From Sea to Sea. National Geographic Society, 1969.

GENTILCORE, R. LOUIS. *Canada's Changing Geography.* Prentice-Hall, 1968.

HUNTER, G. and ROBERTS L. *Canada in Colour.* Clarke, Irwin, 1959.

HUTCHISON, BRUCE. *The Unknown Country.* Longmans, 1942.

IRVING, R. M. (ed.). *Readings in Canadian Geography.* Holt, Rinehart and Winston, 1968.

MAY, C. P. *Great Cities of Canada.* Abelard-Schuman, 1968.

MCDOUGALL, W. D. and FINN, T. G. *Canada in the Western World.* Gage, 1965.

PATERSON, J. H. *North America, A Geography of Canada and the United States.* Oxford, 1965.

PHILLIPS, R. A. J. *Canada's North.* Macmillan, 1967.

SUMMERS, W. F. and SUMMERS, M. E. *The Geography of Newfoundland.* Copp Clark, 1965.

TOMKINS, G. S., TOMKINS, D. M. and SCARFE, N. V. *Discovering Our Land.* Gage, 1966.

WARKENTON, J. (ed.). *Canada: A Geographical Interpretation.* Methuen, 1968.

WEBB, W. P. *The Great Plain.* Ginn, 1931.

2

Discovery and Settlement, 1492-1672

The Norsemen. About A.D. 1000, Leif Eriksson, a Norse captain blown off course while sailing to the Norse colony in Greenland, is said to have reached North America. It is believed that he sailed along the coastlines of present-day Labrador, Newfoundland and the northeastern seaboard of the United States. Eriksson was followed by other Norse sailors and eventually settlements were established on the North American coast. The location of these settlements has been a matter of dispute for some time, but recent archaeological discoveries have provided strong indication that the southern-most area of settlement, Vinland, was on Newfoundland. Encouragement has also been given to this conclusion by the recent discovery of the "Vinland map," which dates from the fifteenth century and is the earliest known map to indicate the discoveries of the Norsemen. The Norse settlements, however, seem to have been short-lived. Even the Greenland settlement mysteriously disappeared sometime before A.D. 1400.

The Fifteenth-Century Urge to Explore. During the fifteenth century, European navigators began to explore southward and westward. There were several reasons for this activity.

(1) A search was being made for an all-sea route to China and India after eastern land routes were severed by the expansion of the Moslem Turks into Asia Minor and southeastern Europe. The great trading centre of Constantinople was captured by the Turks in 1453.

(2) This search was also an attempt to break the trade monopolies held by certain Italian cities, especially Venice and Genoa.

In the fifteenth century, the major trade routes from the East lay overland across Asia to the Mediterranean Sea and then crossed by ship to Europe via distributing centres in Northern Italy. Western European nations strongly resented having to pay heavy "middlemen" prices for the spices, silks and jewels of the Orient. Europe's kings and merchants, therefore, sought to find other routes to the East, sending out explorers to search south around the land of Africa and westward across the Atlantic.

(3) By the end of the fifteenth century, some answers to long ocean voyages had been found. Navigators could calculate their latitude by means of the astrolabe and steer a course by means of the compass. In addition, the Portuguese had developed a seaworthy vessel—the squat, three-masted caravel. It was slower than the galley but was designed to sail into the wind and also offered more space for cargo and more elbow-room for seamen on long voyages.

Christopher Columbus. While the Portuguese sought an eastern route around Africa, Christopher Columbus, a Genoese in the service of Spain, sailed westward in 1492 and discovered an island (San Salvador) which, he believed, lay off the coast of Asia. Columbus made three more westward voyages of exploration and in later years was followed by other Spaniards, who quickly established settlements in the West Indies, Central and South America.

John Cabot. There are suggestions in various historical documents that French and English fishermen may have been fishing off Newfoundland as early as the middle of the fifteenth century. However, not until 1497, when the Genoese navigator, John Cabot (Giovanni Caboto), was sent westward by King Henry VII of England, is there any official record of North American exploration. Cabot seems to have landed on the shores of Newfoundland, Cape Breton Island and perhaps Labrador, although he believed he was in some unknown part of Asia. His discoveries in 1497 and again the following year formed one basis for Britain's subsequent claim to Newfoundland and the Labrador coast. Of more immediate significance to the fishermen of western Europe was his report of the presence of vast schools of fish off the coast of Newfoundland.

The Eastern Shores. In 1500 and 1501, Gaspar Corte-Reale, a Portuguese nobleman, explored parts of Newfoundland and Labrador, sent home two shiploads of Indian slaves and then disappeared to the south. Giovanni da Verrazano, an Italian navigator in French service, followed the North American coastline from present-day Virginia to Newfoundland. He named these shores *Nova Francia* (New France). In the meantime, two more expeditions, one English and the other Spanish, examined the gulfs and bays of eastern Canada, but none attempted to penetrate inland or establish colonies.

JACQUES CARTIER

First Voyage. In 1534, the French king, Francis I, anxious to find a sea route to the Orient, sent a Breton sea captain, Jacques Cartier, on the first of three westward voyages. Sailing from his home port of St. Malo, Cartier made his way across the Atlantic and through the ice-floes of a narrow sea passage (the Strait of Belle Isle), explored the shores of a wide gulf (the St. Lawrence) and anchored in a large bay (Chaleur) on the south side of the Gulf. He went ashore and erected a cross, claiming this new land for France.

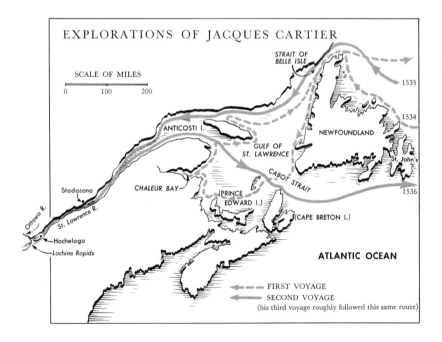

EXPLORATIONS OF JACQUES CARTIER

Second Voyage. On his voyage of 1535, Cartier returned to the Great Gulf and sailed along the north coast of an island (Anticosti), putting in at a small bay on August 10. That day being the feast of St. Lawrence, Cartier named the waters *Baye Sainte Laurens.* (In later years the name St. Lawrence was applied freely to the gulf and to the river.) He continued up a large waterway and visited two large Indian villages, Stadacona (near the present-day Quebec City) and Hochelaga (a site now occupied by Montreal). It was at Hochelaga that Cartier learned from the Indians of a river (the Ottawa) that led to a great series of "fresh-water seas" to the west. The French were hearing for the first time of the Great Lakes.

Cartier was prevented from further exploration of the St. Lawrence by the lateness of the season. He wintered near Stadacona where twenty-five of his one hundred and ten men died of scurvy. The following spring he returned to France, where he gave glowing accounts of the regions he had visited.

Third Voyage. In 1541, Cartier returned to the St. Lawrence region as master pilot of a colonizing expedition under the command of a French nobleman, the Sieur de Roberval. The expedition was to establish a settlement in New France, from which explorers could be sent out to search for a water passage to the East. However, the whole affair was poorly organized. Cartier sailed ahead of de Roberval, spent the winter near Stadacona, and then returned to France. Roberval arrived in 1542 and after he and his followers had endured a North American winter near Stadacona, everyone was glad to abandon the project and return to France.

Although Cartier failed to find a water passage to the East, his discovery of the river that became the main point of entry into the interior of North America was, in later years, to give France a strong claim to the St. Lawrence valley region.

THE FISHERIES

In 1493, the Papacy had tried to prevent conflict between the two pioneers of Maritime exploration, Portugal and Spain, by dividing overseas trade between these rivals. As a result of the Treaty of Tordesillas 1494, Spain was given possession of all lands lying west of an agreed line running north and south through the Atlantic Ocean about a thousand miles west of the Azores. Portugal was given all new lands east of the line.

Newfoundland. Newfoundland was in the area given to Spain, but the Spanish were far too busy exploring the Caribbean and South America to take much notice of French and English fishermen in Newfoundland waters. In spite of Spanish claims, French fishermen landed on the island to refill their water casks and store gear. By 1550 English fishermen were accustomed to going ashore to preserve their catches by drying them in the sun and salting them lightly. (This was "dry fishery," a method of curing used by the English since they could not afford to import large quantities of salt from the Continent. Their fishing rivals employed the "wet" or "green" fishery method, whereby fish were cured and preserved by packing them in barrels of salt.)

In 1583, Sir Humphrey Gilbert, while on his way to establish a colony on the mainland, paused long enough in St. John's harbour to seize supplies from some fishing boats. He attempted to make this action appear legal by proclaiming the sovereignty of Queen Elizabeth I and then trying to collect taxes. Gilbert's piratical visit, however, made no difference to the status of Newfoundland, which remained, nominally, a Spanish possession. However, by 1583, even the Spaniards were sharing the rich hauls of cod being made on the Grand Banks, the great fishing grounds of the continental shelf just south and southeast of Newfoundland. Also, by 1583, England was challenging the growing might of Spain in Europe by preying on Spanish sea commerce wherever it could be found. One result of this policy was the almost complete destruction of the Spanish Newfoundland fishing fleet by an English raiding force in 1585. Thereafter, the south coasts of Newfoundland came to be recognized in practice as belonging to England, with small groups of unsponsored English settlers living in coves along these coasts. The French were gradually forced to fish in other coastal areas of Newfoundland or at the inshore fisheries of the Gulf of St. Lawrence.

THE BEGINNINGS OF THE FUR TRADE

In the latter half of the sixteenth century, there was a casual trade in fur pelts between Indians living along the shores of the Gulf of St. Lawrence and French and Basque fishermen who occasionally came ashore for supplies of fresh water. The chief trading place was Tadoussac, where the Saguenay River joins the St. Lawrence. Here, where codfishers and a few whale and walrus hunters sometimes came to process and pack their catches and refill their water casks, the French met Algonquin Indians. These Indians were more than willing to trade their fur cloaks for brightly coloured European clothing and such items as combs and beads —but, in particular, for iron tools and weapons. The Indians very quickly recognized the superiority of iron weapons and tools over wooden or stone ones.

Beaver Hats. During the latter half of the sixteenth century this casual fur trading changed into a serious business enterprise financed by groups of merchants in France. Fashion had long decreed the use of fur as trimmings for cloaks and gowns. However, when a way was found to utilize the soft, glossy hairs of beaver pelt to make felting for hats, the handsome beaver hat immediately became an essential part of a merchant's or nobleman's costume. A tremendous, continuing demand in Europe for such hats turned the trade in furs into a major business. French merchants began to band together to secure a trade monopoly, that is, the sole right to engage in fur trading. As it happened, the French crown was willing to grant trading rights if a company of merchants applying for a fur monopoly agreed to take settlers out to North America and also agreed to maintain settlement.

The race for the fur monopoly began towards the end of the sixteenth century, and for the next two hundred years the history of Canada is mainly the history of the trade in beaver pelts.

ACADIA

In 1604, the Sieur de Monts, accompanied by Samuel de Champlain, set sail with about 125 settlers for Acadia (roughly the area of today's Maritime provinces). De Monts had secured the fur monopoly, and Champlain was the expedition's cartographer. Champlain had fought for France and later sailed (probably to North America) as an explorer in the service of Spain. The colonists spent the first winter in the Bay of Fundy area, on an island at the mouth of the St. Croix River. However, the site proved to be too exposed to wind and weather so the settlement was moved across the Bay to Port Royal (now Annapolis, Nova Scotia).

Port Royal. Like Quebec a few years later, Port Royal was a single, large *habitation,* in which buildings were placed side by side around a rectangular courtyard and protected by a high palisade mounted with cannon. Crops were sown, roadways were made and a mill was set up to grind grain. However, fishermen along the coast of Acadia could not be prevented from trading with the Indians, and it was impossible for de Monts to enforce his monopoly. With the limited trading he was able to secure, he found he could not support such an expensive venture as Port Royal. When, in 1607, powerful opponents in France had his monopoly cancelled, he moved the entire colony back to France.

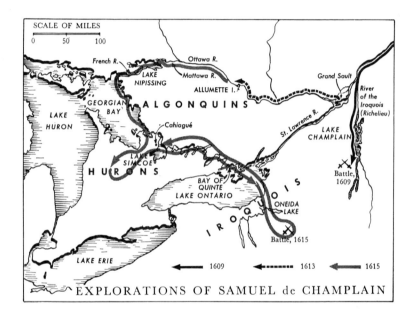

EXPLORATIONS OF SAMUEL de CHAMPLAIN

Encouraged by Champlain, de Monts obtained a one-year renewal of his monopoly and in 1608 sent Champlain and a few men to the St. Lawrence to trade. It was a wise decision. The narrow channel of the St. Lawrence seemed to offer a chance of better control of fur trading. Several large river systems feed the mighty St. Lawrence, and it was the tributaries and back waters of these rivers that were the breeding grounds for many fur-bearing animals. With heavily wooded regions on either side of the St. Lawrence, the river offered the only efficient means of travel. Down its northern tributaries came the Algonquins and Hurons in birch-bark canoes loaded with furs, desperately eager to exchange their pelts for European goods. In addition, the St. Lawrence might prove to be a water passage to Asia.

Nova Scotia. Meanwhile, two other Frenchmen, the Sieur de Poutrincourt and his son continued trading and colonizing in Acadia and, with royal permission, re-established Port Royal in 1610. In 1613, however, Port Royal was attacked and destroyed during a semi-official raid by English settlers from the Virginia colony.

In the ensuing years the colony was claimed by both England and France, both countries sending out colonists and making grants of land. In 1621, James I of England ignored the claims of the French and granted the entire maritime area from Cape Gaspé to the St. Croix River to a Scotsman, Sir William Alexander. In Alexander's land charter, written in Latin, the area was identified as Nova Scotia (New Scotland).

SAMUEL DE CHAMPLAIN, FATHER OF NEW FRANCE

Quebec. Preferring the potentialities of the St. Lawrence, both for colonization and for the fur trade, Champlain chose the towering rock of Quebec as his main base in the early summer of 1608. At the foot of the rock he built the *habitation* that formed the core of the first permanent French settlement in North America, a settlement which was to remain the centre of government throughout the French régime.

The Iroquois. In 1609, Champlain was asked to join a party of Algonquins, Hurons and Montagnais in an attack against their enemies, the Iroquois League, a group of tribes living south of the St. Lawrence. On this expedition, Champlain was able to explore a river (which he named after his powerful supporter at the French court, Cardinal Richelieu) and a large lake to which he gave his own name. Although the war expedition against the Iroquois was successful, it was to cost the French the life-long enmity of the most powerful, well-organized and warlike tribes (the Seneca, the Cayuga, the Oneida, the Onondaga and the Mohawk) in North America. Their undying hatred was to contribute in great measure to the ultimate downfall of New France. The Hurons and Iroquois were enemies of long-standing, and it was probably inevitable that Champlain would sooner or later be forced to agree to support his Indian allies (as he was again in 1615) in order to obtain their furs, for the best furs came from regions north of the St. Lawrence. In any case, the rivalry for furs, quite apart from other long-standing tribal enmities, was to lead to strife between the Iroquois and the Huron.

Monopolies and Exploration. In 1609, de Monts' monopoly expired, and for the next three years Champlain was engaged both in trying to maintain control of the St. Lawrence fur trade against a flood of independent French traders and in striving to have the monopoly renewed. He was finally accorded the monopoly in 1612 and was appointed Lieutenant-General of New France.

In the meantime, with so much of his own time taken up with business, he had encouraged some young men in the colony to explore farther west. Etienne Brûlé, a born adventurer, spent a winter with the Hurons to learn their tongue and find out what they knew of the "Western Sea," which might be the fabled water route to the Orient. Brûlé was later to discover a large bay (the Georgian), leading to what his Indian guides pointed out as the "Sweet Water Sea" (Lake Huron), which in turn led Brûlé to a vast, forbidding-looking stretch of water (Lake Superior). Jean Nicolet, another of Champlain's protégés who lived with the Hurons and learned their language, was destined to explore a great lake (Lake Michigan) and travel up an unknown river (the Fox), a route that would lead ultimately to the headwaters of the Mississippi River. The French were slowly learning the geography of the Great Lakes basin.

In 1613, Nicholas Vignau, another young explorer, reported to Champlain that he had found the wreck of an English ship on the edge of a great salt sea in the north. Champlain was so intrigued that he left Quebec to personally verify the tale. He felt there was a faint chance that this information might be connected with the accounts of the English navigator, Henry Hudson, whose crew had mutinied in 1611 and set him adrift with a few followers in northern waters that we now know as Hudson Bay. Before Champlain had gone very far up the Ottawa River, he found out from a Huron tribe that Vignau had lied to impress him. (It was many years before the English and the French were to appreciate the importance of the bay that Hudson had discovered.)

NEW FRANCE, 1608-1663

Champlain was determined to establish a permanent colony in New France, using some fur profits to subsidize settlement, but it was a constant struggle to secure effective support from his employers. Throughout his career, he found himself at cross-purposes with the mercantile groups upon whom he depended. Most of the settlers who were sent out took up fur-trading rather than farming because two or three good seasons of trading made a man rich. Many of these traders wintered up country in order to be the first to meet and bargain with the Hurons and Algonquins coming down to Quebec with loads of pelts. As early as 1625 several of the Récollet friars and Jesuit fathers who had come out to New France to minister to the needs of Quebec had been drawn up-country to live among and work with the Indians. (In 1615, when Champlain had left Quebec to join the Hurons in another attack upon the Iroquois, there had been a Récollet, Father Joseph Le Caron, preaching the word of God to the Hurons.) In short, Quebec remained a fort and trading post, not a colony.

The Company of New France (1627). By 1620, the monopoly and commission to trade had changed hands in France several times, but on each occasion the promise to bring out settlers and build defences had not been kept. In 1627, Cardinal Richelieu organized *The Company of One Hundred Associates* or *The Company of New France,* a wealthier and more powerful association of merchants than any of its predecessors. It exercised complete control of the government and administration of New France and enjoyed sole trading rights. In return, it undertook to settle 200 to 300 French Roman Catholics every year, to fortify the colony and to protect trade routes. The results, however, were bitterly disappointing to Champlain, for the Company, like its predecessors, proved to be more interested in quick profits than in fulfilling its promises.

English Capture Quebec. Hostilities broke out between France and England in 1628. Three freebooting Englishmen, the Kirke brothers, took advantage of war conditions to intercept the first convoy of settlers and supplies sent to Quebec by the Company. This action deprived the colony of essential supplies and support. By July of the following year the settlement was near starvation. Champlain had to surrender and most of the settlers were returned to France.

Champlain spent the next two years negotiating the return of people to the colony. By the Treaty of St. Germain-en-Laye (1632), New France was surrendered by England and the Scots were recalled from Acadia. The following year, Champlain, now Governor of New France, returned to Quebec with 200 colonists and a few Jesuit priests. Still intent on expanding French power in North America, Champlain made plans for new posts and settlements along the St. Lawrence. In 1634 a trading post was established at Three Rivers at the mouth of the St. Maurice River, which drained a larger fur-trapping area than the Saguenay. Champlain marked out the site of present-day Montreal as a highly desirable location for another fur post. Champlain even intended to build fur posts on Lake Ontario, but he died in 1635 and New France lost its founder and far-sighted administrator.

"The Black Robes."   The work of the powerful religious order called the Society (or Company) of Jesus was almost world-wide in scope. Jesuit missionaries braved hardship, privation and some-times death itself to carry the story of Jesus to people in regions as far apart as South America, Ethiopia, Russia, India and China. Although the Récollet fathers did much good work among the Montagnais and Hurons, they did not have sufficient resources to expand the missionary effort. The Society of Jesus was perhaps the only order of the Roman Catholic Church with sufficient wealth and staff to expend the great efforts necessary in converting the Indians of North America.

The "Black Robes," as the tribesmen called them, began their missionary efforts in North America in 1625. They were most successful in Huronia (the lands of the Hurons between Georgian Bay and Lake Simcoe). By the spring of 1649, eighteen priests were working in this thickly populated area, teaching their faith to the tribes of the Huron nation. Despite many difficulties, the Jesuits won more and more converts with the passing years.

Jesuit Relations.   The Jesuit fathers wrote vivid descriptions of their travels and of Indian life in records known as the *Relations*. These records were eagerly read by churchmen and others in France and aroused tremendous interest in the work and achieve-ments of the Church in the New World. As a result, not only did French priests and nuns volunteer for missionary work in New France, but a society of wealthy and influential people was formed to establish a settlement and mission station in New France.

Founding of Montreal.   In 1642, the Sieur de Maisonneuve, accompanied by workers, priests and soldiers, arrived at the island where about one hundred years before Jacques Cartier had visited Hochelaga and climbed the steep hill he named *Le Mont Royal*. The new settlement, Ville Marie de Montréal consisted of a fort protected by a palisade, a windmill and a few houses. The settle-ment grew slowly because its position close to Iroquois country discouraged many settlers.

The Iroquois. Always dangerous enemies, the Iroquois became an increasingly greater threat to New France after 1614 when they were able to obtain guns and ammunition from Dutch fur traders on the Hudson River. The Iroquois became an even graver menace after fur-bearing animals were trapped out in the regions along the Hudson and those areas immediately north and south of the St. Lawrence. The Iroquois crossed the St. Lawrence and attacked Huron fur fleets coming down the Ottawa from the lands of the northern hunting tribes. In 1648 and 1649, the invaders were so eager to monopolize the fur trade and become the middlemen between the Dutch and the tribes of the north that they raided Huronia itself, wiping out whole villages and, in the process, killing many of the "Black Robes." In 1650, the Jesuits were forced to evacuate their remaining mission stations. The Huron nation, disheartened and fearful, dispersed into groups that fled north, west and southwest. Even Montreal itself was only spared by the heroism of Adam Dollard and sixteen companions who, in 1660, sacrificed themselves in a stand against several Iroquois war parties on the Ottawa River.

By destroying Huronia the Iroquois cut the French off from almost all contact with the tribes north and west of Huronia. In the next ten years the Iroquois raided up and down the St. Lawrence, killing isolated settlers, attacking lone fur posts and ambushing the few fur fleets that ventured down the Ottawa from the north country. Supplies of fur, the life-blood of New France, were slowly but surely being cut off.

ROYAL GOVERNMENT, 1663

By 1663, the situation of New France was so desperate that its affairs were attended to under the direct control and authority of the young King of France, Louis XIV. Determined to increase the strength and prosperity of New France, he proclaimed it a royal colony, to be administered on his behalf by a council of officials. The king then sent the Carignan-Salières regiment, a force of over 1,000 officers and men, to defend the colony. Forts were built on the Richelieu river, an old Iroquois invasion route. In 1666, de Tracy, the lieutenant-governor of New France, marched the regiment into the heart of the Mohawk country and laid waste villages and crops in the fields. He met little opposition, and 1667 saw the signing of a peace treaty. The Iroquois were not yet broken.

They were now too busy warring for furs with tribes in the Ohio and Mississippi valleys. However, they had been shown the force of French arms and were now prepared to leave New France alone —for a time.

The Mercantile System. Jean Colbert, Louis XIV's minister of commerce, viewed overseas expansion as an important part of the development of France's commerce, wealth and power and he therefore adopted Richelieu's policy of mercantilism. Mercantilism characterized Europe's trade with its colonies during the sixteenth, seventeenth and eighteenth centuries. It was a restrictive policy since it involved government control of colonial trade and industry. Industry within the colonies as well as trade to and from the colonies was carefully controlled so that almost complete dependence on the mother country for manufactured goods was maintained. Colonies existed simply as a source of raw materials, offering no competition to domestic industry or trade. Thus, to successive French statesmen, the value of New France lay essentially in its fur potential, in the opportunities to expand the French Empire and in the missionary challenge it offered.

Government of New France. A council of Quebec had been formed in 1647, consisting of the governor, the superior of the Jesuit order (until the arrival of an appointed bishop), the governor of Montreal and persons elected from Quebec, Montreal and Three Rivers. However, the establishment in 1663 of a Sovereign Council of Government under the direct authority of the French crown, ensured that the colony was directed from France. The Council consisted initially of the governor, the bishop and five councillors (appointed at first by the governor and the bishop; later by the king). Two years later, an intendant was appointed and by 1674, when the Sovereign Council was renamed the Superior Council, the intendant had replaced the governor as the presiding official.

The Council had some legislative and administrative control of local affairs, and also acted as a supreme court—but all major laws were decided by the king of France. The governor, as was traditional in the provinces of France, represented the king on ceremonial occasions and had great responsibility in military and diplomatic affairs. The bishop, in addition to his spiritual authority, had a share in civil government as a leading member of the Council. The dividing line between these two spheres of authority was often a matter of conflict. The intendant, a trained official, attended to the administration of law, tax-collection and the control of business, in effect, superintending the whole colony in the light of the laws laid down by his royal master.

JEAN TALON, "THE GREAT INTENDANT"

The first intendant, Jean Talon, arrived in 1665 with royal instructions to encourage the clearing and cultivation of more land and to promote the establishment of local industries. He was told to create a series of populous town and village communities that would form a sturdy colony. Thus Talon came to New France determined to make it a busy, flourishing, agricultural society resembling that of rural France.

Investigation revealed that only a few thousand acres of land were being actively cultivated and that New France held about 3,000 settlers (two-thirds of them men or boys). Talon began his work by offering large land grants to the officers of the Carignan-Salières regiment if they promised to settle discharged soldiers on their land. Talon also offered grants of land to persons of substance in the colony, on the understanding that they would develop the land by the introduction of settlers. Many small settlements were thus started, including a number of soldier-settlements along the Richelieu River. This meant not only the opening of new land but also a further protection of the colony from Iroquois invasions.

Talon next recruited settlers from France, in particular from Normandy, by offers of free passage and the provision of land on modest terms. He also had shiploads of young women—orphaned girls and the daughters of poor families—sent out over the years (perhaps a thousand women in all) in order to provide wives for the men of the colony. As a further encouragement of marriage, wedding presents of money or goods were made by the Council, relief from taxes for a certain number of years was granted young married men and family-allowance payments were made to large families. As a result of all these measures, the census of 1673 showed 6,705 inhabitants, more than double the 1666 population. By 1675, there were 7,833 inhabitants. Thereafter, with little or no immigration from France, the number of French North Americans was to grow towards today's six million.

Talon also gave his attention to the development of natural resources and industries. He was responsible for the clearing of new land, increasing the volume and value of farm products through the use of such crops as hemp and flax, the importing of horses, cows, sheep and pigs. He also introduced the science of stock breeding, decreed the construction of shipyards, encouraged the use of fresh-water and salt-water fisheries and established trade in lumber, fish, furs, peas and corn with the West Indies. When he returned to France in 1672, Talon left behind him a colony whose foundations at last seemed to have been established.

THE SEIGNEURIAL SYSTEM

The pattern of pioneer settlement in New France was designed to create sturdy, self-reliant and co-operative group settlements. An individual of some social standing—an army officer, the son of a prosperous merchant—received a land grant on condition of developing that land by the introduction and supervision of settlers.

The Seigneur.   The landowner or *seigneur* had close ties to the state. His first duty after taking possession of his land was to appear before the governor of New France. There, in the presence of the intendant, he declared himself a vassal of the king, swore to the king all fealty and homage and undertook to honour his many obligations as a seigneur. (It should be noted that the seigneur was only granted the land itself. He undertook to reserve for the king all oak on the seigneury—for shipbuilding—and he agreed to reserve all "mines and minerals" for the crown.) Under his written contract with the state, the newly created seigneur had to maintain a manor house as a residence within the seigneury, cede his lands to *habitants* (residents, i.e. tenants) and build and operate a flour mill. If he had been given judicial rights, he was to establish and maintain a seigneurial court in which to settle local grievances. The seigneur was also required to subscribe to the maintenance of a curé (priest) and a chapel.

Most seigneuries fronted on a river (the rivers being the only reliable highways) and land was divided into long, narrow strips running back from the river. Habitant homes clustered together at the river's edge and near the seigneurial manor, which was often used as a stong point in times of Indian raids.

The Habitant.   In exchange for land the habitant had certain obligations to fulfill. *Cens et rentes* were the yearly dues he paid his seigneur: the *cens* was a nominal money payment, perhaps a few cents in our currency, while *rentes* were more usually paid in produce. (The seigneur was also entitled to *lods et ventes,* a transfer tax, payable when a farm changed hands other than by direct inheritance.) The *droit de banalité* were charges paid for the seigneur's provision of such necessities as a flour-mill, baking ovens and wine presses, the charges being payable in money or in kind. In addition, when the seigneur decreed a *corvée* (hard labour) for his own land, the habitant was required to observe this duty. However, the seigneur's right of corvée was governed by contract to three or possibly four days per year—one for seeding, a second for haying, a third for harvesting and, if included in his contract, a fourth for ploughing—and the habitant could commute his services by a small money payment. Lastly, the habitant undertook by contract with his seigneur to live and cultivate his land, allow a right-of-way to neighbours and permit the building of communal roads on his concession.

The many new seigneuries created by Talon and later intendants spread along the banks of the St. Lawrence (and its tributaries) and thus established a closely knit community of French Canadians. It has often been remarked that those sailing down the St. Lawrence of the French regime gained the impression of passing through one long, continuous village. In this respect the seigneurial system was a success. In other respects the system was less successful. Although less rigid than the feudal system of medieval Europe and designed to attract settlers, it did not do so because its agricultural operations were too small and lacked domestic and foreign markets. The long strips of farmland running back into the bush made it too easy to overwork the land nearest the river and equally easy to neglect the clearing and cultivation of land in the rear. Above all, farming in New France was hard work and yielded small returns. It could not compete with the promise of riches held out by the fur trade.

THE FUR TRADE

In the first half of the sevententh century the main trade in pelts had gradually moved upriver from Tadoussac to Quebec, Three Rivers and Montreal. The St. Lawrence valley had been penetrated by the French, who encouraged the hunting Indians to bring the furs of the *pays d'en haut,* the north country, down the St. Maurice and the Ottawa rivers rather than by the round-about route of the Saguenay.

By 1650 the Ottawa-St. Lawrence supply line of furs was out of operation. The Hurons, the middlemen who had carried iron kettles, knives and axe heads to the tribes of the north and west and brought back pelts, were dead or scattered. The French, therefore, had to go into the interior (avoiding roving bands of Iroquois as best they could) to find the hunting Indians and trade with them. In the years following 1650, individual traders made their way north and west of the St. Lawrence.

Radisson and Groseilliers. The earliest and best known trader-adventurers of this period were Pierre Esprit Radisson and his brother-in-law, Médard Chouart, Sieur des Groseilliers, who made several journeys in the late 1650's in the lands bordering Lakes Michigan and Superior.

Radisson's accounts of their travels are vague and confusing, but it seems clear that on one occasion they paddled via today's Sault Ste. Marie region into Lake Superior and made contact along its southern shores with groups of Hurons and Ottawas driven west by the Iroquois. The two Frenchmen established a fur post at Chequamegon Bay because these Indians were offering to trade beaver pelts heavier and thicker than any Radisson and Groseilliers had seen before. Apparently, the farther north a beaver was trapped, the finer the skin was likely to be since the severe northern winters made beaver grow fine, dense coats of fur.

The two traders also discovered that the Hurons and Ottawas were again ready to act as middlemen, this time between the French and the more remote, primitive tribes of the interior—the Potawatomi, the Illinois, the Sioux, the Chippewa and the Crees. However, Radisson and Groseilliers were told that the French would have to bring trade goods all the way from the St. Lawrence. The Hurons and Ottawas were willing to trade but were not willing to travel through Iroquois country.

Hudson Bay. In the course of their many wanderings, Radisson and Groseilliers claimed to have reached the upper waters of the Mississippi River. They also heard tales of a vast salt sea (Hudson Bay) lying far to the north of the Great Lakes. They discussed between themselves the possibility of French ships sailing into these waters which, of course, would be much closer to the rich fur country of the northwest than Quebec or Montreal. Radisson claims that he and his partner were taken by Indian guides through northern wildernesses to "the seaside," but the vagueness and highly imaginative nature of his reports makes this seem unlikely.

Whether or not Radisson and Groseilliers actually reached the "sea of the north" is not significant. The important fact is that they were now certain that trade with the Indians could be carried on wherever the southern reaches of the salt sea met land. They had heard that there were eastward-flowing rivers running into a great sea and were sure that, with the establishment of fur posts where the rivers met this sea, the Indians would travel downstream and exchange furs for trade goods.

The Hudson's Bay Company.   On their return to Quebec in 1663 with 300 canoe loads of northern pelts, Radisson and Groseilliers were arrested and fined by the governor and their furs were seized. (The previous governor had refused them permission to venture north in 1661 unless he were given one-half of all their future profits from fur trading.) Groseilliers went to France and complained of ill treatment to officials at the French court. Disregarded there, he and Radisson journeyed to England where they received sympathetic hearings from Prince Rupert, a cousin of King Charles II.

Seeing an opportunity to increase English power and influence in North America and also reap fur profits, the prince persuaded friends to finance an expedition to Hudson Bay. When one ship, the *Nonsuch,* returned from the Bay in 1669 loaded with prime pelts, King Charles was persuaded by his cousin to issue a charter of privileges, rights and duties in 1670 to "The Governor and Company of Adventurers of England trading into Hudson's Bay." The Company was given "sole trade and commerce" in the regions whose waters emptied into Hudson Bay (an area now occupied by much of northern Quebec and northern Ontario, Manitoba and Saskatchewan, the southern half of Alberta and the southeast region of the North-West Territories.) The Company was also given the right to govern, to make laws and even to make war. In return for all these concessions, the Company was required to pay the king or his heirs two black elk skins and two black beaver pelts whenever he or his heirs should visit Company territory.

The early Hudson's Bay Company posts on Hudson and James Bays began an immediate and effective competition which was felt at Chequamegon, the French fur posts at Sault Ste. Marie and Michilimackinac and even at Tadoussac on the Saguenay. The favoured position of the Huron and Ottawa middlemen in the French trade was being seriously affected by H.B.C. trade goods available on a large scale and, because of sea access, at much better exchange rates. A fight for control of the Great Lakes fur trade began. This struggle was to develop into a bitter contest between the French and the English for the control of Hudson Bay. Ultimately, the struggle became one for the possession of New France itself.

EARLY HUDSON'S BAY COMPANY POSTS

BIBLIOGRAPHY

BRANDON, W. (ed.). *American Heritage Book of Indians.* Simon and Schuster, 1961.

BURGER, C. *Beaver Skins and Mountain People,* Dutton, 1968.

COSTAIN, T. B. *The White and the Gold.* Doubleday, 1954.

ECCLES, W. J. *Canada Under Louis XIV, 1663-1701.* Canadian Centenary Series, Vol. III. McClelland and Stewart, 1964.

ECCLES, W. J. *The Canadian Frontier, 1534-1760.* Holt, Rinehart and Winston, 1969.

HARRIS, CHRISTIE. *The Ravens' Cry.* McClelland and Stewart, 1966.

JEFFERYS, CHARLES W. *Picture Gallery of Canadian History, Vol. I.* Ryerson, 1967.

JENNESS, D. *The Indian Tribes of Canada.* Ryerson, 1968.

JENNESS, D. *The People of the Twilight.* University of Chicago, 1959.

JURY, WILFRED. *Saint Marie Among the Hurons.* Oxford, 1965.

LANCTOT, G. *A History of Canada.* 3 vols. Clarke, Irwin, 1963-1965.

MEALING, S. R. (ed.). *The Jesuit Relations and Allied Documents.* McClelland and Stewart, 1963.

MINER, HORACE M. *St. Denis.* University of Chicago, 1939.

NISH, C. and HARVEY, P. *The Social Structures of New France.* Copp Clark, 1968.

PERRY, G. *Champlain.* Simon and Schuster.

3

National Rivalries and Conflicts, 1672-1763

THE FRONTENAC REGIME

In 1672, two years after the founding of the Hudson's Bay Company and the year that Talon's second term of office expired, Louis de Buade, Comte de Palluau et de Frontenac, a French soldier and courtier, became governor of New France. Domineering, stubborn and impatient, careless in obtaining and spending money, he was nonetheless a man of immense energy, courage and insight.

Frontenac immediately set out to learn all he could about the colony and the Iroquois. One of his first actions was to send a message inviting the chiefs of the Five Nations to meet him in council at Cataraqui (site of the present-day city of Kingston, Ontario). There, Frontenac cleverly awed the Iroquois by having a fort constructed in the few days that the council was in session. The chiefs, vastly impressed by this display of power, agreed not to interfere with the French fur trade, and peace was secured (for the time being). For several years thereafter Frontenac took care to meet the Iroquois at Cataraqui to impress upon them the virtues of peace.

It was quite clear even by the early 1670's that the only immediate exportable surplus in the colony was fur pelts, which were valuable, light and easily transported to France. It was also becoming clear that furs would continue to be the only exportable surplus. The St. Lawrence seigneuries and the few industries established by Talon were only able to produce a few of the necessities of life, and the lure of the fur trade was not only stealing men away from the seigneuries but was also taking them out of the workshops of Quebec and Montreal. Talon was also very interested in the fur trade when he discovered that its profits paid the salaries of the officials of New France, covered the costs of imports from France and provided government funds with which to establish industry, equip fishing fleets and settle people on the seigneuries of New France. (It is said that he even invested money of his own quite profitably in several trading voyages.)

In several reports he advised the French government to let him build forts on each side of the eastern end of Lake Ontario. These strategically located posts would permit the French to trade with the Iroquois and thus divert pelts away from the English who had now replaced the Dutch on the Hudson River. His advice was ignored.

Frontenac himself was unable to resist the romantic appeal and practical promise of the fur trade. He did not agree with the Council that the number of *coureurs de bois* (independent traders; literally rangers of the forests) should be limited by official *congés* (trade licenses). Instead, he supported the trade, ordering the governor of Montreal to ignore the growing number of coureurs de bois and refusing to join Intendant Duchesneau in cutting down the number of *congés* issued. Frontenac also alienated Duchesneau by encouraging westward exploration and supporting several attempts to discover new trade areas. (His quarrels with Duchesneau became so numerous and so bitter that in 1682 the king was forced to recall both officials.)

The Brandy Dispute.   A very serious problem arising out of the fur trade was the exchange of brandy for pelts with the Indians. The clergy under Bishop Laval threatened spiritual penalties time and again, but the fur merchants claimed that if the practice ended New France would lose the fur trade to the English—who bargained for furs with rum. Frontenac, who was often accused of supporting the merchants for his own private ends, appealed to France for support, and in 1678 received authorization to summon twenty of the leading merchants and seigneurs to meet with the Council to discuss the problem. Since there were no clergy present, the "Brandy Parliament" voted in favour of continuing to supply spirits to the Indians.

The Iroquois.   Despite Frontenac's firm dealings with the Iroquois, they were still determined to monopolize the fur trade in

North America. By 1681, they had crushed the Illinois. By 1682, they were again raiding the Algonquin tribes along the upper reaches of the Ottawa. After 1682 they began a series of attacks on New France itself, and neither of the governors who succeeded Frontenac (de la Barre and de Denonville) proved capable of dealing with the tribes of the League. In 1689 the Iroquois destroyed Fort Frontenac at Cataraqui and massacred the inhabitants at the little settlement of Lachine just up river from Montreal. They harassed outlying seigneuries, cut down men working in the fields, slaughtered cattle, and burned crops, barns and homes. They also began to ambush French fur fleets. When war was declared between France and England in 1689, New France realized that it had to contend not only with the Iroquois but with the English colonists as well, who were already supplying the Iroquois with more guns and ammunition.

King William's War, 1689-1697.   Frontenac was reappointed governor of New France in 1689. The next few years witnessed intermittent but savage attacks by French and English on each other's settlements, but there were no decisive encounters. The French raided New England settlements, looting, burning and killing. Although of little military significance, the French raids were a shrewd move on Frontenac's part because he knew they would restore French prestige with the Indians of the west. French prestige was indeed so restored that as early as the summer of 1690 the western fur trade was once again in operation. The New Englanders retaliated by sending a small fleet to sack Port Royal. They also made an unsuccessful attempt to besiege Quebec.

Frontenac dealt a last, hard blow at the Iroquois. He led an expedition in 1696 against the Onondagas, destroying villages and crops and badly shaking Iroquois confidence. The Treaty of Ryswick (1697) brought an end to hostilities and provided a short respite in the growing struggle between the French and the English.

THE FUR TRADE BEYOND THE LAKES

Extension of the Fur Trade and of French Claims.   During his second term of office, 1670-1672, Talon gave almost all of his attention to countering the English threat in North America. He sent St. Lusson to Sault Ste. Marie and there, with pomp and ceremony intended to awe the Indians, St. Lusson proclaimed the sovereignty of Louis XIV. Talon sent an expedition under Father Albanel to James Bay itself to claim the area for France and to persuade the Mistassini Indians to trade again at Tadoussac. His envoys, however, were unable to persuade the Indians to undertake the difficult trip to Tadoussac.

The Iroquois menace effectively prevented general exploration to the south, but in 1669 Louis Joliet, a fur trader, journeyed by way of Lakes Ontario, Erie and Huron to Sault Ste. Marie. In 1673 he and Father Marquette were sent west by Frontenac. The explorers reached the upper Mississippi valley (via Green Bay and the Fox and Wisconsin Rivers) and journeyed as far down the great waterway as the Arkansas River. They returned, certain that this was a route to the Gulf of Mexico and convinced of its strategic importance. However, it was left to another explorer, La Salle, to complete their initial discovery.

The Compagnie du Nord.   In the meantime, the increasing English competition in the fur trade out of Hudson Bay was causing great concern. In 1682, the French formed a rival company, the *Compagnie du Nord,* and spent a considerable amount of time and money harrying English trading posts. Indeed, in the next thirty years the French and English fought for ownership of the Hudson Bay fur posts. It wasn't until the Treaty of Utrecht, 1713, that the Hudson's Bay Company finally regained undisputed control of the fur trade in the north.

La Salle.   One of the greatest names in the history of North American exploration is that of Robert Cavelier, Sieur de la Salle. Although he was mockingly called the seigneur of La Chine (a reference to his dream of finding a passage to China), he was a fur trader of great ambition, energy and intelligence. La Salle's greatest interest appears to have been in the lands lying to the south and southwest of Lakes Ontario and Erie. He seems to have travelled in these areas between 1669 and 1671 in search of pelts. His writings, along with those of Father Louis Hennepin, a Récollet priest who accompanied him, contain the first known record of the Niagara and Ohio Rivers. In an attempt to revolutionize the fur trade by large-scale business methods, he planned a fleet of sailing ships on the Great Lakes. In 1679, he built the first of them, the *Griffon,* launched her on Lake Erie and sailed to Green Bay in search of furs. When the *Griffon* had been filled with pelts, La Salle sent her back to Niagara, while he himself remained in the interior intending to prepare for a journey down the Mississippi. The ship, unfortunately, was lost on the return voyage and the scheme for a fleet collapsed.

EXPLORATION OF THE MISSISSIPPI

Route of Marquette and Joliet 1673

Route of La Salle 1682

SCALE OF MILES

0   250   500

In 1682, La Salle explored the Mississippi at his own expense, travelling all the way down river to its junction with the Gulf of Mexico. Before returning to France, he raised a wooden cross bearing the arms of France and claimed Louisiana—all the lands and waters of the Mississippi basin—for Louis XIV. His efforts to establish a colony at the mouth of the Mississippi in 1684 ended with his murder in 1687. However, his intention was later fulfilled by others. Frenchmen penetrated large areas of Louisiana and established trade with its Indian tribes. Two great Canadian soldiers of fortune, the brothers Pierre Lemoyne and Jean-Baptiste Bienville Lemoyne, founded settlements in Louisiana by 1700.

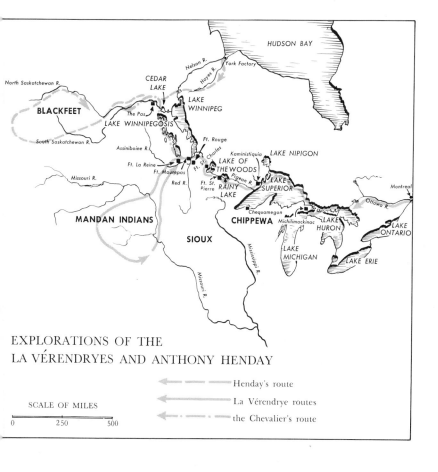

EXPLORATIONS OF THE
LA VÉRENDRYES AND ANTHONY HENDAY

Henday's route
La Vérendrye routes
the Chevalier's route

SCALE OF MILES

0   250   500

With settlements on two of the greatest rivers of North America and forts at such strategic points as Niagara and Detroit, the French appeared to dominate the entire continent.

In the north and northwest, there was also a tremendous burst of French activity in connection with the fur trade. Daniel Grey-solon, Sieur Dulhut, traversed the triangle formed by the upper waters of the Mississippi and Lakes Michigan and Superior, and established fur posts at various points. In 1688 and 1689 Jacques de Noyon pushed on beyond Lake Superior into unknown country to discover Rainy Lake and the Lake of the Woods.

The La Vérendryes. Early in the eighteenth century diminishing supplies of fur (and the continual competition of the Hudson's Bay Company) drove the French trade farther into the north and west. It was the amazing La Vérendrye family that led the search for pelts. Pierre Gaultier de Varennes, Sieur de la Vérendrye, planned a series of fortified trading posts reaching out to the Western Sea, thus neatly combining an extension of his own business interest with the extension of French dominion in North America. As it happened, neither he nor his sons reached the Western Sea. Their real achievement, however, was in breaking out of the Canadian Shield and establishing a series of trading posts on the Great Plains between 1731 and 1743; Fort St. Pierre on Rainy Lake, Fort St. Charles on Lake of the Woods, Fort Maurepas near the mouth of the Red River, Fort Rouge at the junction of the Red and Assiniboine Rivers and Fort La Reine on the present site of Portage La Prairie (Manitoba). Further north Fort Dauphin was erected near Lake Manitoba and Fort Bourbon was erected where the Saskatchewan River enters Cedar Lake.

The tireless exertions of the La Vérendryes proved that the North American continent was much wider than anyone had imagined. Their journeyings also demonstrated that a farther penetration of the Saskatchewan river country could cut off the supply of furs to Hudson Bay.

THE STRUGGLE FOR EMPIRE

The wars of aggression waged by Louis XIV in Europe were followed by a tremendous contest for power between Britain and France. The struggle eventually spread as far as India on one side of the world and North America on the other. The contest in North America, however, was due more to local conditions, intensified by the differences of race, religion and commercial competition. The self-governing British colonies of the Atlantic coast, predominantly Protestant in character, were distrustful of the autocratic, imperialistic regime in New France, a Roman Catholic community. An added source of bitterness was the economic rivalry that stemmed from the fur trade and this was further complicated by the French and British dependence on rival Indian tribes. Ultimately, however, it was the slow westward movement of British settlement into territories claimed by France that precipitated the final war for empire.

THE WARS BETWEEN BRITAIN AND FRANCE

IN EUROPE		IN NORTH AMERICA	
1688-97	War of the League of Augsburg	King William's War (1697—Peace of Ryswick)	1689-97
1701-13	War of the Spanish Succession	Queen's Anne's War (1713—Treaty of Utrecht)	1702-13
1740-48	War of the Austrian Succession	King George's War (1748—Treaty of Aix-la-Chapelle)	1744-48
1756-63	Seven Years' War	French and Indian War (1763—Treaty of Paris)	1754-63

In North America, King William's War (1689-1697), the conflict in which Frontenac played such a prominent role, ended with only nominal peace. Between 1697 and 1763 there were to be three more wars in North America.

Queen Anne's War (1702-1713). When this conflict (known in Europe as The War of the Spanish Succession) broke out, hostilities were also joined in North America. There were the now customary barbarous raids by the French and their Indian allies on New England. New Englanders retaliated by again attacking the Acadian French. In 1710, Port Royal was captured and renamed Annapolis Royal after Britain's Queen Anne. The following year, Quebec was only saved from naval attack by foul weather and the inability of British and colonial commanders to co-operate. The Treaty of Utrecht ended the struggle in favour of the British. France surrendered the forts and territories of the Hudson's Bay Company and gave up all claims to Newfoundland and Acadia, which now became the colony of Nova Scotia. The Iroquois were declared British subjects. However, France was able

LAKE SUPERIOR

Sault Ste. Marie

Michilimackinac

LAKE NIPISSING

Ottawa R.

Ft. Mackinac

GEORGIAN BAY

Montreal

LAKE MICHIGAN

LAKE HURON

F R A N C

Ft. St. Jo

LAKE St. Lawrence R.

Ft. Frontenac

LA CHAMPLA

Ft. Rouillé
(later York)

LAKE ONTARIO

Ft. Oswego

Ft. Ontario

Ft. Frédér

Ft. Carill

LAKE ST. CLAIR

Ft. Niagara

Ft. Stanwix

Ft. William Henry

Ft. St. Joseph

Ft. Pontchartrain
(later Ft. Detroit)

Ft. Herkimer

NEW YORK

Ft. Edwar

Albany

LAKE ERIE

Ft. Presqu'Ile

Hudson R.

Ft. Le Boeuf

Ft. Miami

Ft. Sandusky

Ft. Venango

M O U N T A I N S

Susquehanna R.

Delaware R.

Ft. Augusta

New York

N E W

Ft. Duquesne
(later Ft. Pitt)

PENNSYLVANIA

Ft. Harris

Philadelphia

NEW JERSEY

Ft. Bedford

Ohio R.

Ft. Necessity

Ft. Cumberland

Potomac R.

MARYLAND

DELAWARE

DELAWARE

VIRGINIA

A P P A L A C H I A N

Mt. Vernon

James R.

Richmond

CHESAPEAKE BAY

N

SCALE OF MILES
0   50   100

FOR POWER

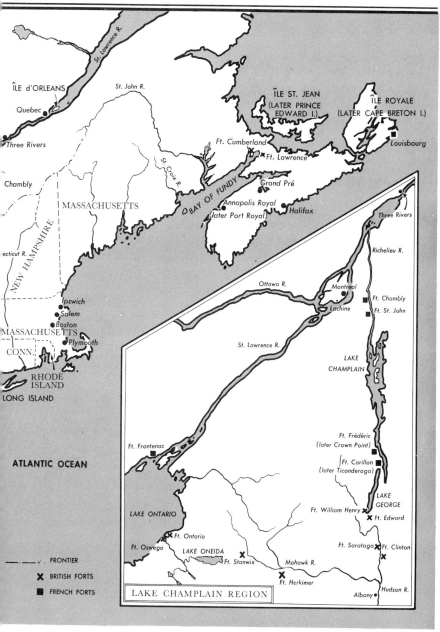

ÎLE d'ORLEANS
Quebec
Three Rivers
Chambly
St. Lawrence R.
St. John R.
MASSACHUSETTS
NEW HAMPSHIRE
ecticut R.
Ipswich
Salem
Boston
MASSACHUSETTS
CONN.
Plymouth
RHODE
ISLAND
LONG ISLAND

ATLANTIC OCEAN

Ft. Cumberland
St. Croix R.
×Ft. Lawrence
Grand Pré
BAY OF FUNDY
Annapolis Royal
(later Port Royal)
Halifax

ÎLE ST. JEAN
(LATER PRINCE
EDWARD I.)

ÎLE ROYALE
(LATER CAPE BRETON I.)
Louisbourg

Three Rivers
Richelieu R.
Ottawa R.
Montreal
Lachine
Ft. Chambly
Ft. St. John

St. Lawrence R.

LAKE
CHAMPLAIN

Ft. Frontenac

Ft. Frédéric
(later Crown Point)

Ft. Carillon
(later Ticonderoga)

LAKE
GEORGE
Ft. William Henry×
×Ft. Edward

LAKE ONTARIO

Ft. Ontario×
Ft. Oswego
LAKE ONEIDA
×
Ft. Stanwix
Mohawk R.
×
Ft. Herkimer

Ft. Saratoga×
×Ft. Clinton

Albany•
Hudson R.

———·— FRONTIER
× BRITISH FORTS
■ FRENCH FORTS

LAKE CHAMPLAIN REGION

to qualify these surrenders in that the boundaries of Hudson Bay and Acadia were not clearly defined. In addition, the islands of the Gulf of St. Lawrence remained in French hands.

Louisbourg.   The French decided to establish a naval base on Île Royale (Cape Breton Island). There, in 1719, they began the construction of a great fortified port designed to protect the St. Lawrence fisheries and guard the water entrance to New France.

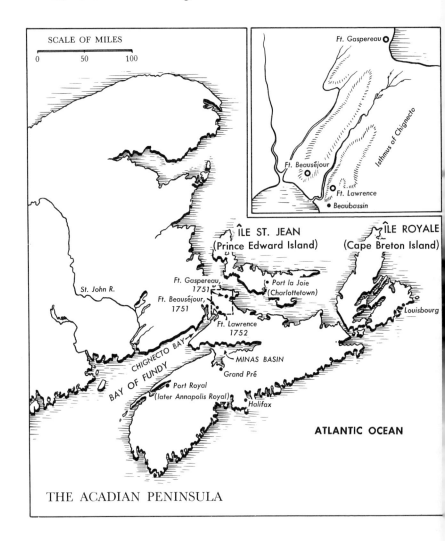

SCALE OF MILES

0   50   100

Ft. Gaspereau

Ft. Beauséjour

Ft. Lawrence

Beaubassin

Isthmus of Chignecto

ÎLE ST. JEAN
(Prince Edward Island)

ÎLE ROYALE
(Cape Breton Island)

St. John R.

Ft. Gaspereau,
1751

Ft. Beauséjour,
1751

Port la Joie
(Charlottetown)

Louisbourg

Ft. Lawrence
1752

CHIGNECTO BAY

BAY OF FUNDY

MINAS BASIN

Grand Pré

Port Royal
(later Annapolis Royal)

Halifax

ATLANTIC OCEAN

THE ACADIAN PENINSULA

The massive stone fortress of Louisbourg, guarding a protected anchorage, would also permit the French to menace British trade and fishing interests in Acadia and in Newfoundland. Elsewhere in North America, the French set about strengthening their empire. Now that Hudson Bay was again English, the old Lake Superior fur posts of Chequamegon and Kaministiquia were reoccupied, and direct contact with the western tribes was renewed. The establishments of Michilimackinac (at the junction of Lakes Huron and Michigan), Fort Frontenac and the newer posts of Niagara and Detroit were strengthened, while additional posts were built in the Mississippi valley. New Orleans was founded near the mouth of the Mississippi to guard the southern water entrance to New France.

King George's War (1745-1748). When war again broke out in Europe (The War of the Austrian Succession), the border skirmishes between French and British settlements in Nova Scotia— an area that then included today's province of New Brunswick— developed into full-scale raids. Early in 1745, Colonel William Pepperell led an expedition of New England colonists against Louisbourg and captured it. In 1746, a French naval attempt to retake Louisbourg and harass the British in Nova Scotia came to nothing.

Once again, peace failed to bring a lasting settlement. The Treaty of Aix-la-Chapelle in 1748 returned Louisbourg to the French in exchange for the port of Madras in India. Thus, the British colonists were needlessly angered and the French were given back a fortress that would continue to menace British colonials.

THE SEVEN YEARS' WAR, 1756-1763

Pre-War Preparations. The Treaty of Aix la-Chapelle was, in effect, no more than a truce. Both sides strengthened their defences. New France added extra links to the chain of forts and trading posts stretching south from the Great Lakes to the mouth of the Mississippi. In Nova Scotia, Britain established the port of Halifax in 1749 to offset the threat of Louisbourg and to act as a base for future war operations. Both sides fortified the Lake Champlain-Hudson River route.

The Expulsion of the Acadians. After the Treaty of Utrecht, under which Acadia became British (1713) the bulk of the

Acadian French had remained in the new province of Nova Scotia. Most of them lived along the Fundy coast, tilling the soil as their forefathers had done before them. They did not mix or intermarry with British settlers, preferring their own customs, language and faith. Although they refused to accept several half-hearted British demands for an oath of allegiance, they were a peaceful folk who gave the British no trouble or cause for alarm and simply wished to remain neutral.

As late as 1775 British officials in Nova Scotia still distrusted the Acadians, finding suspect their refusal to take an oath involving military service in time of war. When deputies from Acadian villages once more refused to take the oath of allegiance, Charles Lawrence, the acting governor of Nova Scotia, abruptly ordered the deportation of the Acadians. In the course of the next few years, hundreds of Acadian families were deported and then scattered, often with unintentional but tragic consequences, among the British colonies.

Colonial Comparisons. By 1775, the French had made magnificent efforts at expansion in North America. They had pushed west as far as the upper reaches of the Saskatchewan River. They controlled the fur resources of all those lands drained by the Mississippi and the St. Lawrence rivers, which meant, in effect, the greater part of eastern North America. But these regions had a population of barely 60,000 people living either on the seigneuries of the St. Lawrence and one or two of its tributaries or in the chain of trading posts and settlements scattered between Montreal, the Manitoba basin and New Orleans.

The British colonies, on the other hand, were almost forty times as populous, formed much more compact settlements and enjoyed a prosperous agriculture and a flourishing export trade. As British settlement pushed steadily westward, the spearhead of population gradually moved through the passes of the Appalachian mountains and into the Mississippi basin—territory claimed by France but only weakly held.

The Ohio Frontier. It was this British expansion into the interior which brought on the last battles for empire. By 1750, the Ohio River valley was being claimed by both French and British, and when a group of Virginians formed the Ohio Company and announced their intention to establish settlement in the upper Ohio valley, the French hastened to construct a number of forts below Lake Erie. A colonial emissary (the young George Washington) was sent to protest, but the French refused to move out and seized two British strongpoints, Fort Necessity and the site of Fort Duquesne. The same year the British general Braddock marched on Fort Duquesne with 1,550 regulars and 450 Virginian militiamen. He was disastrously defeated and lost his own life. In 1755, both France and Britain sent reinforcements to North America.

Major-General Montcalm.   Britain, as always, was poorly prepared for war when it finally broke out in Europe in 1756. The Royal Navy was strong, but the army was under-strength and lacked competent commanders. Even the government of the day was indifferently led. The French were better prepared for the war and quickly set about defending themselves in North America.

In the spring of 1756, Louis-Joseph, Marquis de Montcalm-Gozon, arrived in Quebec with two fine regiments. Despite the handicaps of having to work with the corrupt intendant, Bigot, and the domineering Governor General of New France, the Marquis de Vaudreuil-Cavagnal, Montcalm quickly secured the southern frontier of New France. In 1756 he captured the British fort, Oswego, on the south shore of Lake Ontario, thus clearing the way to the northern end of the Ohio valley. The following year he took Fort William Henry, a British encampment in the upper valley of the Hudson. Montcalm then retired to the southern end of Lake Champlain to strengthen the defences of Fort Carillon (later known as Ticonderoga), which he successfully held against attack by a superior British force.

William Pitt.   In 1757, William Pitt, the new British Secretary of War, sought to defeat France by engaging her with his allies in Europe while stripping her of colonial possessions. He ordered the capture of Louisbourg, Fort Duquesne and Montreal in 1758. Only the first French strongpoint was taken after prolonged bombardment from land and sea. Its inhabitants were sent back to France. In 1758 Montcalm, entrenched at Ticonderoga, shattered the Montreal invasion force led by General Abercrombie.

Pitt's strategy for 1759 was again a three-pronged assault on New France—the capture of Fort Niagara, Montreal and Quebec. Niagara was taken, but its attackers were too spent to continue. There remained Quebec.

Quebec.   Montcalm fell back on Quebec to strengthen its defences because by this time he was suffering from lack of reinforcements and supplies from France. This situation was partly due to the

British naval blockade but also to the very limited co-operation of Vaudreuil and Bigot.

General James Wolfe, the commander of the British forces sent against Quebec, quickly gained command of the St. Lawrence above and below the city and effectively blockaded Quebec and New France for the rest of the 1759 campaign. After weeks of siege work Wolfe finally found a poorly guarded path leading up the cliffs just west of the town and was able to muster his well-

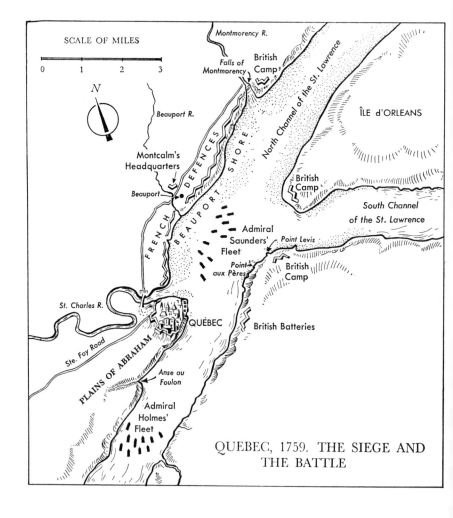

QUEBEC, 1759. THE SIEGE AND THE BATTLE

disciplined regiments. On the famous Plains of Abraham outside Quebec, Montcalm gave battle with his force of regulars, militiamen and Indian allies but was quickly routed. Both Montcalm and Wolfe were mortally wounded in the battle. Quebec was taken.

The End of New France. The British force spent a miserable winter in Quebec. The following April, French forces from Montreal defeated the British at Ste. Foy, just outside Quebec, and then besieged the town. However, British ships arrived shortly afterwards with supplies and reinforcements, and the French were forced to withdraw. In September the British marched into Montreal, and Vaudreuil surrendered New France, thus ending the war in North America.

In February, 1763, the Seven Years' War came to an end with the signing of the Treaty of Paris. All French possessions in North America became British with the exception of the tiny islands of St. Pierre and Miquelon off Newfoundland's south coast (retained by France), and Louisiana (granted to Spain). In North America, Britain had won a tremendous sweep of empire, stretching from Hudson Bay to the Gulf of Mexico and from the Atlantic to the Mississippi. It was a gigantic area, occupied by thousands of Indians, French and British colonists.

BIBLIOGRAPHY

BIRD, HARRISON. *Attack on Quebec—1775.* Oxford, 1968.

ECCLES, W. J. *Frontenac.* McClelland and Stewart, 1965.

EIFERT, V. S. *Louis Jolliette, Explorer of Rivers.* Dodd, Mead.

JEFFERYS, CHARLES W. *The Picture Gallery of Canadian History, Vol. I.* Ryerson, 1968.

KAVANAGH, M. *La Verendrye: His Life and Times.* Kavanagh Press, 1968.

NISH, C. and HARVEY, P. *Social Structures of New France.* Problems in Canadian History Series. Copp Clark, 1968.

OSLER, E. B. *La Salle.* Longmans, 1967.

PARKMAN, FRANCIS. *A Half Century of Conflict.* Collier, 1962.

PARKMAN, FRANCIS. *La Salle and the Discovery of the West.* New American Library, 1962.

PARKMAN, FRANCIS. *Montcalm and Wolfe.* Collier, 1962.

RUTLEDGE, J. L. *Century of Conflict.* Doubleday, 1956.

STACEY, C. P. E. *Quebec, 1759.* Macmillan, 1959.

STANLEY, C. F. G. *New France: The Last Phase, 1744-1760.* Canadian Centenary Series, Vol. V. McClelland and Stewart, 1968.

STEELE, IAN. *Guerillas and Grenadiers.* Ryerson, 1969.

TERRELL, J. U. *La Salle: The Life and Times of an Explorer.* Clarke, Irwin, 1968.

WADE, M. *The French Canadians, 1760-1967.* 2 vols. Macmillan, 1968.

4

The Formative Years, 1760-1791

Military Rule (1760-63). When Britain occupied New France in 1760, she was faced with the problem of governing some 70,000 French-speaking Roman Catholics accustomed to their own laws and way of life. Since plans for governing the colony could not be made until the conclusion of peace (1763), military governors were appointed at Quebec, Three Rivers and Montreal. Supreme authority over these three districts was nominally placed in the hands of the British commander-in-chief, General Jeffrey Amherst.

The affairs of the colony were run with as little change as possible. Authority was exercised with consideration and restraint during these years, and the French settlers appreciated this sympathetic treatment. Economic stability was restored, and the currency was stabilized. Although the army had to be billeted, the people were paid in cash.

Pontiac's Rebellion, 1763. When the Treaty of Paris was concluded two problems demanded immediate British attention: the Indians and the fur trade.

Following France's defeat, the Indian allies remained fiercely loyal to her. They resented the flow of eager British fur traders into their territories and they feared that settlers from the seaboard colonies would occupy their lands. By 1763, Pontiac, an Ottawa chieftain, had rallied the tribes south and west of the Great Lakes against the British, and war parties captured all British forts west of Niagara with the exception of Detroit. It took General Amherst several months of wilderness campaigning to remove the threat of further Indian raids. Five years were to pass before a peace treaty was accepted by the Indians. Pontiac's rebellion forced the British to recognize the Indian problem and to consider a policy for the settlement of the interior.

The Royal Proclamation of 1763. The Proclamation followed closely on the heels of the Treaty of Paris. It was desgned with two

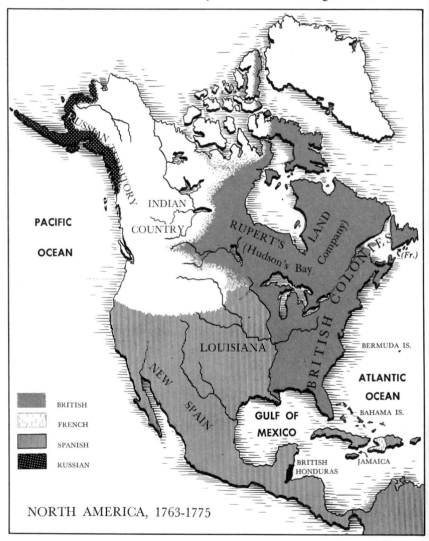

NORTH AMERICA, 1763-1775

goals in mind. One of these goals was to reassure the Indians and thus to avoid further uprisings. To do this the Proclamation created boundaries for Quebec that confined the colony to a small irregularly shaped area on both sides of the St. Lawrence River from the Gulf of St. Lawrence to a line north and east of Lake Ontario (see map on page 52). The Proclamation also established the Appalachian watershed as a boundary for Britain's Atlantic colonies. The territory beyond these boundaries was reserved for the Indians. Settlement was prohibited in this Indian territory and only licensed traders were permitted to enter it.

These territorial arrangements were satisfactory to the Indians, but they caused a great deal of anger among the fur traders in Quebec and in particular among the American colonists. Had the Americans not fought in the recent war primarily to take the west from France and to open it up for settlement?

The second goal of the Proclamation was designed to encourage migration from the Atlantic colonies to Quebec. The hope was to create in Quebec a Protestant, English-speaking colony, similar in pattern to the established royal colonies on the Atlantic seaboard. Land was offered free to ex-soldiers and on easy terms to others. An English legal system and an elected assembly were promised.

The Proclamation was distinctly unsuccessful in achieving this second goal. Few settlers entered Quebec. The American colonists were more interested in moving into the fur-rich and fertile Ohio valley. Quebec was not an acceptable substitute. The *Canadiens,* on the other hand, were Roman Catholics and, according to British law, were therefore ineligible to sit or vote in an assembly. Since most of them were unfamiliar with the English common law, they were also unable to take an active part in judicial or legal affairs.

The "Montrealers."   In spite of the failure of the Proclamation of 1763 to encourage settlement in Quebec, a small group of British and American merchants (many of them Scots) did immigrate to the colony after 1760. They originally came as army contractors and their arrival had an important effect on the colony. Their shrewdness and energy, when combined with the knowledge and skill of the Canadian voyageurs, soon gave a strong boost to the fur trade, the colony's chief economic support. As a centre for the trade, Montreal became more important than Albany and Philadelphia. Even the Hudson's Bay Company lost ground to its Montreal competitors and was forced to abandon its "Stay on the Bay" policy.

The "Montrealers," or "pedlars," as they were contemptuously called by the Hudson's Bay Company, lost no time in undermining the Company by dealing directly with the Indians. By 1776, they had reached La Vérendrye's domain—Lake Winnipeg, the Red River, the Assiniboine River and Lake Winnipegosis. Aggressive traders such as Alexander Henry the Elder, James Finlay and Peter Pond went into the Saskatchewan country and discovered the rich, heavy winter pelts that it produced. Thence they journeyed northwest to a region even wealthier in furs, a region where winter lasted seven, eight or even nine months of the year and where furs were correspondingly heavy, rich and glossy. This was the Athabasca country. It was here that the Montrealers explored, built fur posts and established contact with the Chipewyans, the Red Knives, the Dog Ribs, the Caribous and the Stoneys.

The arrival of English-speaking merchants in Quebec not only revived the fur trade, it also created new tensions in the colony. The way of life, the interests, attitudes and opinions of the newcomers differed sharply from those of the conservative, agricultural, Roman Catholic communities of New France. Control of commercial affairs was soon largely in the hands of the British. Agriculture remained, for the most part, an occupation of the French-speaking people along the St. Lawrence and its tributaries. The English-speaking colonists agitated for an assembly and English laws, but the French were unfamiliar with, and therefore wary of, both. In whose favour would such questions be settled?

Civil Rule and Governor Murray. In 1764, civil rule replaced military rule in Quebec, and James Murray (one of Wolfe's officers and the famous military governor of the Montreal district) became the first governor-general. Murray's dislike of the British business community in Quebec was such that his conservative interpretations of the terms of the Proclamation helped to preserve the French-Canadian character of the colony. Under the Proclamation, the benefits of English law had been promised to new settlers, but the Court of Common Pleas continued to settle French-Canadian litigation according to French law. Likewise, English freehold tenure had been promised, but land grants continued to be made *en fief et seigneurie*. Murray saw the Roman Catholic Church in Quebec as potentially a strong support to British sovereignty in the colony. For this reason he interfered in its affairs very little. In fact, he gave the Church active behind-the-scenes assistance in overcoming a grave threat to its welfare. In 1760, Bishop Pontbriand had died. British law forbad relations with the Vatican and, therefore, appeared to prevent the appointment of a new bishop. But Murray devised a means whereby the French Canadians were allowed to choose a new bishop from their midst with the approval of Rome. He also permitted priests to revive the collection of the tithe.

Sir Guy Carleton. Sir Guy Carleton, Murray's successor, not only disliked the merchant groups of Montreal and Quebec, he thoroughly distrusted them. He suspected that they wanted a provincial assembly in order to further their own interests in defiance of the Proclamation. (In this opinion he was probably correct. Like the leading French merchants before them, the British merchants of Quebec were determined to monopolize the western fur trade.) In addition, Carleton, an English aristocrat, was opposed to—and fearful of—the whole idea of an elected assembly. He knew, for example, that the assemblies in the Atlantic colonies were already very much at odds with their governors.

The Quebec Act, 1774. The individuality and separateness of Quebec was at last officially recognized by the British Parliament in the *Quebec Act of 1774.* This statute has been called the "Magna Carta of the French-Canadian race." Its main provisions were as follows:

(1) The boundaries of Quebec were extended northeast to Labrador and west to include the Great Lakes and the vast territory between the Mississippi and Ohio rivers—the rich, fur area in which trade had been restricted under the Proclamation of 1763.

(2) The "free exercise" of the Roman Catholic religion, and the right of the Church to collect tithes and dues, were given legal recognition.

(3) The seigneurial system was recognized.

(4) Civil suits were to be tried by "the Laws of Canada" (French law). Criminal cases were to be tried in accordance with British law, which was thought to be more humane than the French criminal code. (Two amendments were never carried out: the introduction of *habeas corpus,* and the introduction of British law in commercial lawsuits.)

(5) Government was to be by a governor and an appointed legislative council. (The Proclamation's promise of an elected assembly was abandoned.)

(6) Roman Catholics were made eligible for public office including the legislative council. (This was unique in the British Empire.)

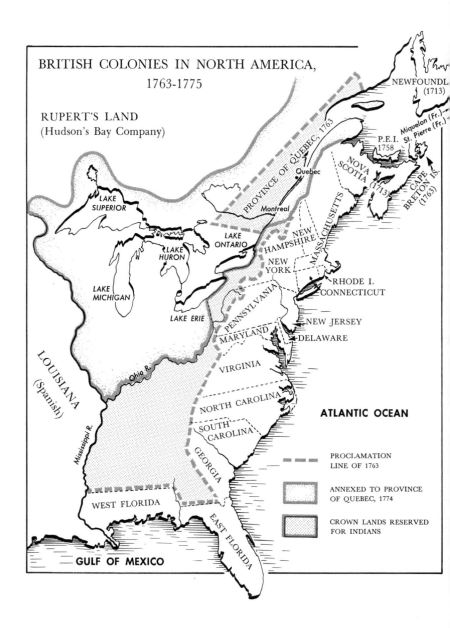

BRITISH COLONIES IN NORTH AMERICA,
1763-1775

RUPERT'S LAND
(Hudson's Bay Company)

NEWFOUNDL
(1713)

Miquelon (Fr.)
St. Pierre (Fr.)

P.E.I.
1758

NOVA
SCOTIA
(1713)

CAPE
BRETON IS.
(1763)

PROVINCE OF QUEBEC, 1763

Quebec

Montreal

LAKE
SUPERIOR

LAKE
ONTARIO

LAKE
HURON

LAKE
MICHIGAN

LAKE ERIE

NEW
HAMPSHIRE

MASSACHUSETTS

NEW
YORK

RHODE I.
CONNECTICUT

PENNSYLVANIA

NEW JERSEY

MARYLAND

DELAWARE

LOUISIANA
(Spanish)

Ohio R.

VIRGINIA

NORTH CAROLINA

ATLANTIC OCEAN

SOUTH
CAROLINA

Mississippi R.

GEORGIA

PROCLAMATION
LINE OF 1763

ANNEXED TO PROVINCE
OF QUEBEC, 1774

CROWN LANDS RESERVED
FOR INDIANS

WEST FLORIDA

EAST FLORIDA

GULF OF MEXICO

Effects of the Quebec Act.   In general, the Act was acceptable to
the French Canadians, although they were somewhat unhappy with
the continuance of seigneurial dues and church tithes. Needless
to say, however, the seigneurs and clergy were quite pleased with
these terms. Control of the fur trade within the boundaries set by
the Act pacified the English-speaking, Quebec merchants, although
they were annoyed at there being no elected assembly. The Act,
in effect, restored many of the traditional customs and practices of
New France. The one basic change was that they now looked to
London, not Versailles, for decisions. The Quebec Act, however,
played an important part in aggravating the grievances of the
Thirteen Atlantic Colonies and in hastening their rebellion.

THE AMERICAN REVOLUTION, 1775-1783

Events Leading up to the Revolution.   By 1775, several genera-
tions of British descendents lived in the Thirteen Colonies. For
many years there had been little interference by successive British
governments in North American affairs. However, trade and
navigation acts after 1651 provoked much dissatisfaction.

It was the policy of mercantilism, as expressed in these acts, that
became an excuse for revolution. Mercantilism was an economic
system supporting the monopoly of empire trade and shipping and
dependent on colonies for its survival. Mercantilism restricted
the manufacture of certain goods that might compete with British
products. It forced the colonies to use British ships, limited the
sale of certain colonial products to Britain only and required that
all colonial imports of foreign goods be obtained only through
Britain. Mercantilism, however, was far from being one-sided.
The colonies enjoyed a protected market in Britain and in other
British colonies, and colonial goods were not subjected to restrictive tariffs. Yet, in the long run, mercantilism seemed to be a great
handicap to the development of trade and manufacturing in the
seaboard colonies. Many colonists regarded it as nothing less than
economic bondage.

The existence of British garrison forces in North America
which had been welcome during the French wars now irritated the
colonists. In particular, they were annoyed that the Westminster
Parliament passed acts designed to raise within the colonies one-
third of the money necessary to support these forces. The colonists
themselves were given no opportunity to approve or disapprove of
these taxes.

The first of these statutes, the *Sugar Act of 1764* and the *Stamp Act of 1765,* raised initial protest in colonial assemblies. When the *"Townshend Acts"* of 1767 placed duties on such items as paper, glass, lead and tea, several colonies observed non-importation agreements and British imports dropped by nearly two-thirds. The Townshend Acts were hastily repealed—with the exception of the duty on tea. This duty sparked a revolution!

The Tea Act. From 1770 to 1773, there were few difficulties between Great Britain and her colonies. Having won the repeal of some taxes, the colonists allowed the British to collect others, including the duty on a pound of tea. However, in 1772, Parliament passed the *Tea Act,* which gave the East India Company, the great British trading concern, the sole right to sell tea in North America.

This legislation only served to remind the colonists of a tax about which they had never been consulted. Colonists, in their anger, prevented Company tea ships from entering the harbours of New York City and Philadelphia. At Annapolis, a Company vessel and its cargo were burned. At Boston, three Company ships were raided and their cargoes of tea destroyed.

Parliament's answer to the "Boston Tea Party" was to close the port of Boston and to suspend some of Massachusetts' rights of self-government. There followed other "Intolerable Acts " (as the colonists branded them) that restricted town meetings and billeted troops in the colony.

Unfortunately, the Quebec Act of 1774 was also passed at this time. It was immediately viewed by the colonists as a British revival of the former French policy of confining the English colonies to the Atlantic seaboard by preventing their expansion into the Mississippi basin. In the eyes of the colonists this was a defeat for their democratic ideals and their aspirations for western expansion. In addition, the stern Protestants of New England were disturbed by the "establishment" in Quebec of the Roman Catholic Church. If anything, the Quebec Act was regarded by the colonists as the most intolerable of the "Intolerable Acts." It seemed to hurt not only Massachusetts, but all the Atlantic colonies.

One momentous result of the Intolerable Acts was the calling of a Continental Congress at Philadelphia, which produced a *Declaration of Rights and Grievances* ("No taxation without representation"). The other result came in April, 1775, when armed colonists and British troops clashed at Lexington and Concord and blood was spilled. One month later, a second Continental Congress met and issued a *Declaration of the Causes and Necessity of Taking Up Arms*.

The Attitude of Quebec and Nova Scotia. At this time, Quebec and Nova Scotia showed very little interest in the affairs of their southern neighbours. There were a few, isolated protests and demonstrations in reply to appeals for support from the Thirteen Colonies, but no organized uprisings. The restrictions of the mercantile system weighed less heavily on the Quebec and Halifax merchants, who, in any case, were more dependent upon the British market. There was no boycott of East India Company tea or, for that matter, embargoes on British goods or non-importation agreements.

New England, in particular, hoped that the Nova Scotians would join the Revolution; but various factors produced a neutralist attitude—the strong commercial and family ties of British immigrants, the deterrent of a strong military and naval base at Halifax, the isolation within the province of much of its population. The Nova Scotians also had a keen eye for the profits to be reaped by selling war supplies to both sides. Quebec also showed no desire to join in the revolt. Some of the British merchants in Montreal were sympathetic to the revolution, but the French Canadians were unwilling to take part—on either side. When Quebec was invited to send representatives to the First Continental Congress, the offer was politely declined.

The Invasion of Quebec. In 1775, the American patriots decided to invade Quebec. They hoped to win the colony over to the revolutionary cause and also to remove a military threat in the north. In May, they captured Ticonderoga and Crown Point. In November, a force under Richard Montgomery took Forts St. John's and Chambly on the Richelieu and accepted the surrender of defenceless Montreal (almost capturing Governor Carleton in the process). Montgomery then joined Benedict Arnold's army outside Quebec.

In a blinding, December snowstorm, the fortress-city commanded by Carleton was assaulted by ill-equipped, hungry and near-exhausted troops. The results were disastrous for the attackers. Montgomery was killed and Arnold was wounded, 100 Americans lost their lives and 400 were taken prisoner. When a British fleet arrived in the spring with reinforcements for Carleton, the besiegers were forced to withdraw.

The Americans had received only half-hearted support from some merchants and habitants, who were moved more by local grievances than revolutionary ideals. By the time the invaders left, Quebec opinion was unanimously against the "liberators" who had mocked the Roman Catholic faith and had sought to buy supplies with worthless paper money.

The War of Independence. In July 1776, the Second Continental Congress issued the *Declaration of Independence,* and fighting began in earnest. Governor Carleton did not make use of the large army sent to him in 1776, possibly because he was more interested in a last attempt to reach agreement with the colonists. The British general, Burgoyne, led these troops south a year later, but was forced to surrender when trapped and surrounded in the wilderness near Saratoga.

In 1778, a vengeful France and her partner, Spain, signed treaties of alliance with the revolutionaries. (A family quarrel now became a war.) With supplies from France of men, money, and weapons, and with French naval support, the colonists were able to stave off defeat and wear down Britain's will to win. In 1782, the British government favoured opening peace negotiations and agreed to recognize the independence of the united colonies.

The Treaty of Versailles, 1783. Detailed agreement was secretly reached in 1783. Neither Britain nor the United States wished to see France return to North America. Britain, anxious to restore friendly relations with her former colonies and utterly weary of colonial problems, casually conceded vast areas of North American territory as part of the price of peace. An international boundary line was drawn from the mouth of the St. Croix River on the Bay of Fundy, north to the watershed between the St. Lawrence and the Atlantic, and southwestward to the headwaters of the Connecticut River. From there it ran westward along the 45th parallel to the St. Lawrence and then through the middle of Lakes Ontario, Erie, Huron and Superior to the northwest corner of Lake of the Woods. The line was then supposed to run due west to the Mississippi (whose headwaters were actually much to the south).

When she put her signature upon the Treaty of Versailles, Britain gave away a western fur empire that it had taken the French a century and a half to build. Every important fur post from Montreal to Grand Portage at the western end of Superior was now in American territory. (Spain was conceded east and west Florida and all lands west of the Mississippi.) In addition, the United States was given fishing rights not only on the banks off Newfoundland and in the mouth of the St. Lawrence, but also within the three-mile limit of British North American territorial waters. It also had rights to dry and cure fish on any unsettled shores, bays and inlets of British North America. This Treaty established a precedent that has affected Canadian-American relations—particularly regarding offshore rights—ever since.

POST-WAR PROBLEMS

The United Empire Loyalists. The greatest problem that remained after the treaty of 1783 was that of the British supporters in the United States—"Tories" to the Americans, and "United Empire Loyalists" to the British. During the war, many of them had been persecuted by the revolutionaries and many had had their homes and property confiscated. The United States' government agreed to "earnestly recommend" to the individual states the return of Loyalist property, but this recommendation was largely ignored. The trials and tribulations of eight years of war had left much bitterness in the minds of Americans against Britain and everything British.

Not content with ousting government officials, businessmen and prosperous landowners during the war, Americans badly abused those Loyalists who returned after the war to re-settle or claim compensation for land and property confiscated during the Revolution. Many Loyalists were unwilling to endure such abuse and determined to leave the United States.

Some of the wealthiest citizens, and almost all former colonial officials, returned to Britain. Other Loyalists went to the West Indies or to the Floridas. But for the majority, North America was their homeland and Britain was almost a foreign country. These people naturally looked to the remaining British North American colonies as a place of refuge.

The exact number of persons involved in the Loyalist migration is hard to determine. It is estimated that some thirty-five to forty thousand made their way to Nova Scotia and that another five to seven thousand moved to the western end of Lake Ontario, in the Niagara and Detroit regions. Some of those who first went to Nova Scotia continued their migration, finally settling down in the area west of Montreal, along the St. Lawrence and the eastern shore of Lake Ontario.

58

LOYALIST SETTLEMENTS
BEFORE 1800

GULF OF ST. LAWRENCE

CAPE BRETON

Sydney

Guysborough

PRINCE EDWARD I.

Charlottetown

Parrsboro

NOVA SCOTIA

Halifax

NEW BRUNSWICK

Fredericton

St. John R.

Saint John

BAY OF FUNDY

Annapolis

Liverpool
Shelburne

ATLANTIC OCEAN

SCALE OF MILES

0   100

MAIN ROUTES OF THE LOYALISTS

AREAS OF LOYALIST SETTLEMENT

MASSACHUSETTS

MASSACHUSETTS

NEW HAMPSHIRE

Boston

LOWER CANADA

Quebec City

Three Rivers

St. Lawrence R.

Montreal

Ottawa R.

Cornwall

LAKE CHAMPLAIN

Hudson R.

Williamstown (Brockville)

Kingston

Smiths' Creek (Port Hope)

York (Toronto)

LAKE ONTARIO

Newark (Niagara-on-the-Lake)

Niagara R.

NEW YORK

New York

PENNSYLVANIA

UPPER CANADA

Grand R.

Dover Mills (Port Dover)

LAKE ERIE

LAKE ST. CLAIR

Sandwich (Windsor)

LAKE HURON

Creation of New Brunswick.   In the winter of 1782-3, Sir Guy Carleton organized mass migrations to Nova Scotia from the port of New York City.   Among these emigrants were some well-educated men and women, and some people of distinction.   The majority, however, were tradesmen, storekeepers, farmers, and discharged soldiers.   Many Loyalists found homes in Nova Scotia, Cape Breton Island and Prince Edward Island, but a large number settled in the St. John River valley.   Here, like Loyalists elsewhere in British North America, they were given land and supplied with provisions, tools, seed and livestock.   Their efforts were so successful and their demands for self-government so vocal and persistent that in 1784 the new province of New Brunswick was created.   Its jurisdiction ran from the St. Croix River to the Northumberland Strait and from Quebec's eastern boundary to the old dividing line between French and British, the Isthmus of Chignecto.   The New Brunswickers quickly became prosperous by exporting timber and such agricultural products as potatoes and wheat.

Post-War Politics.   After 1783 Britain reverted to her old conservative, mercantilist policies.   In doing so she was warmly applauded by the merchants of British North America.   As far as government was concerned, the trend in British North America was toward political division into a number of small colonies, as has been noted in the case of the Loyalist immigrants in the St. John River valley.   Prince Edward Island (Île St. Jean) had been a separate colony since 1769 and in 1784 Cape Breton Island was given colonial status.

In Quebec, however, British merchants were still petitioning for English law, a representative assembly and the repeal of several clauses of the Quebec Act.   The Loyalists, together with Carleton, were opposed to merchant ambition, but also sought a more liberal system of government for the province.   Some concessions were made.   Habeas corpus was established in 1784, and shortly afterwards juries were permitted in civil suits.   The new settlers in the western half of the province wanted government separate from that of Quebec, English law, local courts, freehold land tenure and, particularly, financial help for building roads and for establishing schools and churches. However, Carleton (now Lord Dorchester) found it impossible to carry anything through the Council in Quebec, which was dominated by men from the French-speaking eastern half of the province.

The Constitutional Act of 1791. In 1791, the British government passed the *Constitutional Act,* or *Canada Act,* in an attempt to satisfy the French Canadians as well as both the English merchants and newly arrived Loyalists.

The main provisions of the Act were:

(1) The office of Governor-in-Chief of British North America was instituted.

(2) Quebec was divided into the provinces of Upper and Lower Canada, with the Ottawa River as the dividing line, except for two seigneuries on its southwest bank. As a result of this division there were some 20,000 people (most of whom were of Loyalist extraction) in Upper Canada and some 100,000 French and 10,000 British in Lower Canada. In effect, the Act created a political division that emphasized the racial division.

(3) Each province was given a government consisting of a British lieutenant-governor, an appointed executive council, an appointed legislative council and a legislative assembly elected by property owners. It was hoped that the legislative councils and the assemblies, or "lower houses," would work together in a legislative partnership similar to that of Parliament's House of Lords and House of Commons. Governors were to be appointed by the British Parliament. The executive and legislative councils, in turn, were to be appointed by the governors. Legislative assemblies and legislative councils were empowered to make laws and to vote certain monies. Governors and executive councils, however, could summon or dissolve legislative assemblies at will, veto bills and control finance. Britain had the power to disallow any law passed by a colonial government.

(4) Upper Canada was given freehold land tenure and English law while Lower Canada retained the seigneurial system (though freehold tenure was permitted if requested) and French civil law.

(5) The status given the Roman Catholic Church under the Quebec Act was confirmed.

(6) The Church of England was "established" as the state church. An Anglican bishop was appointed to Quebec. One seventh of all Crown lands in both provinces were set aside as endowment "reserves" for the support of "the Protestant clergy."

Effects of the Constitutional Act. On the whole, the Act of 1791 altered very little. It did give Roman Catholics the right to vote and hold elected office yet it also tended to strengthen conservatism in both politics and society. It preserved many characteristics of the old French regime in Lower Canada, and established a British colonial regime in Upper Canada. It introduced an element of representative government, but not responsible government, since the reins of government were still held by a British governor and his executive council. In Lower Canada the English-speaking merchants, who were in the minority, remained dissatisfied for they were unable to get their proposed economic measures passed in the assembly. At the same time, French Canadians suspected that assembly and council would become nothing more than taxing bodies. The provision of reserved land for the support of a Protestant clergy was open to abuse. Anglican governors of Upper Canada tended to give funds obtained from clergy reserves exclusively to the Anglican Church, ignoring the other rapidly increasing Protestant denominations.

The Act, in short, introduced into Canada a modified system of the royal colonial government that had operated in the Atlantic colonies until the War of Independence. Although there were elected assemblies, there were still appointed councils. Although the peoples of the Canadas could, to some extent, regulate their lives and tax themselves, they were still subject to the veto powers of councils, governors and the British Parliament.

BIBLIOGRAPHY

COHEN, S. S. (ed.). *Canada Preserved*. Copp Clark, 1968.

EVANS, G. N. D. *The Loyalists*. Copp Clark, 1968.

FITZGEORGE, PARKER. *Famous Indians*. Canadian Portrait Series. Clarke, Irwin, 1956.

JEFFERYS, C. W. *Picture Gallery of Canadian History, Vol II*. Ryerson, 1968.

KLASSEN, H. G. *Thrust and Counterthrust*. Longmans, 1965.

LANCTOT, GUSTAVE. *Canada and the American Revolution*. Clarke, Irwin, 1967.

5

Expansion and Adjustment, 1791-1818

British-American Relations. Tension between Britain and her former colonies, the United States, did not disappear overnight. Following the treaty of 1783, American traders and settlers had hoped to move west into former British fur territory south and southwest of the Great Lakes. The British, however, refused to surrender such posts as Michilimackinac, Detroit and Niagara until the Americans had satisfactorily provided for displaced and dispossessed Loyalists and had arranged the settlement of pre-Revolutionary British debts. American refusal to honour fully the 1783 treaty may well have justified this stand, but the British were reluctant to leave for two main reasons. First, Britain did not want to lose some half to two-thirds of the Great Lakes' fur trade. Second, Britain was afraid that the Indians might rise up in protest against the violation of British guarantees that Indian lands would remain untouched.

Jay's Treaty, 1794. Several attempts by American frontiersmen and farmers to move westward into the Ohio valley were bloodily stopped by the Indians. Since the British continued to occupy the interior posts and were suspected of using the Indians to wipe out American settlements, anti-British sentiment increased to the point where there was talk of invading British North America. John Jay was sent by the American government to London to negotiate a settlement and avert a war. As it happened, Britain had become involved in the French revolutionary wars and wanted to avoid complications.

Under Jay's Treaty the British were required to withdraw from the interior posts, though both nations were to have free use of the Great Lakes and could pass freely over the new international boundary. For some years Upper and Lower Canada benefited from this arrangement, but the Americans gradually placed more and more restrictions on Canadian fur traders, who were ultimately forced to depend on the regions north and west of the Great Lakes in their search for pelts. A further western expansion was clearly essential if the fur trade was to survive.

THE FUR TRADE

The Pacific Coast.   Under Russian sponsorship the Danish navigator, Vitus Bering, had crossed the Pacific in 1741 to the Aleutian Islands and the Alaskan coast. In these regions he had discovered a wealth of fur-bearing animals, especially sea otter. Russians soon established trading posts in these areas, but did not publicize Bering's discoveries.

Captain James Cook, on his famous third voyage around the world in 1778, was the first European to be recorded on the Pacific coast of present-day Canada. Soon after the record of his voyages was published (1784), British and American traders were sailing northwest Pacific waters in search of the sea otter.

Disturbed by the fact that foreigners were invading waters which they considered their own, the Spanish sent several expeditions northward from Mexico. In 1789 a Spanish patrol seized several ships and also a trading post owned by John Meares at Nootka Sound. Meares appealed to the British government, and the subsequent furore almost resulted in war. However, the incident was settled peacefully and, under the Nootka Convention of 1791, Spain surrendered her claim to own the Pacific coast north of the 42nd parallel. The North Pacific gradually came under the control of British and American traders, while the Russians continued to obtain furs from Alaska.

In 1791, another British navigator, Captain George Vancouver, was sent by the British government to make an accurate survey of the North Pacific coast and to find a water passage through North America from the Pacific to the Atlantic. Vancouver spent three years exploring, mapping, charting and surveying the northwest coast of the continent. He circumnavigated a large island (Vancouver Island) behind Nootka Sound, but failed to recognize the

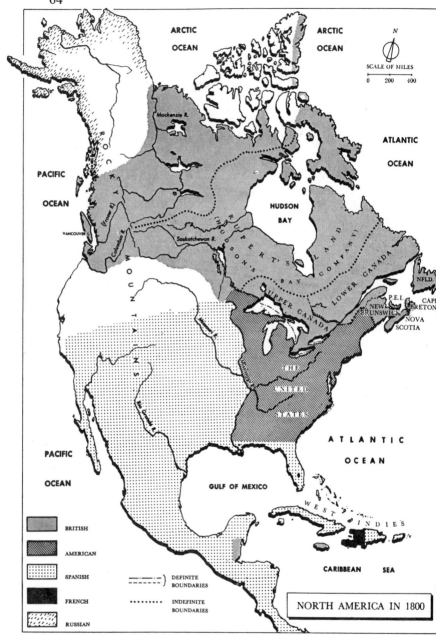

ARCTIC OCEAN

ARCTIC OCEAN

N

SCALE OF MILES

0   200   400

ATLANTIC

OCEAN

Mackenzie R.

PACIFIC

OCEAN

HUDSON

BAY

VANCOUVER

Saskatchewan R.

NFLD.

UPPER CANADA

LOWER CANADA

P.E.I.

CAPE BRETON

NEW BRUNSWICK

NOVA SCOTIA

THE

UNITED

STATES

ATLANTIC

OCEAN

PACIFIC

OCEAN

GULF OF MEXICO

W E S T   I N D I E S

CARIBBEAN   SEA

BRITISH

AMERICAN

SPANISH

FRENCH

RUSSIAN

DEFINITE BOUNDARIES

INDEFINITE BOUNDARIES

NORTH AMERICA IN 1800

mouth of a large river (the Fraser). Vancouver was unlucky in that he found an important river mouth farther south but claimed it too late for Britain. An American ship's captain, Robert Gray, had discovered the river five months earlier and had named it after his vessel, the *Columbia*.

The Hudson's Bay Company. In the north, the Hudson's Bay Company had observed the policy of "Stay on the Bay" for many years until competition from the Montrealers finally forced it to change this attitude. By 1774, the "pedlars" from Montreal were making such inroads upon the trade of York Factory that the Bay Company sent Samuel Hearne to establish its first inland trading post, Cumberland House, on the Saskatchewan River. Other inland posts followed, and competition between the Company and the Montrealers became keener. It was to reach a climax shortly after 1811 when the Hudson's Bay Company made a land grant for settlement in the Red River area, an area that lay across the western route of the traders from Montreal.

The "Nor'Westers." Individual British "Pedlars from Quebec" had, with the help of French voyageurs, extended the fur trade as far west as the Rockies and as far north as the lands bordering the Arctic. By 1787, however, the cost of such extended trading operations had risen so drastically that a number of Montreal traders joined forces and pooled resources to form the *North West Company*. The "Nor'Westers" boasted such famous names as Simon McTavish, Joseph Frobisher (these two held a controlling interest in the North West Company), James McGill, Peter Pond, Alexander Mackenzie, Simon Fraser and, later, David Thompson. McTavish, a businessman rather than an actual trader, often travelled to Fort William to meet his wintering partners and plan trade expansion. (Grand Portage, the old meeting-place, was American territory after 1783.)

In 1789 Alexander Mackenzie discovered the river that bears his name and followed it to the Arctic Ocean. In 1793, he started up the Peace River and by following numerous rivers reached Dean Channel, thus becoming the first European to cross the continent and to reach the Pacific.

Between 1805 and 1808, Simon Fraser established Forts St. James, McLeod, Fraser and George, west of the Rockies in what is now British Columbia. In 1808 he led an expedition down what he believed to be the Columbia River to the Pacific. It was in

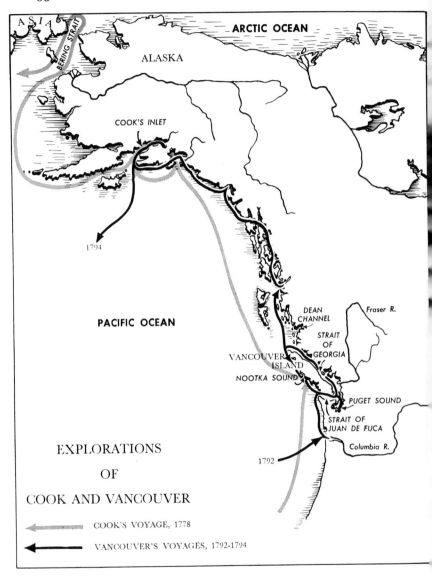

ARCTIC OCEAN

ASIA

BERING STRAIT

ALASKA

COOK'S INLET

1794

PACIFIC OCEAN

DEAN CHANNEL

Fraser R.

STRAIT OF GEORGIA

VANCOUVER ISLAND

NOOTKA SOUND

PUGET SOUND

STRAIT OF JUAN DE FUCA

Columbia R.

1792

EXPLORATIONS

OF

COOK AND VANCOUVER

COOK'S VOYAGE, 1778

VANCOUVER'S VOYAGES, 1792-1794

ARCTIC OCEAN

Mackenzie R.

GREAT
BEAR LAKE

GREAT SLAVE LAKE

Slave R.

Fort Chipewyan · LAKE ATHABASKA

Peace R.

Parsnip R.

Blackwater R.   Athabaska R.

Bella
Coola R.
VANCOUVER I.   Fraser R.

PACIFIC

OCEAN

EXPLORATIONS

OF

ALEXANDER MACKENZIE

SCALE OF MILES

0   200   400

fact a new route, the Fraser River, but it proved too perilous to
provide the fur trade with a Pacific outlet.

In 1811 David Thompson, perhaps the greatest land geographer
that ever lived, finally found his way from the Kootenay to the
mouth of the Columbia River. Thompson had served with the
Hudson's Bay Company from 1784 to 1797, during which time he
made a series of journeys from the Great Lakes and the Mississippi
to the Rockies and north of the Peace and Athabasca Rivers. He

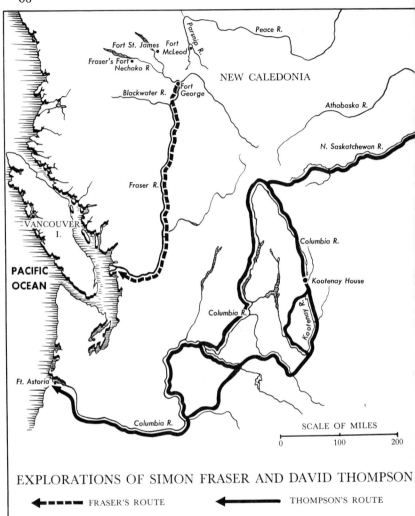

EXPLORATIONS OF SIMON FRASER AND DAVID THOMPSON

◄ ----- FRASER'S ROUTE   ◄————— THOMPSON'S ROUTE

joined the North West Company in 1804, and in 1807 crossed the Rockies and spent some years establishing trading posts and mapping large areas of present-day British Columbia. He later spent ten years surveying the International Boundary between Canada and the United States from St. Regis, Quebec, to the northwest corner of the Lake of the Woods.

The Fur Trade on the Pacific Coast. When Thompson arrived at the mouth of the Columbia in 1811, he found an American trading post, Fort Astoria, built by men of John Jacob Astor's Pacific Fur Company. However, Astor was not long able to compete with the vigorous Canadian traders, and just after the War of 1812 broke out he wisely sold his post to the North West Company. Jay's Treaty had given the historic fur lands south of the Great Lakes to the United States, but by 1813 the North West Company had gained substantial control of the Pacific fur trade from the Columbia River to Alaska.

THE NORTH-WEST

Separated from the busy St. Lawrence basin by the bulk of the Canadian Shield was the North-West. This was a vast area that included the Hudson Bay basin, the prairies and thousands upon thousands of square miles of forest, muskeg and tundra stretching north and west up to and beyond the Arctic Circle. The few thousand inhabitants of the North-West were Indians and Métis. The Indians roamed the plains and the northern forests. The Métis, the half-breed descendants of Indian women and French or Scottish fur traders, lived mainly in an area of several thousand square miles surrounding the junction of the Red and the Assiniboine Rivers.

Some Métis were traders and some were farmers, but the principal Métis occupation was the buffalo hunt. The Hudson's Bay Company and the North West Company traded and hunted in the Assiniboia region and both companies were dependent upon the Métis of the region for supplies of pemmican. (Pemmican was made by pounding dried buffalo meat into powder and then mixing it with melted buffalo fat and wild berries. A highly concentrated, nourishing food, it was the staple provision carried by traders and explorers.) It was to this centre of the buffalo hunt and the pemmican trade that immigrant Highland Scots, sponsored by Lord Selkirk, came to farm in 1812.

Lord Selkirk. In Scotland, at the turn of the century, many Scottish landowners were anxious to convert their estates into profitable sheep ranges. To do this they found it necessary to evict the crofters (tenant farmers) who lived on their lands. Thomas Selkirk, fifth Earl of Selkirk, was concerned with the plight of the many hundreds of people who were forced to leave their small

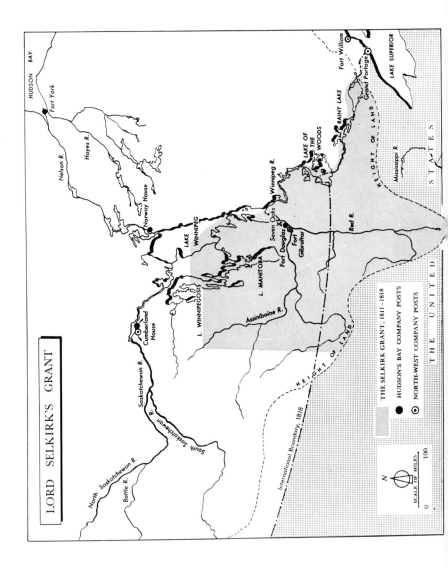

LORD SELKIRK'S GRANT

THE SELKIRK GRANT, 1811–1818

● HUDSON'S BAY COMPANY POSTS

◉ NORTH-WEST COMPANY POSTS

HUDSON BAY

Fort York

Nelson R.

Hayes R.

Norway House

LAKE WINNIPEG

L. MANITOBA

L. WINNIPEGOSIS

Cumberland House

Saskatchewan R.

South Saskatchewan R.

North Saskatchewan R.

Battle R.

Assiniboine R.

Fort Douglas

Fort Gibraltar

Seven Oaks

Winnipeg R.

Red R.

LAKE OF THE WOODS

RAINY LAKE

HEIGHT OF LAND

Grand Portage

Fort William

LAKE SUPERIOR

Mississippi R.

HEIGHT OF LAND

International Boundary, 1818

THE UNITED STATES

N

SCALE OF MILES

0   100

holdings. Between 1803 and 1809 he arranged passage for many Highland families to Prince Edward Island, and, later, to Baldoon, an area near Lake St. Clair in Upper Canada. The settlers he brought to Prince Edward Island prospered. The Baldoon settlement, however, was not successful because of malaria and intermittent floods.

The Selkirk Settlement. In 1809, Selkirk turned his attention to an idea he had once had of settling people on land in the Red River valley. As it happened, in 1810 a period of depression in the fur trade enabled Selkirk both to buy Hudson's Bay Company stock and to acquire ownership of thousands of square miles of H.B.C. land. His tract stretched from Lake Winnipeg south to the headwaters of the Mississippi and from the Lake of the Woods to the upper reaches of the Assiniboine River. This small empire came to be known as Assiniboia.

It soon became apparent that settlement in Assiniboia was going to cause trouble. The arrival of white settlers in 1812 (and 1813-1815) angered the Métis, who considered the Assiniboia region their own. The ultimate spread of farming would obviously interfere with the buffalo hunt and the pemmican trade. The colonists were bound to come into conflict with the North West Company since Lord Selkirk's grant lay directly (and by no means accidentally) across the Company's prime route into the North-West.

When Miles Macdonnell, Governor of Assiniboia, issued his "Pemmican Proclamation" forbidding food supplies to be taken out of Assiniboia (due to the low level of supplies in the colony) and then seized a quantity of pemmican belonging to the North West Company, the result was violence ("The Pemmican War"). Macdonnell was seized by Nor'Westers and sent to Montreal. Fort Douglas in the Red River settlement was attacked and some buildings burned. Fort Gibraltar, a Nor'Wester post, was destroyed. In 1816 an encounter—the "Massacre of Seven Oaks"—between a party of Selkirk settlers and a group of Métis and North West Company voyageurs resulted in the death of twenty settlers and a Company employee. One of the dead was Robert Semple, who had been appointed governor of Assiniboia in succession to Macdonnell.

Selkirk himself became personally involved. He journeyed to Red River with a hundred mercenaries and seized the North West Company's centre of Fort William on his way. For months thereafter, the British Colonial Office, the Hudson's Bay Company, the North West Company and Lord Selkirk were all involved in a con-

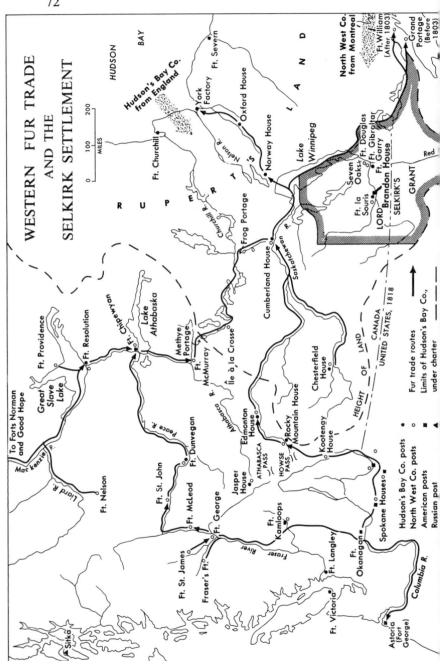

WESTERN FUR TRADE
AND THE
SELKIRK SETTLEMENT

HUDSON BAY

Hudson's Bay Co. from England

MILES
0   100   200

North West Co. from Montreal

Ft. William (After 1803)

Grand Portage (Before 1803)

Ft. Severn
York Factory
Oxford House
Ft. Churchill
Norway House
Lake Winnipeg

Seven Oaks
Ft. Douglas
Ft. Gibraltar
F. Garry
Ft. la Souris
Brandon House
LORD SELKIRK'S GRANT
Red

Nelson R.
Churchill R.
Frog Portage
Cumberland House
Saskatchewan R.

R U P E R T 'S   L A N D

Ft. Providence
Ft. Resolution
Great Slave Lake
To Forts Norman and Good Hope
Ft. Chipewyan
Lake Athabaska
Methye Portage
Ft. McMurray
Île à la Crosse
Athabasca R.

Mackenzie R.
Liard R.
Peace R.
Ft. Nelson
Ft. Dunvegan
Ft. St. John
Ft. McLeod
Ft. George
Ft. St. James
Fraser's Ft.
Fraser River

Jasper House
ATHABASCA PASS
Edmonton House
HOWSE PASS
Rocky Mountain House
Kootenay House
Chesterfield House

HEIGHT OF LAND
CANADA
UNITED STATES, 1818

Kamloops
Ft. Langley
Ft. Okanagan
Spokane House
Ft. Victoria
Astoria (Fort George)
Columbia R.
Sitka

Hudson's Bay Co. posts ●
North West Co. posts ○
American posts ■
Russian post ▲

Fur trade routes
Limits of Hudson's Bay Co., under charter

fused mass of charges and countercharges in the courts of Upper Canada. Selkirk finally lost his civil action and had to pay heavy damages. His health broken, he returned to Britain where he died in 1820.

Selkirk's death did not end the Red River colony. The settlement survived, prospered and grew. Its difficulties with the North West Company virtually disappeared after the Hudson Bay Company absorbed its rival in 1821 because the fur trade was now centred on Hudson Bay. (The "Pedlars from Quebec" simply could not compete in the long run with the much cheaper and much more direct sea route of the wealthy H.B.C.)

THE PROVINCES BEFORE 1812

Lower Canada. By the end of the eighteenth century it was clear that France and the French Canadians had finally parted company. At the beginning of the nineteenth century the French Canadians had emerged clearly as a separate people. The seigneurial class and the Roman Catholic clergy were still wary of the long-term effects of British representative government in the province, but were also strongly opposed to the Revolution in France. However, the philosophy of the Revolution did make itself felt to some extent among many *Québéçois*. Their discontent led to efforts to take executive control from the predominantly British ruling class. This struggle was to develop within a few decades into a conflict between the two "races."

Immigrants from the United States continued to enter British North America. Although the majority settled in Upper Canada, some 9,000 moved into that part of the Eastern Townships lying east of the Richelieu River, where, like most French Canadians, they led an agricultural existence. A few of the newcomers founded small businesses. Elsewhere in the province, the French-speaking population rose from 65,000 in 1763 to 335,000 in 1814.

Lower Canada's large population, situated as it was, on a natural highway and trade route, the St. Lawrence, was able to develop trade and commerce far beyond that of the other provinces. The fur trade still came down to St. Lawrence ports, notably to Quebec City and to Montreal. Enormous rafts of white pine were also floated down the Ottawa River to these centres for export to Britain. At Quebec City, the new centre of the timber trade, thousands of feet of sawn lumber were loaded annually on board ships bound for British ports.

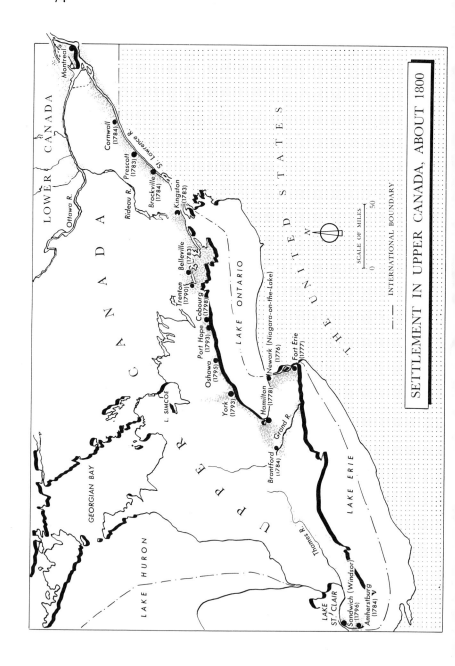

SETTLEMENT IN UPPER CANADA, ABOUT 1800

LOWER CANADA

Montreal

Ottawa R.

Cornwall
(1784)

St. Lawrence R.

Prescott
(1783)

Rideau R.

Brockville
(1784)

Kingston
(1783)

Belleville
(1783)

Trenton
(1790)

Cobourg
(1798)

Port Hope
(1793)

Oshawa
(1795)

York
(1793)

Hamilton
(1778)

Newark (Niagara-on-the-Lake)
(1776)

Fort Erie
(1777)

Branford
(1784)

Grand R.

LAKE ONTARIO

THE UNITED STATES

N

SCALE OF MILES

0   50

INTERNATIONAL BOUNDARY

C A N A D A

U P P E R

L. SIMCOE

GEORGIAN BAY

LAKE HURON

Thames R.

LAKE ERIE

LAKE
ST. CLAIR

Sandwich (Windsor)
(1796)

Amherstburg
(1784)

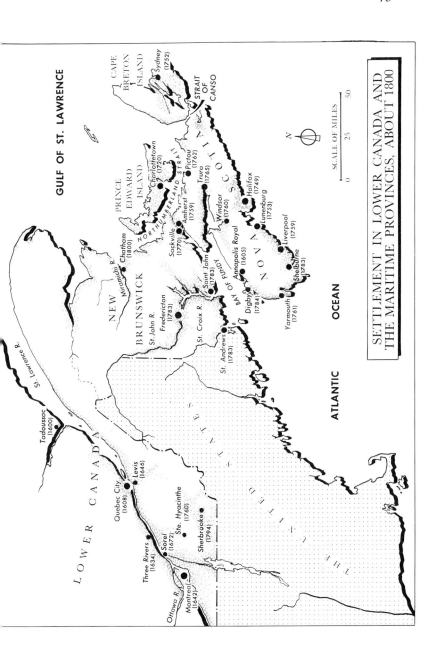

GULF OF ST. LAWRENCE

CAPE BRETON ISLAND

Sydney (1752)

STRAIT OF CANSO

PRINCE EDWARD ISLAND

Charlottetown (1720)

Pictou (1767)

Truro (1765)

N O V A   S C O T I A

Halifax (1749)

Windsor (1760)

Lunenburg (1753)

Amherst (1759)

Liverpool (1759)

Sackville (1770)

Annapolis Royal (1605)

Shelburne (1783)

Saint John (1783)

Digby (1784)

Yarmouth (1761)

Chatham (1800)

Miramichi R.

NORTHUMBERLAND STRAIT

BAY OF FUNDY

NEW BRUNSWICK

Fredericton (1783)

St. John R.

St. Croix R.

St. Andrews (1783)

ATLANTIC OCEAN

St. Lawrence R.

Tadoussac (1600)

LOWER CANADA

Quebec City (1608)

Lévis (1646)

Three Rivers (1634)

Sorel (1672)

Ste. Hyacinthe (1760)

Sherbrooke (1794)

Ottawa R.

Montreal (1642)

THE UNITED STATES

SETTLEMENT IN LOWER CANADA AND
THE MARITIME PROVINCES, ABOUT 1800

N

SCALE OF MILES

0   25   50

The Atlantic Coast. Newfoundland remained a fishing colony. Farming was impossible in its rocky, forested interior or along its bare, wind-swept shores. Cape Breton Island, too, was a rock-strewn, rolling countryside that drove its inhabitants to the sea to fish for a living. There was some further immigration to Prince Edward Island, Nova Scotia, and New Brunswick following the Loyalist influx at the end of the War of Independence. Prince Edward Island's rich, red soil made agriculture the principal occupation. In Nova Scotia and New Brunswick the main industries were fishing, lumbering, ship-building and maritime trade. (Preferential trade agreements between British North America and the West Indies effectively excluded trade with the United States.) With its enormous forests, New Brunswick in particular benefited from the timber trade and ship building. At this time, New Brunswick white pine was in great demand in Britain for ships' masts and spars.

Upper Canada. By far the greatest number of immigrants from the United States journeyed to Upper Canada. Out of a population of 94,000 in 1813, it has been estimated that some eighty per cent were of American origin, and only one-quarter of these of Loyalist stock. A steady stream of English, Irish, Scots, Dutch and German immigrants became quite marked after 1800.

The influx of Americans was destined to produce considerable discontent. The immigrants were markedly individualistic and independent; many of them were avowed republicans. They protested against the many minor restrictions which remained on the old colonial system of government and urged the need for new roads, schools and churches.

Upper Canada was still a frontier province, depending principally for its living upon exporting its wheat and the products of mixed farming. It was a land of small scattered farms, few towns of any appreciable size, and little commercial or industrial development. Its settlers, however, were energetic and anxious to improve themselves and their province.

THE WAR OF 1812

Napoleon's Blockades. When Napoleon Bonaparte's navy was practically destroyed at the battle of Trafalgar (1805), he had to resort to other means to crush the power of Britain. In an effort to destroy her commercial foundations he launched his "Continental

Policy." In 1806 and 1807, he effectively sealed off the whole of Europe from trade with Britain. Britain retaliated with Parliamentary orders-in-council which virtually closed the continent to neutral commerce. In an effort to uphold the commercial rights of neutrals, the United States government responded by forbidding American trade with foreign countries. This policy was continued by the Non-Intercourse Act of 1809, which was imposed at different times against both Great Britain and France. It proved to be an ineffective protest against Britain's orders-in-council and led to division of opinion within the United States.

The embargoes of both France and the United States effectively created a British North American economy. Since American trade with the West Indies was severed, the Canadas and the Maritimes became for the first time the real source of West Indian supply. At the same time, when Russia joined the Continental Blockade, Britain was faced with an acute shortage of timber. The British government immediately raised the colonial preference on timber and encouraged firms which began to trade with British North America. At a single stroke, one of British North America's staple products had become a vital raw material.

Causes of War. The reasons for President Madison's declaration of war against Britain in 1812 are difficult to explain but they included a desire to uphold the freedom of the seas and the goal of extending the United States' empire to the west.

At sea, British warships had been searching American vessels for British deserters, and there had been a number of cases in which Americans had been forced to serve on British ships against their will. (In 1807, a British frigate, the *Leopard,* had attacked an American warship, the *Chesapeake,* killing and wounding some of her crew and making off with five men suspected of being deserters from the Royal Navy.)

In the West, the Shawnee chieftain, Tecumseh, succeeded in inducing many tribes to revolt against American intrusion into Indian territory until he was defeated in 1811 at Tippecanoe by an American force. The United States assumed that the British were behind the uprising. From the frontier areas an anti-British party, the "War Hawks," pressed for war. The "War Hawks" hoped not only to end the Indian menace, but to obtain control of the fur trade and to annex British North America.

The United States' declaration of war was well timed. Napoleon was on his way into Russia, and Britain had gathered almost all her forces in Europe. There were fewer than 5,000 regular British soldiers in British North America to defend a border that stretched for a thousand miles south and west of Montreal. From Britain's point of view, there was a largely Loyalist population that could certainly be depended upon; but the French Canadians and the fringe of American immigrants in Lower Canada were considered potential trouble-makers. In Upper Canada the original Loyalist groups had been submerged by more recent immigrants from the United States, whose loyalty was far from certain. On the other hand, many New Englanders refused to fight and continued to trade and maintain friendly contacts with Nova Scotians and New Brunswickers. The United States suffered another disadvantage as well, for she had reduced her regular army and had to depend on forces composed of poorly trained militiamen and volunteers.

The Invasions of the Canadas.   If United States' forces had followed the line of the Richelieu River and had taken Montreal, it is unlikely that the Canadas could have survived. Successive American generals, however, concentrated their attacks on other points. One, General Hull, was easily defeated at Detroit by Isaac Brock, Lieutenant-Governor of Upper Canada. Following this victory, Brock marched his small force, composed of regulars, some militia and some Indian allies, back to Niagara. There he beat back another American invasion at the battle of Queenston Heights. (Brock himself was killed in this encounter.) The British also attacked and captured the post of Michilimackinac in 1812.

The following year, an American force attacked and burned part of the town of York (Toronto). The British were defeated at Put-in-Bay on Lake Erie, and again on land at the battle of the Thames near Moraviantown (where Tecumseh was killed). But the effects of these defeats were purely local. A two-pronged American attack on Montreal late in the season was more serious but it fizzled out. At Chateauguay an American force was repulsed by British regulars and French Canadian militia, and at Crysler's Farm British soldiers and Upper Canada militia turned the enemy back.

In 1814, the Americans launched a final attack on the Niagara peninsula as a preliminary to moving on to Kingston and Montreal. They won an engagement at Chippawa but, failing to secure naval support, were unable to achieve a decisive victory at the battle of Lundy's Lane and were forced back to Fort Erie. Meanwhile, Napoleon Bonaparte had been defeated in Europe, and Britain was able to send troops to British North America. A British raid on

79

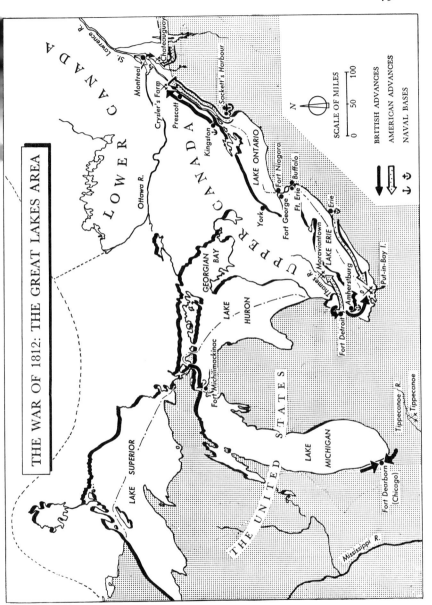

THE WAR OF 1812: THE GREAT LAKES AREA

CANADA

St. Lawrence R.

LOWER CANADA

Ottawa R.

Chateauguay

Montreal

Crysler's Farm

Prescott

Sackett's Harbour

Kingston

UPPER CANADA

LAKE ONTARIO

Fort Niagara

Buffalo I.

Fort Erie

York

Fort George

Ft. Erie

Erie

GEORGIAN BAY

Moraviantown

LAKE ERIE

Put-in-Bay I.

LAKE HURON

Thames R.

Amherstburg

Fort Detroit

Fort Michilimackinac

LAKE SUPERIOR

THE UNITED STATES

LAKE MICHIGAN

Fort Dearborn (Chicago)

Tippecanoe R.

Tippecanoe

Mississippi R.

N

SCALE OF MILES

0   50   100

BRITISH ADVANCES

AMERICAN ADVANCES

NAVAL BASES

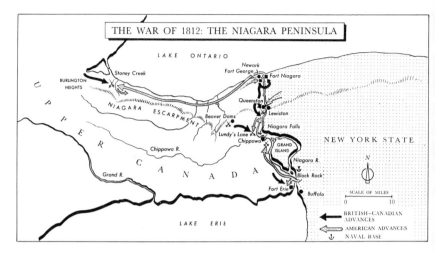

THE WAR OF 1812: THE NIAGARA PENINSULA

Washington was a success and, in the north, a British force took over the whole of Maine east of the Penobscot River. Before news arrived in North America that a peace treaty had been signed, one final bloody battle occurred in which the British failed dismally in an attack on New Orleans.

On Lake Champlain, British and American naval forces had remained evenly matched throughout the war. When Sir George Prevost, Governor of Lower Canada, marched 7,000 of the Duke of Wellington's peninsula veterans down to the American base at Plattsburg, he had to march them back again without striking a blow because the tiny British flotilla supporting him on the lake had been overcome.

The British Navy.   It was the power of the Royal Navy that decided the outcome of the war. On the Atlantic, the small American navy could only mount isolated attacks on single vessels. It concentrated, as did privateers, on capturing merchant ships. (Nova Scotians and New Brunswickers copied this example and sent out privateers to capture American ships.) Little by little, the Royal Navy hunted down American frigates, privateers and merchantmen, and systematically imposed a blockade that extended the full length of the American coast. By 1814, the United States was virtually on the defensive.

Treaty of Ghent 1814.   Both sides were weary of the inconclusive conflict and were happy to bring it to an end in 1814 by the

Treaty of Ghent. All territory taken in the war was restored. Commissions were appointed to settle outstanding problems, and as a result negotiations dragged on over a period of four years. The British finally agreed to leave the boundary as it had been determined in 1783. Under the Convention of 1818, it was agreed that the 49th parallel would be the boundary from the Lake of the Woods to the Rockies. The disputed territory on the Pacific Coast was to be jointly occupied by both countries for ten years (later extended to 1846). American fishermen were to be allowed ashore in British North American bays and harbours only for fuel, shelter and repairs. They were definitely excluded from the inshore fisheries, except those of Labrador and of southern and western Newfoundland.

The Rush-Bagot Agreement, 1817. After the war, American naval forces on the Great Lakes ceased to exist practically overnight, but the British kept a number of small ships in commission. In 1817, the United States' Secretary of State, Richard Rush, and the British minister in Washington, Sir Charles Bagot, signed a formal agreement to dismantle all warships and allow only one small patrol vessel per nation on Lakes Champlain and Ontario, and a total of two vessels per nation on the upper lakes.

Effects of the War. The peace negotiations were hammered out in the interests of Anglo-American friendship. Maine was handed back to the United States, although the Maine-New Brunswick boundary was left undefined, to be the object of negotiation, arbitration and local violence until 1842. Forts Niagara, Detroit and Michilimackinac were declared American possessions. A large portion of the Great Lakes region was confirmed as American territory. British North America was driven back to subsist upon the fur trade and a primitive economy and was now penned behind an international border that had been finally drawn and firmly fixed. As a Canadian historian has remarked, "All that British North America gained from the War of 1812 was simply the right to remain British."

BIBLIOGRAPHY

CAMPBELL, M. W. *McGillivray, Lord of the Northwest.* Clarke, Irwin, 1962.

CAMPBELL, M. W. *The Saskatchewan.* Clarke, Irwin, 1965.

COLES, H. L. *The War of 1812.* University of Chicago, 1965.

CRAIG, G. R. *Upper Canada, 1784-1841*. Canadian Centenary Series, Vol VII. McClelland and Stewart, 1964.

DANIELS, R. *Alexander Mackenzie and the North West*. Faber and Faber, 1969.

DRUCKER, PHILIP. *Cultures of the North Pacific Coast*. Science Research Associates, 1965.

GRAY, J. M. *Lord Selkirk of Red River*. Macmillan, 1963.

HAIG-BROWN, RODERICK. *The Whale People*. Collins, 1962.

HUTCHISON, B. *The Fraser*. Clarke, Irwin, 1965.

KAYE, LAMB, W. (ed.). *Simon Fraser—Letters and Journals 1806-08*. Macmillan, 1960.

MCKAY, DOUGLAS. *The Honourable Company*. McClelland and Stewart, 1949.

MACKENZIE, A. *Voyage to the Pacific in 1793*. Citadel Press, 1967.

MCLOUGHLIN, FLORENCE. *The First Lady of Upper Canada*. Burns and MacEachern, 1968.

MASON, P. P. (ed.). *After Tippecanoe*. Ryerson, 1963.

RICH, E. E. *The Fur Trade and the Northwest to 1857*. Canadian Centenary Series, Vol. XI. McClelland and Stewart, 1967.

SEWID, J. *Guests Never Leave Hungry*. University of Yale, 1969.

SHEPPE, WALTER. *The First Man West*. Cambridge University, 1962.

WOLCOTT, H. F. *A Kwakiutl Village and School*. Holt, Rinehart and Winston, 1967.

WOOD, E. A. *The Mapmaker*. Macmillan, 1962.

ZASLOW, M. (ed.). *The Defended Border*. Macmillan, 1964.

6

British North America, 1815-1850

British Influx. For several decades after 1815 a large number of immigrants came to British North America. These newcomers were almost exclusively from the British Isles, where unemployment and distress, aggravated principally by the effects of the Industrial Revolution, encouraged emigration. In 1828, only about 12,000 persons arrived, but in 1830 the number of immigrants had doubled. Between 1815 and 1842, 560,000 people came from the British Isles. The "hungry forties," and especially the terrible Irish potato famine of 1846 further increased British immigration. In the nine years between 1842 and 1851, 433,000 people arrived. Unfortunately, cheap land and high wages in the United States also attracted immigrants and about 50 per cent of the newcomers moved on. The population of British North America in 1820 was 750,000, but by 1851 it had leaped to 2,436,000. Of this number 70 per cent lived in the St. Lawrence-Great Lakes region.

The Maritimes. In Nova Scotia, the population which included Acadians, Loyalists, pre-Revolutionary Yankees and a small pocket of Germans at Lunenburg increased after 1815 by the arrival of 40,000 Catholic and Presbyterian Highland Scots. By the time immigration slackened off in 1838, the province had a population of nearly 200,000.

New Brunswick probably had the greatest change. This Loyalist province received some 5,000 to 6,000 immigrants a year after 1815. The 1840's and early 1850's brought many "famine Irish" and semi-destitute English and Scots.

The Canadas.   To this area came the greatest number of immigrants. In particular there was a tremendous influx in the late 1840's and early 1850's of nearly half a million Irish men and women.

In Lower Canada the British held more than two-thirds of the seigneurial rights and were unwilling to grant land to settlers. Unfortunately, the unclaimed land was often practically impossible to reach because of lack of roads and transport. A few British immigrants did pioneer settlements in previously unsettled parts of the province, but the majority moved on to Upper Canada, leaving French-Canadian life comparatively undisturbed.

Large numbers of British, German, Dutch and American immigrants settled in Upper Canada. Here the population reached 150,000 in 1824, and soared to almost 400,000 by 1838. Philanthropists and the activities of colonizing companies were responsible for much of the immigration. (Lord Selkirk's endeavours have been noted in Chapter 5.)

The ambitious and aggressive Colonel Thomas Talbot obtained a grant of 5,000 acres on the north shore of Lake Erie at the beginning of the century and worked heroically, if dictatorially, in the cause of settlement. For each settler he placed on a farm, Talbot received another 200 acres of land. He directed the settlement of half a million acres, organized schools (by 1830 there were twenty schools on his land) and in 1809 began to build the Talbot Road that was intended to run from the Detroit River in the west to York in the east. By 1837, there were 50,000 people on his lands.

In 1823, John Galt, a business-minded poet and novelist from Ayrshire, Scotland, founded the Canada Company, with shares held by some of the ablest businessmen in London. By 1824 he had helped to settle some 2,000 people on the Huron Tract (one million acres north of the Talbot Settlement and bordering the southeastern shore of Lake Huron) in and around such prospering communities as Guelph and Goderich. The Company paid half the cost of improvements such as schools, roads and bridges constructed by settlers, and Galt organized the construction of the Huron Road, which ran for most of its length through Canada Company land. By 1832, over 1,000 people lived in the Guelph area. There were mills, taverns, stores and churches, and the settlement grew as fast as the Company extended its land holdings.

The British America Land Company, directed by Galt's son, Alexander Tilloch Galt, received over 800,000 acres in Lower Canada in 1833. The settlement of the Eastern Townships made the province more than one-fifth English-speaking, a great change from the one-fiftieth of 1791.

PIONEER LIFE AND PROGRESS

Early immigrants often lived in tiny isolated clearings far from their nearest neighbours. There were few roads, no regular system of transportation, no regular mail service, few newspapers and often no schools, churches or doctors within several days' journey. First homes were often little more than a log shanty with the simplest wood furniture and with oiled paper in the one window. As conditions improved, houses were built of stone, clapboard, stucco, or brick, with several rooms, glassed windows and better furniture. By the 1830's brick homes, stores and other buildings were becoming quite common in the villages and towns of Upper Canada.

The Land. The virgin forests of British North America were usually viewed simply as something to combat, rather than as a source of income. As a result, thousands of valuable trees were cut down and burned in order to clear the land for farming. The ashes of hardwood timber, however, had a commercial value—they could be sold as potash for use in the manufacture of soap. Many centres in Upper Canada had potash works, and potash was shipped in large quantities to Great Britain.

In the lower Great Lakes-St. Lawrence area, farming remained the most important industry. Farming methods were still comparatively primitive, especially in Lower Canada, where the habitant continued to work his long narrow strips of land. Such food as a farmer grew, he grew for family consumption; only a few farmers near towns were able either to produce a surplus or find a market within reach.

Only gradually did the production of wheat reach a point where the export of grain to Britain became possible. Often the farmer had to thresh and winnow his own grain, but most settlers transported their wheat to a nearby grist-mill to be ground. These mills were powered by wind, water or oxen; not until the middle of the nineteenth century did steam mills come into use.

The Timber Trade. During the French period in North America, the Richelieu River district had been the main lumbering area. However, lumbering operations gradually shifted (particularly after the arrival of the United Empire Loyalists) to the St. John River area of New Brunswick, the Ottawa River Valley, the upper reaches of the St. Lawrence and the eastern end of Lake Ontario.

Lumbering was often found to be more profitable than farming (with subsequent ill effects on the settlements). There was a steady demand in the main ports for squared timber, ships' masts, planks and barrel staves. In 1807 the first timber raft was floated down the Ottawa River to the St. Lawrence and thence to Quebec City, a journey of thirty-five days. Sixteen years later there were more than 300 rafts making the journey annually.

Lumbering began in Upper Canada as a family affair, but soon developed into large-scale operations involving a number of employees. The timber trade encouraged the establishment of so many small sawmills that by 1845 Upper Canada alone had two thousand.

Growing shipbuilding industries drew on the vast supplies of timber in the Maritimes, and as trade with Great Britain, the West Indies and the Mediterranean expanded after the War of 1812, Nova Scotia built up her merchant fleet until it became one of the largest in the world.

Religion.   While the French in Lower Canada were served by a large number of Roman Catholic priests, the English of Upper Canada had few clergymen to whom they could turn. In 1791, there were only two Protestant clergymen in the whole province, both of whom (one Anglican, one Presbyterian) were United Empire Loyalists.

The Anglican Church was not legally the established Church in Upper Canada. Nevertheless, it enjoyed many of the privileges of such a position. For example, all important government posts were held by Anglicans, as was the case in England. The Anglican Church also claimed sole right over the Clergy Reserves established under the Constitutional Act of 1791. These two factors were major sources of discontent among the numerous other Protestant denominations. In 1822, the Presbyterians laid claim to a share of the income from the Reserves on the grounds that the Presbyterian Church of Scotland had been recognized as an established Church in the Act of Union of 1707. Later a few other denominations claimed a share.

In spite of, or because of, its privileges, the Anglican Church displayed little zeal or energy in comparison with other Protestant denominations. The Anglican clergy tended to avoid the discomforts of the bush and seldom went the rounds of their rural parishioners. The Methodist circuit riders, on the other hand, travelled around to out of the way communities and gave religious leadership and comfort to many a backwoods pioneer community and family. The movement spread widely. Indeed, the Methodist Church became, in 1828, the first autonomous Canadian church.

Education. Few persons in Europe and North America at the beginning of the nineteenth century considered that the government was responsible for education; this responsibility lay in the hands of the church and the home. In British North America there was no compulsory school attendance, no means of training teachers (who were, with certain notable exceptions, itinerant, ill-educated misfits who had failed in other occupations) and no taxation with which to support schools. The only local elementary or common schools that existed had been established by the people themselves, without government support. Wealthier children were taught at home by private tutors, or in the district grammar schools. It was not until 1816 that small government grants were given to local common schools in the province. However, attendance at that time was not compulsory and teaching did not improve for many years. Both Loyalists and later American immigrants were active in their demands for some kind of organized educational system in Upper Canada.

In Lower Canada, education had suffered from the suppression of the Jesuit Order in 1773 and did not improve until its return in 1842. During the intervening years the French Canadians opposed strongly the English move toward secular education. They saw it as another attempt to undermine their position in the province.

Universities. The churches were the first promoters of higher education. The first university, the Anglican King's College of Nova Scotia, was founded in 1802 at Windsor, and was followed by the Baptist academies of Pictou and Horton (the latter became Acadia University), and in 1818 by the non-sectarian Dalhousie University. The Anglican King's College of New Brunswick was founded in 1829. In Upper Canada the Anglicans established King's College (later the University of Toronto), the Methodists founded Victoria College (later Victoria University), and the Presbyterians, Queen's College in Kingston. In Lower Canada, lack of racial agreement retarded development, and although McGill University was founded in 1821 it was virtually undeveloped until the middle of the century. The Roman Catholic college of Laval in Quebec City was not founded until 1852.

DEVELOPMENTS IN TRANSPORT

Roads. Lack of efficient methods of transport was one of the major obstacles to settlement and development in the early part of the nineteenth century. In 1802, there was no adequate highway in the whole of British North America, and the immigrants, many of whom had settled in remote areas, were unable either to spend time building roads or to pay taxes for this purpose. In the late eighteenth century, Col. John Graves Simcoe had constructed rough military roads, but it was left to such men as Colonel Talbot and John Galt to initiate the first proper highways to serve settlers. By 1816, Montreal and Kingston were connected; the following year this link was extended to York, and stagecoaches appeared. By 1827, it was possible (although extremely uncomfortable) to travel all the way from Halifax, Nova Scotia, to Amherstburg on the Detroit River. But it was not until the 1830's and 1840's that the mud and corduroy roads (and the stagecoaches themselves) were improved sufficiently to make road travel even tolerable.

Steamships. Just as the fleets of canoes and the French bâteaux had given way to the larger York and Durham boats as transport boats on the major rivers and lakes, so these vessels gave way to the steamship. The year 1807 saw the first steamship in North America, the *Clermont,* built on the Hudson. Two years later, John Molson's paddle-wheeler, the *Accommodation,* appeared on the St. Lawrence. By 1818, six more powerful craft were plying regularly between Montreal and Quebec City. In 1816 the *Frontenac* was built on Lake Ontario. It was the first steamship on the Great Lakes. By the 1830's steamship service was in full swing, speeding up communications, and soon canals were needed to extend the service. In 1833, the *Royal William,* built at Quebec City, became the first ship to cross the Atlantic entirely on steam power. (It was the first of Samuel Cunard's great Cunard Steamship Company fleet.) By 1845 iron vessels were coming into use.

Canals. As the province of Upper Canada developed and water transportation became more efficient, the question of canals, especially on the St. Lawrence, became ever more urgent. It was vital to Upper Canada's economic development to have an efficient canal system linking her with the Atlantic. After the absorption of the North West Company by the Hudson's Bay Company in 1821 had removed the fur trade from the St. Lawrence, merchants and traders in both provinces saw a canal system as a main trade route to and from the American midwest. However, the political separation of Upper Canada and Lower Canada placed obstacles in the way. French Canadians viewed the building of a canal system as a move to further the prosperity of the Montreal and Upper Canadian merchants at their expense and they refused to sanction the project. Nevertheless, Lower Canada did complete the shallow Lachine Canal in 1825, while the far less prosperous upper province began work on one at Cornwall and in 1829 opened the Welland Canal across the Niagara Peninsula. In 1832, British army units completed the Rideau Canal from Bytown (the present-day Ottawa) to Kingston on Lake Ontario but its purpose was basically military.

The Long Sault Rapids of the St. Lawrence, a great barrier to shipping, were not by-passed until 1843, when the government of Upper Canada completed fourteen years of off-and-on construction. In the meantime, the Americans had built a network of hundreds of miles of inland waterways and in 1825 had opened the Erie Canal. This provided, for the first time, a direct waterway from the American midwest to the Atlantic and thus destroyed the two Canadas' hope of serving that area by way of the St. Lawrence.

ECONOMIC DEVELOPMENTS

Exports.   Throughout most of the nineteenth century, British North America depended largely on the export of trade staples—and on their export to imperial markets. In spite of agitation to obtain more local autonomy, most of British North America recognized fully the advantages of the old colonial system with its preferential markets and financial aid. As a result the colonies were reluctant to sever the British connection. Lumber in various forms (masts, barrel staves, etc.) remained the chief export until the middle of the century, when wheat from Upper Canada took first place. Other exports included flour, potash, furs and fish. As time went on, the ship-building industry and the carrying trade grew to the point where British North America had one of the largest merchant fleets in the world. This increased trade resulted in the expansion of business firms, improved business methods and the opening of banks.

Manufacturing.   Towns grew rapidly in the provinces. Montreal and Quebec City were large, busy commercial centres. York (renamed Toronto in 1834), which had been a mere village in 1812, became the commercial as well as the administrative centre of

Upper Canada. In the Maritimes, Halifax was a flourishing seaport and garrison town, while Saint John was the centre of trade commerce in New Brunswick.

The earliest secondary industries in British North America included flour mills, breweries, shipyards, and a small iron foundry near Three Rivers, which had been operating since the eighteenth century. By the 1830's there was a paper mill in Upper Canada at Belleville, and at York there was the York Foundry and Steam Engine Manufactory and a large firm of carriage makers. In the industrially more advanced Lower Canada, paper, leather, glass, rope, stoves, and steam-engines were being produced.

THE END OF THE OLD COLONIAL SYSTEM

Britain's Attitude Toward Her Colonies. In their plans for developing the St. Lawrence route to the midwest, the Canadian merchants and traders had hoped to be able to ensure free markets in the United States and protected ones in Europe. These hopes were not fulfilled. While the United States was attempting to establish new protective measures, the rise of capitalism in Britain was demanding an end to the mercantile system and encouraging the establishment of free trade. Many political economists had for years denounced the Empire as a "millstone" and praised the moral aspects of free trade. Britain's expenses in British North America were indeed still considerable. Quite apart from preferential trade agreements, she was financially responsible for the defence of the colonies, which involved a standing army and the construction of forts, strategic canals and roads.

Reform of the Navigation Acts. As competition from the United States grew stronger, the British Navigation Acts came under constant attack. Between 1822 and 1826 reforms in the British Navigation Acts brought about the repeal of certain colonial trade privileges.

In 1845 the Irish potato crop failed, and the English wheat crop was disappointing. The need for cheap bread was desperate, and in 1846 the British government repealed the Corn Laws. Thus the old preference rates that had applied to colonial grains were eliminated. The preference on colonial timber had already been cut back by 50 per cent; it was now further reduced and was to vanish by 1860. The Navigation Acts were finally repealed in 1849, thus permitting ships of other nations to enter British North American ports and compete in the carrying trade.

THE FIGHT FOR RESPONSIBLE GOVERNMENT

In the British North America of the early 1800's, the head of government in each colony and the representative of the British monarch was an official appointed by the imperial government. In Newfoundland and in Lower Canada he was known as the Governor, while in each of the other colonies he was called the Lieutenant-Governor. (The Governor of Lower Canada was also the senior appointee or Governor-in-Chief for all of British North America.) Within their colonies governors and lieutenant-governors controlled administrative appointments, the military forces and legislation. They could rule upon such matters as land grants and banking without consulting the elected representatives of the people, and they could suspend and dissolve the elected assemblies at will. These officials were responsible solely to the British government.

The Executive Council. The governor, who frequently held his post for a very short time, turned for advice and assistance to the Executive Council. The members of this council were directly responsible for their actions to the governor (for he had personally appointed them), not to the elected representatives of the people in the legislative assembly. Thus, there was no way of imposing popular will on the highest, most powerful and influential ruling body in the colony. The American colonies had rebelled under this system of government. In England, a solution had slowly been developing; in answer to the demand for responsible government, a cabinet composed of advisers and leaders was formed from the party holding a majority of the seats in an elected assembly. These cabinet members could have seats in either the House of Commons or the House of Lords.

In British North America powerful local groups of Tories had formed in the aftermath of the War of 1812 in order to keep the government in their own hands. They favoured the appointment method of selecting members to the Executive Council because it was through the Executive Council that they exercised power. In Upper Canada these groups were given the name "Family Compact" (in Lower Canada *Château Clique*)—an unflattering reference to their tendency to promote the political and financial welfare of close relatives and friends.

The Compacts were essentially urban groups. They gained control of such areas as political appointments, Crown land grants (in provinces that were primarily rural), banking, business and education. The Compacts also had the power (via the executive councils) to authorize laws, regardless of the recommendations of legislative assemblies. They believed that they were working in the best interests of the mother country, of the Anglican religion, and of the colonies. However, they failed to grasp the idea of democratic government (toward which Britain herself was slowly moving) and viewed it with distaste and dislike as just another Americanism.

It became increasingly obvious that the abuses, patronage and unpopular policies of local governments would lead to demands for improvement. Many of the colonists had already experienced the benefits of democratic government in the United States, and a further spur to action was the Reform Act of 1832 in Britain which gave the middle classes the right to elect representatives to Parliament who would then be responsible to their electors. The period from 1820 to 1849 comprises the story of the Reformers' struggle in British North America to establish a form of government that would be responsible to the people for its actions and capable of passing laws desired by the people.

The Maritimes.   There were perhaps fewer abuses in the governments of the Maritimes than in Upper and Lower Canada. However, the upper class society in the Loyalist, conservative stronghold of Halifax allowed the Assembly little effective authority and attempted to impose cultural and religious standards upon the Nova Scotian community. This society included merchants, military officers, naval officers and politicians; one of its most brilliant men was Thomas Chandler Haliburton—lawyer, Assembly member, judge and author of the immensely humorous and satirical "Sam Slick" series. "Responsible government," wrote Haliburton, "is responsible nonsense."

In Nova Scotia, opponents of the government found a leader in the hot-tempered newspaperman, Joseph Howe. He earned the anger of the ruling class and the support of the people of Nova Scotia through his witty, penetrating articles in his paper, the *Novascotian*. In 1835, he defended himself against a charge of libel by the government, and was triumphantly acquitted. The following year Howe was elected as a Reform member to the Assembly and was soon recognized as the spokesman of the Reform party in the province.

Unrest in the Canadas.   In Upper Canada, supposed abuses in government and popular discontent were widespread. The Family

Compact, the Clergy Reserves, inadequate roads, Crown grants of land to a favoured few, the lack of popular education and attempts to bring all education under Anglican control, the prestige and power of the Anglican Church, all were features that gave rise to grievances and ever increasing demands for reform. There was also a loss of confidence in the law courts, arising largely from the trial and banishment of Robert Gourlay. He had been a land agent who had organized a convention which seemed to cast doubt upon official land grant policies.

In Lower Canada there was superficially the same struggle, but it was a racial and religious struggle at the same time. The rural French-Canadian majority in the Assembly resented the power of the urban, English Château Clique in the executive. In both Upper and Lower Canada the basic struggle was that of the small farmer and town worker against powerful individuals, vested interests or cliques. Whereas in Upper Canada, the struggle was motivated by a desire for political reform, in Lower Canada the political attacks upon banks, land companies and English merchants were inspired by a conservative attitude which opposed all change and progress because it threatened old institutions and old ways. French Canada had remained unaffected by the American and French revolutions.

The British proposal in 1822 for a united legislature for the two Canadas (while retaining separate administrations) caused a mighty storm of protest in French Canada. The proposal was designed, (1) to help the growing English minority in Lower Canada, (2) to solve the revenue disputes between the two provinces (Upper Canada felt that Lower Canada was benefiting unfairly from revenue from international trade, most of which came into the country via Montreal or Quebec), and (3) to anglicize Lower Canada.

The Rebellion in Lower Canada. The leader of the French-speaking majority in the Legislative Assembly of Lower Canada was the eloquent but immoderate Louis Joseph Papineau. After a series of clashes between executive and assembly, Papineau issued *The Ninety-Two Resolutions* in 1834. This was a list of grievances, some of which were so extreme that he lost the support of many moderates as well as the leaders of the Roman Catholic Church.

By 1837, government in the province had ground to a virtual standstill. The British government passed *The Ten Resolutions,* which refused to allow an elected legislative council and empowered the executive to raise and spend government monies without the consent of the Assembly. That same year, the wheat crop failed, exports declined, and unemployment spread.

Papineau and his *Patriote* followers felt that armed rebellion was the only course left to them, and the rebellion began accidentally in a Montreal street brawl in November. Papineau left the city the next day, and warrants that went out for his arrest sparked further violence. On November 22, a small British force attacked half-armed, untrained *Patriotes* at St. Denis on the Richelieu River but were forced to retreat. However, two days later, at St. Charles, the rebels were defeated and Papineau fled to the United States. Further minor clashes occurred, and in December there was a fierce battle at St. Eustache, northwest of Montreal. The rebellion was disorganized and quickly fizzled out, but it caused a considerable amount of bloodshed, disrupted trade on the St. Lawrence, caused widespread emigration to the United States and demonstrated to the British government that the reform movement would have to be taken seriously.

Rebellion in Upper Canada.   In 1826, the many Loyalist Methodists in Upper Canada were provoked into supporting the Reformers' cause. At that time the Anglican Archdeacon John Strachan, an eminent member of the Family Compact, had charged them with disloyalty to the Crown. However, they later broke away from the more radical policies of the Reformers under the leadership of Egerton Ryerson, the Methodist teacher and preacher. The leader of the moderate Reformers was Robert Baldwin, a man noted for his political honesty and moderation and a champion of responsible government. Under the moderates the party gradually gained strength until, by 1828, it held a majority in the Assembly.

By the mid-1830's the Reformers were being spurred on by a radical leader three times expelled from the Assembly by the Compact, the fiery William Lyon Mackenzie. He was owner and editor of the *Colonial Advocate*, in which he published biting attacks on the Family Compact. In 1835, Mackenzie brought in *The Seventh Report on Grievances,* which listed the demands of the extreme Reformers. One important demand was that the Legislative Council be elected by the people. In 1836 the new lieutenant-governor, Sir Francis Bond Head, who had persuaded the moderate leaders (including Baldwin) to join him for a short period, dissolved the Assembly because it refused to vote government monies, and then led the Tory party to victory in the following general election.

Mackenzie, however, enraged by the British government's *Ten Resolutions*, and encouraged by reports of rebellion in Lower Canada, issued his *Declaration of Toronto Reformers*. In this declaration he set out the justifications for the use of force in the name of "social democracy . . . and political democracy." Mackenzie, like Papineau in Lower Canada, advocated American-type popular institutions rather than the British model of the moderates.

The rebellion in Upper Canada was just as poorly planned and managed as that in Lower Canada. On December 7, the lieutenant-governor finally decided to send a militia force against the mustering rebels, and on Yonge Street north of Toronto (close to the present-day site of Maple Leaf Gardens) a band of ill-organized rebels was routed. Mackenzie fled to the United States where he roused support for his cause. Patriot Societies and "Hunters' Lodges" were organized along the border to aid the rebel cause. Half a dozen raids on Canadian soil were conducted in 1838. Mackenzie was finally arrested by the United States' government and imprisoned for a brief period. (He later received a pardon and returned to Upper Canada to be re-elected to the Assembly.) In the meantime, the rebellion in Upper Canada faded out just as its counterpart in Lower Canada had done.

LORD DURHAM

Thoroughly disturbed by the rebellions in Upper and Lower Canada, the British government appointed Lord Durham as governor-general of the five provinces in 1838. He was given orders to investigate the causes of the recent disturbances, to win the support of the people in British North America, to improve relations with the United States and to recommend improvements in colonial government.

John George Lambton, first Earl of Durham was liberal in outlook, a superb orator and possessed a fiery temper. He carried out his orders successfully and soon managed to restore the prestige of Britain in the colonies. When he arrived in Lower Canada, the province had a suspended constitution, it was tired of ineffectual rebellion and was embarrassed by the number of political prisoners; Durham sensibly banished the leaders to another colony (though he had no authority to do so) and freed the rest. Later the same year he was attacked for this in the British House of Commons and he resigned.

The Durham Report.   Two months after his return to London, Durham, with the assistance of his secretary, Charles Buller, and an English colonial statesman, Gibbon Wakefield, produced his famous *Report on the Affairs of British North America.* This was one of the most remarkable documents in British colonial history, and one that laid the foundations of responsible government in British North America.   In his *Report,* Durham advocated:

1. that the British government retain control of foreign relations (including the armed forces), external trade, the constitutional framework and the disposal of public lands (in all other matters, particularly the development of municipal government, provincial governments would be responsible);
2. that all money bills originate with the governor but be submitted to provincial assemblies for discussion and approval;
3. that the two Canadas be reunited in one legislative union, while retaining local autonomy in other fields (thus the French Canadians would gradually be absorbed and anglicized);
4. that the old Executive Council be made responsible to the Legislative Assembly rather than to the governor, with members of the new Council or Cabinet being chosen from the party with a majority in the Assembly, and that these ministers be each responsible for a department of government (this suggestion was, in fact, based on proposals made by Robert Baldwin and Charles Buller to Lord Durham, who then promoted them).

Durham criticized the British Colonial Office for blundering and accused the Family Compacts of dishonesty and self-interest. Durham's *Report* was, in fact, advocating responsible government.

THE ACHIEVEMENT OF RESPONSIBLE GOVERNMENT

Durham's proposals were loudly condemned by the Tories in British North America and by Lord John Russell, who had just taken over the Colonial Office. Russell could not understand how a governor could be responsible to an assembly when he was already responsible to the imperial government. The Reformers, on the other hand, greeted the proposals with enthusiasm, and supported the union of the Canadas, to the alarm of both the Tories and the French Canadians.

The Act of Union, 1841. In 1840, the British government passed the Act of Union, which created the United Province of Canada. The Lower and Upper Canadas came to be called Canada East and Canada West respectively. The Act came into effect in 1841. The new government was to consist of:

1. a governor appointed by the Colonial Office and responsible to the Colonial Office in London;
2. a Legislative Council (or Upper House appointed by the governor);
3. an Executive Council appointed by the governor and still responsible to him;
4. a Legislative Assembly (or Lower House) consisting of 84 elected members (42 from Canada East and 42 from Canada West). Members of the Executive Council were to hold government departments for a period depending on the governor's wishes, but the Legislative Council would consist of life members.

Canada East with its greater population was naturally dissatisfied with its representation. Nor did Canada East relish the idea of having to help pay debts incurred in earlier years by Canada West. For the first time, however, French and English groups were able to meet on an equal footing when the House opened in Kingston in June, 1841.

In spite of Governor Sydenham's tactful handling of affairs, the English and French Reformers remained restless and, under the leadership of Robert Baldwin and Louis Hippolyte Lafontaine, continued to press for responsible government. The struggle primarily concerned the Executive Council. Sydenham was anxious to control it for the purpose of strengthening his government, while the Reformers sought to subordinate it to the control of the Assembly.

Sydenham, who died late in 1841, was succeeded by the diplomatic Sir Charles Bagot. Faced with a Reform majority, Bagot soon appointed an executive council which consisted wholly of French and English Reformers or moderates, under Baldwin and Lafontaine. This first recognition of a cabinet consisting of members from the majority partly lasted less than two years. In the elections of 1844 under an unsympathetic new governor, Sir Charles Metcalfe (Bagot had died in Canada in 1843), the Tories returned to power.

In 1846, the Whigs were returned to office in England under
Sir John Russell, whose new Colonial Secretary, Earl Grey, was
a brother-in-law and disciple of Durham and his concept of
responsible government. (Grey was a friend of Buller and Wakefield, but, like them, disagreed with Durham's assumption of Anglo-
Saxon superiority and the gradual assimilation of the French
Canadians.) Under the sympathetic guidance of Lieutenant-
Governor Sir John Harvey in Nova Scotia and of Governor-General
Lord Elgin (a son-in-law of Durham) in the Province of Canada,
this policy was quickly carried out and self-government in all
domestic affairs was granted in 1848.

Nova Scotia.   In Nova Scotia, Joseph Howe had early supported
Baldwin's proposals for responsible government and in his *Open
Letters* of 1839 to Lord John Russell, he gave a brilliant exposi-
tion of its advantages. The Reformers won the election held in
August, 1847. Early in 1848 Howe and J. B. Uniacke were asked
to form a ministry, the first reponsible ministry in British North
America or in any British Colony.

The Province of Canada.   In Canada, things did not run so
smoothly. Lord Elgin immediately let it be known that he would
himself take no part in election campaigns but was ready to work
with any party elected by the people. In March, 1848, after the
Reform party had returned triumphantly to power in both parts
of the province, he called on Robert Baldwin and Louis Lafontaine
to form a ministry. (The "Great Ministry" came to an end in
1851, but by that time it had reformed the system of municipal
government, improved the judicial system, laid the foundations for
the great decade of railway building, and assumed control of postal
services.)

The "Rebellion Losses Bill."   In 1849, Elgin sanctioned the *Act
of Indemnification*, or the *Rebellion Losses Bill* as it has come to
be called. This Bill was designed to compensate *any* person (rebel
or otherwise) in Canada East whose property had been damaged
during the rebellion of 1837 (a more conservative Bill had already
been passed in Canada West). The Bill roused the fury of the
merchants who were disturbed because colonial preference had
ended and alarmed by the new power of "unprogressive and anti-
commercial" French. They acted by assaulting Lord Elgin and
burning the Parliament Buildings in Montreal.

The Westminster Parliament, however, refused to intervene, in
spite of protests calling for the resignation of Lord Elgin. In sign-

ing the Bill, Elgin accepted the principle of responsible government —that a governor is independent of political parties; makes cabinet appointments only with the approval of his prime minister, the leader of the majority party; and acts upon the advice of his ministers.

New Brunswick.   Progress toward responsible government in New Brunswick was held back by the fact that revenue from Crown lands provided enough money to pay the salaries of government officials, with the result that such officials were not dependent upon monies voted by the Assembly. Gradually, however, the power of the Anglican Church was diminished and the Assembly slowly gained control of revenues. In 1848, the Reform party won the election and by 1854, with the support of the British government, responsible government was achieved.

Prince Edward Island.   The struggle in Prince Edward Island was between wealthy absentee landlords and their tenants. The island had received nominal representative government in 1773, and by 1850 the Assembly had gained control of revenues. However, responsible government was only attained in 1862 when, for the first time, the Legislative Council was freely elected.

Newfoundland.   In 1832, Newfoundland had achieved representative government. The second election, 1837, brought a leading Reformer, Dr. William Carson, into the Assembly. In 1844, agitation for responsible government began. Eleven years elapsed before, in 1855, under Governor C. H. Darling, an executive council distinct from the legislative council was created. In the same year the Liberal or Reform party gained a majority in the Assembly and its leader, P. F. Little, became the first prime minister. Responsible government had been achieved.

With the introduction of responsible government in domestic matters, the provinces of British North America reached a new stage in their development. The achievement of responsible government in 1849 was followed directly by administrative, judicial and financial reforms, and by the railway boom and the rapid development of manufacturing industry.

Yet responsible government was not the solution to all the political ills of the provinces. It did not, for example, lessen the bitterness of politics in Nova Scotia. It did not resolve the racial and sectional divisions within the Province of Canada. More important, local responsible government could not influence the forces at work in Britain and North America during the 1850's and 1860's that threatened to draw the provinces into the American union.

BIBLIOGRAPHY

ABRAHAMSON, UNA. *God Bless Our Home*. Burns and MacEachern, 1966.

BREDIN, T. *River of Canada*. Longmans, 1962.

CRAIG, G. M. (ed.). *Lord Durham's Report*. McClelland and Stewart, 1963.

GLAZEBROOK, G. P. DE T. *Life in Ontario, A Social History*. University of Toronto, 1968.

GUILLET, E. C. *Pioneer Days in Upper Canada*. Canadian University Paperbacks. Macmillan, 1964.

JEFFERYS, C. W. *The Formative Years*. Ryerson, 1968.

JEFFERYS, C. W. *Picture Gallery of Canadian History, Vol. II*. Ryerson, 1968.

JOHNSON, P. M. *Canada's Pacific Province*. McClelland and Stewart, 1968.

KILBOURNE, W. *The Firebrand*. Clarke, Irwin, 1964.

KLASSEN, H. G. *Thrust and Counterthrust*. Longmans, 1965.

LANGTON, A. (ed.). *A Gentlewoman in Upper Canada*. Clarke, Irwin, 1967.

LOWER, J. A. *Self-government*. McClelland and Stewart, 1968.

MCDONALD, T. H. (ed.). *Exploring the Northwest Territory,* University of Oklahoma Press, 1966.

MARIOTT, ALICE. *Kiowa Years*. Collier-Macmillan, 1968.

MORRIS, AUDREY Y. *Gentle Pioneers*. Hodder and Stoughton, 1968.

NEATBY, L. H. *Conquest of the Last Frontier*. Longmans, 1966.

PARKMAN, FRANCIS. *The Oregon Trail*. New American Library, 1950.

RADDALL, T. H. *The Path of Destiny*. Doubleday, 1957.

RASKY, F. *The Taming of the Canadian West*. McClelland and Stewart, 1967.

TRAILL, CATHERINE P. *The Backwoods of Canada*. McClelland and Stewart, 1966.

WADE, M. *The French Canadians, 1760-1967*. 2 vols. Macmillan, 1968.

WISE, S. F. and BROWN, R. C. *Canada Views the United States*. Macmillan, 1967.

7

The Struggle for Confederation, 1843-1867

The proximity of the United States remained a constant and definite factor in the economics and politics of British North America. This was true even after the failure of the 1837 rebellions had established the fact that the provinces would not adopt the American-type government advocated by Papineau and Mackenzie. After 1837, relations between the two countries suffered recurrent strains for many years.

NATIONAL BOUNDARIES

The Maine-New Brunswick Boundary. Border disturbances emphasized the importance of settling certain boundary controversies, especially that of the Maine-New Brunswick boundary which had been defined in 1783. The line was to follow the St. Croix River to its source and thence directly north to the highlands that divided the watershed between the Atlantic Ocean and the St. Lawrence River. It was to continue along the highlands to the northwest of the source of the Connecticut River, and down that river to the forty-fifth parallel. This agreement had shown itself open to misinterpretation in almost every detail, for example: Which river was the one referred to as the St. Croix? Were rivers flowing into the Bay of Fundy to be considered as flowing into the Atlantic?

The location of the St. Croix was agreed upon in 1798. The Treaty of Ghent left the other problems to a later commission, which struggled for eight years with boundary problems but failed

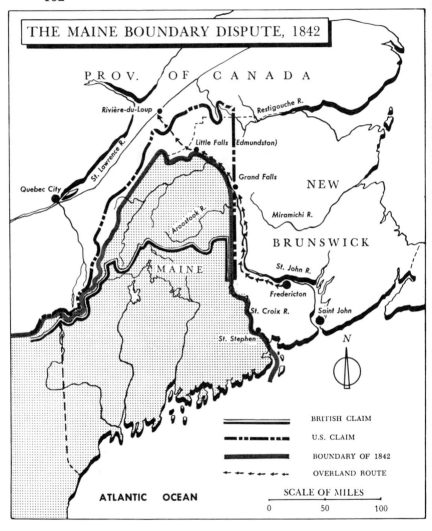

to reach agreement. In 1831, the affair was referred to the King of the Netherlands for arbitration. Although his decision would have given the United States about two-thirds of the disputed area, his decision was refused by the American government.

Meanwhile, people from both countries had settled in the disputed areas. The British, for example, occupied a section of

what is now northern and eastern Maine, while Americans claimed a section of western New Brunswick and a narrow strip of Canada East south of the St. Lawrence. Clashes between British and American settlers in disputed areas became more frequent and finally flared up as the "Aroostook War" of 1839 when sparked by an incident between rival logging groups in the Aroostook Valley. Police and militia were dispatched from both Maine and New Brunswick to prevent an outbreak of violence.

In 1842, Lord Ashburton, the British envoy, and Daniel Webster, the American Secretary of State, met to negotiate a solution to the dispute. (Both men suppressed maps supporting the other's claims, and these discussions have been called the "battle of the maps.") Minor adjustments were made to the common boundary between the St. Lawrence and the Lake of the Woods, and a "give-and-take" agreement was finally reached to produce a definite boundary between Maine and New Brunswick. For New Brunswick it was an unpleasant compromise, but it did leave the Temiscouata Road—a vital military communication with Lower Canada—within British territory.

The Oregon Boundary.   Large numbers of Americans had moved into the Oregon area which was still held jointly by the British and the Americans. As a result, the Hudson's Bay Company became involved in a conflict over the administration, and it became necessary to establish a boundary between British and American territory. The British held out for the Columbia River as the boundary (roughly the forty-fifth parallel), until the United States threatened war. (President James Polk was elected in 1844 with the slogan "Fifty-four forty or fight.") In 1846 a compromise was reached, in which the forty-ninth parallel was extended from the Rockies to the Pacific coast—but leaving the whole of Vancouver Island as a British possession. The situation in Oregon was a useful object lesson. It emphasized the fact that unless British North Americans effectively occupied the empty lands north and west of the Great Lakes, American infiltration would bring about other situations similar to that in Oregon.

TRADE

By 1849 the old British mercantile system had ended. The question then arose as to whether the British provinces would turn to the rest of the British Empire or to the United States to replace their lost trade.

The Annexation Manifesto.   The British merchants of Montreal had been especially hard hit by the introduction of free trade. Infuriated at the power given French Canadians by responsible government, and outraged by the apparent desertion of the merchant class in Britain, they sought help from the United States and its large market. In October, 1849 over 1,000 of them signed a manifesto advocating union with the United States. They gained disappointingly little American support in this enterprise (which was strongly opposed by French Canadians). The Americans were not anxious to endanger Anglo-American relations. This, together with an improvement in the economic position of the Canadas, caused the movement to collapse, but it was a theme that was to recur from time to time throughout the years.

Reciprocity.   The United States' market appeared to be the only one likely to compensate for the loss of the British market, and after 1846, attempts were made by the Canadas to establish some form of reciprocal trade. The United States government was more interested in excluding competition in lumber, coal, fish and agricultural products than in gaining access to the limited British North American market. However, it was anxious to settle a long-standing dispute with Britain over the inshore fisheries and to gain access to these rich fisheries.

By 1854 negotiations for a trade and fishing agreement were under way. Lord Elgin was sent to the United States where his brilliant diplomacy and lavish hospitality won over all the delegates —southerners saw the treaty as a means of delaying the annexation of British North America and therefore limiting the power of the north, and northerners supported the treaty as a natural move toward annexation.

In June, 1854, a twelve-year treaty was signed. It made provision for reciprocal free trade in coal and fish, and farm and forest products; United States' vessels were granted inshore fishing rights and were allowed on the St. Lawrence and Canadian canals in exchange for Canadian access to Lake Michigan. Interestingly enough, while the treaty undoubtedly strengthened economic ties between the two countries and increased the prosperity of British North America (American trade with the provinces trebled in value), it also strengthened political separatism and helped establish a permanent British North America.

THE THREAT OF MANIFEST DESTINY

By the middle of the nineteenth century American expansionists talked of the United States' "Manifest Destiny" to form a continental nation encompassing both Mexico and British North America. The United States had already organized much of the West. Iowa was made a state in 1846, Minnesota received statehood in 1858, Oregon became a state in 1859. In 1852 the railroad reached Chicago, in 1854 the Mississippi and by 1859 the Missouri. As land became scarcer Americans looked north and the better communications and markets in the United States helped draw attention to the vast relatively unsettled territory north of the forty-ninth parallel.

Pacific Coast. The many former North West Company posts were being operated by "The Bay." Fort Victoria had been built on Vancouver Island in 1843 as the western headquarters of the Company in anticipation of the loss of Fort Vancouver in the Oregon territory. Vancouver Island had been created a Crown colony in 1849 (the year that Fort Victoria became the western base of the H.B.C. under the command of James Douglas). In 1858 the British governors legalized Douglas' proclamation of jurisdiction over the mainland by creating the Crown colony of British Columbia. This was done in an effort to prevent the repetition of an Oregon problem in the wake of a gold rush and an influx of American settlers.

Red River. By 1850 the Red River settlement at Fort Garry (the site of modern Winnipeg) numbered over 5,000 persons, but the community's mail and commerce were being carried out via the United States. A further threat to British North America was the United States' purchase of Alaska in 1867.

Canadian Interest in the West. If the North-West was not to be lost to the United States, some action had to be taken to annex the area to British North America and to improve communications between the various provinces. The Reformers or "Clear Grits" of Canada West encouraged this idea in order to expand the farming economy of the province (by 1850, farmers in Canada were already moving into the United States because of a shortage of usable land). Slowly, manufacturers, railway interests, financial and commercial groups began to add their support as well.

In 1858, the Reformers made the incorporation of the North-West a plank of their party platform, and that same year, a committee was formed to investigate the whole matter, especially since the Hudson's Bay monopoly was due to expire in 1859. The committee's report recommended that the Red River and Saskatchewan River districts be given to the Province of Canada, and that the Hudson Bay Company's rights on the Pacific coast be terminated. Unfortunately, the Province of Canada still lacked the necessary communications, population and financial resources to permit the take-over of the North-West.

War Between the States. Civil strife in the United States only increased the threat of annexation. The Americans were overly sensitive to interference by Britain (or British North Americans). The North resented Britain's sympathies with the South and wrongly assumed that the British provinces as a whole held the same view. In fact, the social make-up of the provinces naturally encouraged support for the North. (For many years the "Underground Railway" organization had brought slaves from the South to the safety of the Province of Canada.) Although a small Tory group in the Province openly supported the South, thousands of Canadian volunteers served with Northern armies.

When a Northern warship held up a British mail steamer and removed two Confederate diplomats who were travelling to Britain, the *Trent* Crisis of 1861, as it was called, threatened to precipitate war between Britain and the United States. Ten thousand British troops were hurriedly sent over to protect the provinces, but President Lincoln apologized and released the prisoners, and the crisis was smoothed over.

Another naval situation at the end of the war caused considerable alarm. Several Confederate warships built in Britain, notably the *Alabama* and the *Florida,* had wrought much havoc upon Northern shipping during the war. Lincoln's government claimed that Britain was responsible and many Northerners threatened to seize the British provinces by way of compensation. Eventually, in 1871, Britain agreed to arbitration of the claims and the scare died down.

The Fenians.   Anglo-American relations were at their worst by the time the War Between the States ended in 1865. During the war there had been several Confederate raids on the North from British North American soil, with the result that the United States government had remained indifferent to the activities of the Fenians. The Fenians were a group of Irish Americans organized in New York City in 1857 to revive the struggle for Irish independence and to raise support for this cause in the United States. Between 1866 and 1870 the Fenians conducted several raids across the border into Canada, having decided to attack the British government via its North American provinces. These "invasions" did not prove serious in themselves (although the Fenians succeeded in taking Fort Erie at one stage), but they occurred at the height of the anti-Canadian feelings in the United States and caused five years of border uneasiness before the movement finally collapsed in 1871.

Economic Reprisals.   The most serious threat from the United States was an economic one. In spite of inshore fishing rights, hostility to the Reciprocity Treaty steadily grew in the United States, together with agitation for protective tariffs. In 1866 the

Treaty was allowed to lapse. The ten years of its duration had been prosperous ones for British North America. By refusing to renew the agreement, annexationist forces in the North hoped to force British North America to consider union with the United States. Added to all this, was the quite serious competition of American railroads.

Railway Difficulties. By 1846 there were nearly 5,000 miles of railroad in the United States. Railroad transport helped to develop the economy of the country at an astounding rate. It moved goods quickly and efficiently to export points, encouraged settlement and generally played an important part in fostering a sense of national unity. British North America, with its newly developed ideas of

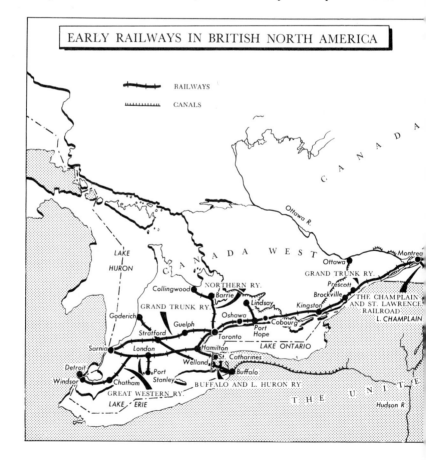

EARLY RAILWAYS IN BRITISH NORTH AMERICA

economic self-sufficiency, and with its plans for increased trade within the provinces and with the United States, saw the vital importance of building a similar transportation system. But the enormous amounts of money necessary for railway building were not available, and by 1846 British North America had only the fifteen and a half miles of the Champlain and St. Lawrence Railroad—a "portage railroad" built to facilitate transportation between Montreal and New York City.

Although railways, which held such great promise for the movement of goods, were expensive to build, this did not prevent several from being promoted. In 1849, Francis Hincks, inspector-general during the Baldwin-Lafontaine ministry of 1848-51, was responsible for the passage of a bill by which the government of

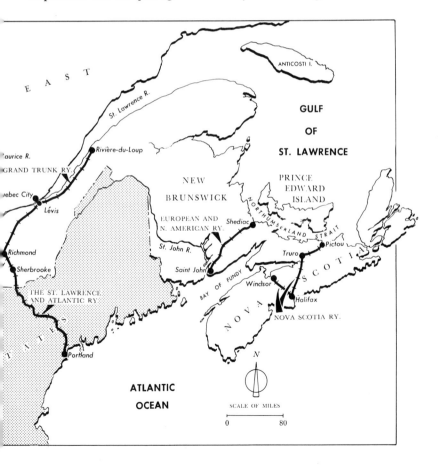

the Province of Canada guaranteed the interest on one-half of the bonded debt of any railway that was at least seventy-five miles long. This promise of government assistance resulted in a flurry of commercial activity to obtain railway charters and to construct numerous short lines. (By 1860 railway mileage in British North America, mostly in the Province of Canada, had increased to 2,065.)

However, many of the lines were highly speculative ventures, and soon went bankrupt. Others amalgamated until only a few comparatively large lines remained. The St. Lawrence and Atlantic, built primarily to improve Montreal's communications with the Eastern Townships, was opened between Montreal and Portland (an ice-free port) in Maine in 1853.

Two years later, two other lines had been built: the Great Western, linking Hamilton with the Niagara River and with Windsor; and the Northern, running from Toronto to Collingwood on Georgian Bay. Yet between western Lake Ontario and Montreal there was still no railway connection, and American railroads —the New York Central at Buffalo, the New York and Erie, and the Ogdensburg Railway running to Boston—diverted much of the commerce from the St. Lawrence to American ports. American railroads even linked up with local lines in Canada West to reach Lake Huron and the Ottawa valley.

Short branch lines were being constructed about this time in the Maritimes. However, it was only after the failure of a major scheme to link all the provinces by an "intercolonial" railway that work on a Grand Trunk Railway, a rail link between Toronto and Montreal, from Lake Huron to the Atlantic was planned. The Grand Trunk's central section from Montreal to Toronto was completed in 1856, and the line eventually ran from Sarnia in the west to Quebec City and Rivière du Loup. From here the St. Lawrence and Atlantic line was leased to reach Portland in the east.

Construction costs forced railway promoters to appeal time and again to the Canadian legislature for money. British capital made wary by a British railway boom and collapse in the forties, was not available to British North Americans until the middle eighties, and the British government refused all appeals for railway capital. The competition of American railroads was too severe and many of the provincial lines continually operated at a loss or went bankrupt. Railways in British North America brought into being such industries as iron and steel foundries, rolling mills and locomotive shops, and quickly transported such domestic manufactures as boots, shoes, cotton goods and agricultural implements. Even with all this, the Province of Canada alone incurred a crushing debt of $30,000,000, and was still not linked by rail with the Maritimes. As long as the provinces remained politically divided, they found it impossible to work together and lacked the financial resources to maintain rail links. As a result they were not able to maintain a British North American identity.

TOWARD CONFEDERATION

The possibility of economic or political federation among the provinces had been raised at intervals since the end of the eighteenth century. In 1789, Governor-General, Lord Dorchester (Guy Carleton), had written the British government suggesting a "general government for His Majesty's dominions upon this continent . . . to the general interest and to the preservation of the unity of the Empire." Radicals such as Robert Gourlay and William Lyon Mackenzie had favoured federation, and even Lord Durham had written that "The North American colonist needs some nationality of his own." Events in the mid-nineteenth century led to further talk and serious consideration of some form of union among the colonies.

The repeal of the Navigation Acts in 1849 brought free trade and an end to the favoured position that colonial markets had enjoyed under the old mercantile system. Further dislocation of the colonial markets was threatened by growing dissatisfaction in the United States with the Reciprocity Treaty, that was in fact allowed to lapse by the United States in 1866. Together these two blows to the economics of British North America forced the colonies to depend more upon each other. This growing mutual interest made the question of union more urgent. The threat of American annexation in the west and a new inter-provincial interest that followed the introduction of the railways also lead to a renewed interest in political union. The question remained, however, what would be the nature of this union? Would it be a series of local unions—the Maritimes, the Canadas, and the western territories—all with regional and external trade interests? Would it be a federal union? Or would it be a legislative union of all the British colonies?

The union of the two Canadas in 1841 had not proved to be the success that Lord Durham and others had hoped it would be.

As a result the concept of local union became unacceptable in the Canadas. To understand how this became the case one must understand the complex political history of the Canadas during the 1850's.

The Baldwin-Lafontaine administration had brought about several progressive and constructive reforms in local government, in education, and in the position of French Canada. It remained, however, under constant attack from the more radical reformers of the party and in 1851 was forced to resign. There followed a reform administration led by Francis Hincks and Augustin Morin. During their three years in power the Reciprocity Treaty with the United States was signed and an impetus was given to railway building through the Municipal Loan Fund Act which allowed municipalities and railway companies to borrow money on the credit of the provincial government. Many of the new railways went bankrupt. Hincks became too involved financially with railway development and his administration was forced to resign.

The Liberal-Conservatives.   In Canada West, after the fall of their government, Francis Hincks and Augustin Morin joined with Sir Allan MacNab and John A. Macdonald, thus forming an unusual coalition composed of moderate reformers and Tories. A similar group in Canada East, composed of moderate reformers (the *Bleus*), united under George Etienne Cartier. In 1854, during the confused situation following indecisive election results, Macdonald, joined with his fellow-lawyer, Cartier, to bring the groups from the two provinces together. Under the new title of the Liberal-Conservative party, this new party was a province-wide coalition of interests.

Among the first reform measures enacted by the new administration was the secularization of the clergy reserves. Existing rectories were provided for and funds from the reserves were given to municipalities in proportion to their population. Seigneurial tenure was also abolished; the province bought the rights of the Seigneurs; and habitant farmers were permitted to buy or rent small holdings. (Roman Catholic Church lands, one-quarter of Seigneurial holdings, were exempt from the act.)

"Clear Grits."   Following the death of the Baldwin-Lafontaine administration in 1851, the Reformers gradually developed a new appearance. Led by George Brown of Canada West, the *Clear Grits* (that is "men of clear grit" determined to fight for reform) advocated democracy of the American frontier type—universal suffrage, the secret ballot, elected officials, biennial elections—and, in general, opposed urban commercial interests. Their antagonism towards big business, often reflected in the editorials of George Brown's Toronto newspaper, *The Globe,* became quite marked (especially over public monies given to Grand Trunk interests). They distrusted Cartier's followers, who had allied themselves with Liberal-Conservative businessmen in order to have a full share of economic benefit. With increasing frequency the Reformers called for "Rep by Pop" (representation in the legislature according to population). Such a demand, if granted, would diminish the power of French Canadians in the Assembly and give political strength to the larger and faster growing population of Canada West.

The Parti Rouge. Meanwhile, Canada East was witnessing the rise of a small but vigorous radical party of young democrats, the *Parti Rouge.* Under the leadership of Antoine Aimé Dorion the party advocated American-type republicanism and French anti-clerical radicalism. They agreed with the Clear Grits in their opposition to the union of 1841, but resented strongly the Grits' cry of "Rep by Pop." Indeed the *Parti Rouge's* hatred of every-thing English ultimately led them in the unexpected direction of seeking annexation with the United States, where they felt they would have fairer representation. Their party's political centre was the *Institut Canadien,* originally founded as a literary club. How-ever, the formal condemnation of the *Institut* and of the radical policies of the *Parti* by the Roman Catholic Church severely weak-ened Dorion's following. His quarrel with the Church robbed the *Rouges* of any claim to speak for French Canadians.

Deadlock. These various parties were so evenly balanced in the Canadian Assembly that effective government was fast becoming impossible. Politics in the provinces was plagued with racial and political complications. The Liberal-Conservative party consisted mainly of French-Canadian members and the Reform party was composed mainly of English-speaking members. Conflicts of material interests became entangled in a confused mixture with religious and racial differences. Canada East considered itself taxed for too many English-Canadian projects. For example, four-fifths of all municipal loans went to municipalities in Canada West. Canada West, which now had a larger population, raised two-thirds of all taxes and resented using these monies for such things as compensation to seigneurs due to the abolition of seigneurial tenure and the institution of the township system in 1854. The "Double Majority" procedure, under which any important measure had to receive a majority of votes from the representatives of both Canada East and Canada West became almost completely unworkable. By the early 1860's government in the Province of Canada had reached a complete deadlock.

The "Great Coalition." By 1860, partly lines had become hopelessly blurred as ministry after ministry sought to hold together to govern the Province. Between 1861 and 1864 there were two elections and four further changes of ministry. After these successive breakdowns of government, George Brown, who controlled enough votes to overthrow any ministry, suggested a coalition government in order to solve the recurrent deadlock. Basic to this offer, of course, was the necessity of framing a new constitution for the Province. Brown, Macdonald and Cartier also agreed to consider at the same time, the possibility of some form of federal union.

In the meantime, Queen Victoria had already resolved another deadlock. Ever since the Parliament buildings in Montreal had been burned in 1849 at the time of the riots over the Rebellion Losses Bill, there had not been a permanent meeting-place for the Canadian legislature. The members had been unable to decide upon a site and the legislature had been meeting alternately at Toronto and Quebec City. The Queen was asked to choose a location and in 1857 selected Ottawa (formerly Bytown), at that time a lumber town.

The Interest in Federation. After the breakdown of government became obvious, the party of Macdonald and Cartier (which had a far stronger tradition of political centralization than the Reformers) started in 1858 to seriously promote British North American unity. In the same year, Alexander Tilloch Galt (of the British America Land Company and, more recently, a promoter of the St. Lawrence and Atlantic railway) indicated where business and railway interests lay by accepting the position of minister of finance in the Macdonald-Cartier ministry. This he did on condition that the Liberal-Conservatives made a British North American federation party policy, one of his aims being to promote an intercolonial railway. Unfortunately, two delegations to Westminster seeking British approval for discussion of such a federation proved fruitless.

The Clear Grits too were advocating some form of British North American unity. They proposed a "federative system" of either the two Canadas or one general union applied to the whole of British North America. They were stimulated by the vision of western expansion and aware that the Hudson Bay Company's trade monopoly was about to expire.

The Charlottetown Conference. Maritime leaders as well had been considering federation for a number of years. In September 1864, political leaders in the Maritimes were planning to hold a conference at Charlottetown, Prince Edward Island. It was their intention to discuss the feasibility of a federal union among themselves for economic and defence purposes. Macdonald, having agreed with Brown to support a policy of a general union of all British North American provinces, requested permission for a group from the Province of Canada to be heard. Permission was granted, and seven Canadian delegates, led by Macdonald, arrived at Charlottetown on September 1, 1864. Macdonald, Cartier, Brown and Galt made persuasive speeches outlining their vision of provincial union in North America. The Conference's final decision, made after an adjournment to Halifax, was to convene a conference at Quebec City the following month to discuss confederation.

The Quebec Conference. On Sunday, October 9, 1864, thirty-three representatives (the "Fathers of Confederation" as they have been called) of five provinces (this time including delegates from Newfoundland) gathered at Quebec City. The Conference opened on October 10, and at the end of the second day, after a brilliant and moving address by Macdonald, a motion was quickly passed in favour of federal union. The remainder of the Conference was spent reconciling the many conflicting views on the duties and powers of a federal government. In particular, the touchy question of provincial representation in a federal parliament had to be solved.

The Seventy-Two Resolutions. After several days of heated debate (during which the affable, diplomatic Macdonald was at his persuasive best), the Conference summarized its proposals for federation in The Quebec Resolutions or Seventy-Two Resolutions as they are often called. These resolutions were to be submitted to the provinces for examination and approval and to the British government and Colonial Office for approval and authorization.

The Opposition to Confederation.   The Quebec Resolutions were debated in each of the provincial legislatures. After initial opposition on the part of the *Rouges* and extreme English-Canadian Reformers, the Province of Canada approved them. In Nova Scotia, Joseph Howe attacked the Resolutions as being unworkable and as being unprofitable to the province. The premier, Charles Tupper, who had represented the province at Quebec City, was unable to rouse enough support for Confederation in the legislature. In New Brunswick, all the federalist cabinet ministers—including Leonard Tilley, the premier—were defeated in the elections the following year; candidates who opposed Confederation were swept into office. In Prince Edward Island, Confederation was promptly rejected. In Newfoundland, the Resolutions were ignored because trade ties were much closer with Britain than with the other provinces.

Despite these set-backs, Macdonald, Brown, Galt and Cartier journeyed to Britain in 1865 to appeal for support. The Colonial Office, having decided that Confederation was necessary for the future well-being and safety of the provinces and having noted its strong support in the Province of Canada, brought pressure to bear on Maritime lieutenant-governors. More effective in changing the climate of opinion, however, were certain events in 1866—the Fenian raids upon New Brunswick and the ending of reciprocity. That year Leonard Tilley was returned to power in New Brunswick, and Charles Tupper was finally able to marshal enough popular support in Nova Scotia for Confederation. Canada and two of the Maritime provinces were now ready for discussions with the Colonial Office.

THE FEDERATION OF THE PROVINCES, 1867

The British North America Act.   At a conference in the Westminster Palace Hotel, London, in December, 1866, sixteen delegates from the three provinces discussed proposals for Confederation with representatives of the British government.

In March the following year, Parliament passed the *British North America Act*. The Act described the new constitution as "similar in principle to that of the United Kingdom." British parliamentary and monarchical forms were to be preserved. (Nobody at Quebec City had questioned this matter, which had really been settled years before by the grant of responsible cabinet government.)

The central government was made as strong as possible (the Fathers of Confederation were deeply suspicious and wary of the numerous rights and privileges given to the individual American states by the Constitution). The Act followed the lead of the twenty-ninth of the seventy-two resolutions which gave the federal parliament general and all-embracing powers "to make Laws for the peace, welfare and good government of the Federated Provinces (saving the Sovereignty of England)."

The division of powers between the federal and provincial levels was based on the principle that matters of national interest would be legislated by the central government and those of a local interest by provincial governments. The powers of the provinces were carefully enumerated. For example, direct taxation, appointment and payment of provincial officers, the management and sale of public lands belonging to the province, the development of railways, canals, telegraph, roads, steamship lines, education, the administration of justice, property and civil rights, and a number of lesser matters were all given to the provinces.

Under the terms of the British North America Act, the new state, the Dominion of Canada, was to consist of the four provinces of Ontario (formerly Canada West), Quebec (formerly Canada East), New Brunswick and Nova Scotia.

The Parliament of the Dominion of Canada was to be composed of three elements: the head of government (the monarch who was to be represented by a governor-general) and a two-chamber legislature (an Upper House corresponding to the old legislative council, and a Lower House corresponding to the old legislative assembly). Members of the Upper House or *Senate* were to be *appointed* for *life* in accordance with the following *regional* representation: Ontario 24, Quebec 24, and Nova Scotia and New Brunswick together 24. The Lower House or *House of Commons* was to consist of 181 members *elected* (for a maximum term of five years) in proportion to provincial population. Quebec, however, was guaranteed under the Act a total, permanent representation of 65 members.

Since the expansion of railway communication was considered vital to the growth of the Dominion (and of the Maritimes in particular, whose representatives at Quebec had insisted on a rail link with the St. Lawrence basin), the British North America Act made special provision for the construction of an intercolonial railway. This task took nine years to complete, and in 1876 the whole line

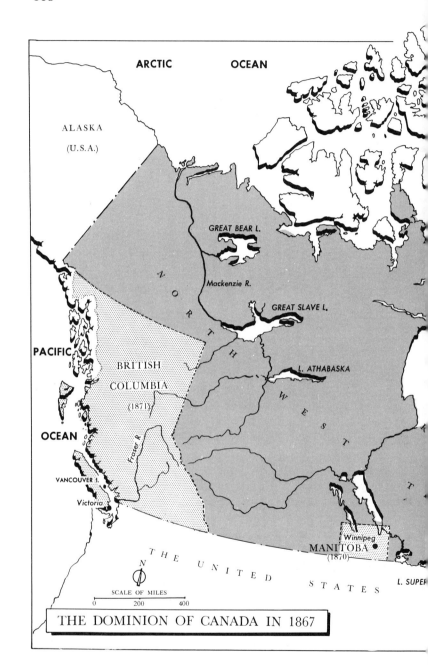

THE DOMINION OF CANADA IN 1867

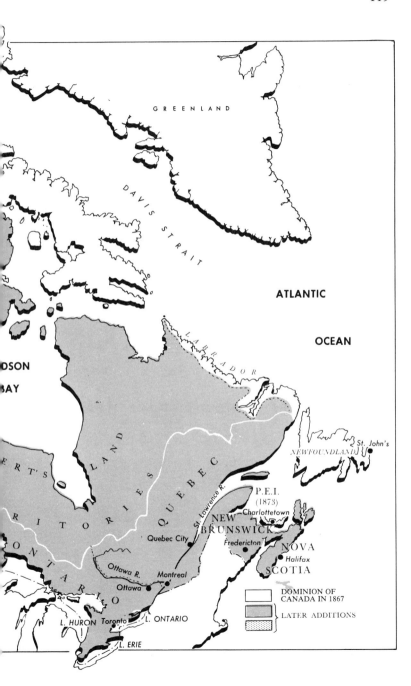

GREENLAND

DAVIS STRAIT

ATLANTIC

OCEAN

DSON

BAY

LABRADOR

St. John's

NEWFOUNDLAND

RT'S   LAND

ERT'S

RITORIES

QUEBEC

St. Lawrence R.

P.E.I.
(1873)

Charlottetown

NEW
BRUNSWICK

Quebec City

Fredericton

NOVA

Halifax

SCOTIA

ONTARIO

Ottawa R.

Montreal

Ottawa

L. HURON   Toronto   L. ONTARIO

L. ERIE

| | DOMINION OF CANADA IN 1867 |
| | LATER ADDITIONS |

was in service over its 700-mile length, thus joining six Atlantic ports with Quebec and Ontario.

It is important to note that the BNA Act did not grant complete independence to the Dominion of Canada. Among other things, the Act was a statute of the Westminster Parliament and therefore could not be changed or amended in any degree except by the Westminster Parliament. In addition, the new dominion could not have direct dealings with other states, could not control immigration, could not command Canadian armed forces—except through British officers—and could still have any of its parliamentary measures disallowed by the Westminster Parliament. Even Macdonald's wish to name the new nation the "Kingdom of Canada" was changed to "Dominion" in case the United States might be offended by any obvious suggestion of monarchy.

Thus, legally, the Dominion was just as much a dependent colony as its component provinces had been. Yet British North America had been given, through Confederation, a chance to solve the problems that had plagued the provinces for decades. These problems included sectional and religious conflict, political instability, economic stagnation and isolation, and military weakness. Confederation was a natural step forward after the achievement of responsible government. The next step forward would be to use Confederation to create a nation.

BIBLIOGRAPHY

BREDIN, T. *Confederation, 1867*. McClelland and Stewart.

COPP, J. *Confederation: 1867*. Copp Clark, 1966.

CREIGHTON, D. G. *The Road to Confederation*. Macmillan, 1964.

CREIGHTON, L. *The Elegant Canadians*. McClelland and Stewart, 1967.

DAWSON, R. M. *Democratic Government in Canada*. University of Toronto, 1963.

FITZGEORGE, P. *Gold Rush Justice*. Canadian Vignette Series. Burns and MacEachern, 1968.

GRAHAM, W. H. *The Tiger of Canada West*. Clarke, Irwin, 1962.

HAYES, J. F. *Nation Builders*. Copp Clarke, 1968.

JEFFERYS, C. W. *The Formative Years*. Ryerson, 1968.

MACNUTT, W. S. *The Atlantic Provinces, 1712-1857*. Canadian Centenary Series, Vol. IX. McClelland and Stewart, 1965.

MILLER, E. F. *Ned McGowan's War*. Canadian Vignette Series. Burns and MacEachern, 1968.

PETHICK, D. *Victoria, the Fort*. Mitchell Press, 1968.

RAMSEY, BRUCE. *Barkerville*. Mitchell Press, 1961.

RAMSEY, BRUCE. *Ghost Towns of B.C.* Mitchell Press, 1963.

SCHULL, J. *The Nation Makers*. Macmillan, 1967.

SCOTT, I. G. *The Trek of the Overlanders*. Canadian Vignette Series. Burns and MacEachern, 1968.

SLATTERY, T. P. *Assassination of D'Arcy McGee*. Doubleday, 1968.

THORBURN, HUGH G. *Party Politics in Canada*. Prentice-Hall, 1967.

WAITE, P. B. (ed.). *Pre-Confederation*. Canadian Historical Document Series, Vol. II. Prentice-Hall, 1965.

8

The Dominion of Canada, 1867-1873

With the passage of the British North America Act, the task of building a new nation in the northern half of North America had just begun. A new government had to be formed. Even before July 1, 1867, John A. Macdonald had been asked by Governor-General Monck to form a cabinet. The choice of Macdonald as prime minister was an obvious one, but the task of selecting cabinet ministers was much more complicated. With sound political foresight and skill, Macdonald formed a ministry that included seven Conservatives and six Reformers. Of these, five came from Ontario, four from Quebec, and two each from Nova Scotia and New Brunswick. Not only did Macdonald account for the demands of coalition and regionalism by this choice, but he arranged for the representation of the Protestant English of Quebec and the English Roman Catholics outside Quebec. Indeed, by his selection, Macdonald cleverly succeeded in taking into consideration all the significant and potentially divisive political, racial, religious and regional forces within the new Dominion.

The First Dominion Parliament. Elections to the House of Commons in the summer of 1867 brought several surprises. Because the Reform party lacked a policy that provided a constructive alternative to Macdonald's coalition, its leader George Brown, who in fact had been a Father of Confederation, was defeated. In Nova Scotia there was a strong anti-Confederation feeling and although Charles Tupper, a coalitionist, was elected, all other supporters of Confederation were defeated.

The first months after Confederation were by no means easy ones for the new government. There was still considerable antagonism to Confederation in some areas and steps had to be taken to weld the existing federation and its diverse peoples into a stable economic, social and political community. In addition, Newfoundland, Prince Edward Island, British Columbia, Rupert's Land and the North-West Territories still remained outside the federation and plans had to be made to bring them within the jurisdiction of the federal government. Arrangements for the promised Intercolonial Railway between Halifax and the St. Lawrence River also had to be made.

THE PROVINCES

Nova Scotia. Despite the best intentions of Macdonald and his colleagues, divisive problems still existed in the new Dominion. Under the leadership of Joseph Howe, Nova Scotian anti-Confederationists expressed considerable dissatisfaction with the way Confederation had been imposed on them. In some quarters frustration resulted in threats of secession to the United States. Howe, although certainly not an annexationist himself, visited England in an attempt to secure the secession of Nova Scotia. When this proved impossible because of diplomatically deaf ears in Britain, Howe began to demand "better terms." After prolonged negotiations, Nova Scotia was given "better terms" (federal assumption of an additional $2,000,000 of the province's debt and an annual subsidy of $82,698 for ten years), and Howe entered the federal cabinet. The Nova Scotian "antis" were thus silenced, if not pleased, and open dissatisfaction subsided.

Rupert's Land and the North-West Territories. With Confederation an accomplished fact, many Canadians began to consider more seriously the annexation of Rupert's Land and the North-West Territories—that vast stretch of Hudson Bay lowland, muskeg and prairie lying north of the new Dominion and west to the Rocky Mountains. When the Montreal-based North West Company had been absorbed by the Hudson's Bay Company in 1821, the eastern colonies had lost their contact with the North-West. Consequently, this vast region had developed very slowly under the monopolistic control of the Hudson Bay Company with its outlet and headquarters located on the Hudson Bay.

The few thousand inhabitants of the North-West were Indians, a few white fur traders, and, historically more significant, the Métis.

For the Métis, life centred on the buffalo hunt and, to a lesser extent, the fur trade and farming. Fort Garry, the H.B.C. post at the junction of the Red and Assiniboine Rivers, was the seat of the Roman Catholic bishop as well as the Company's local government.

It was the area around Fort Garry (formerly known as the Red River Colony but now more frequently called Assiniboia) that was particularly attractive after 1867 to those Canadians in the East being forced to look farther afield for new land upon which to settle. There were also interests in the United States who were casting covetous eyes in the direction of the Canadian North-West. Canadians became concerned with the increasing infiltration of American settlers into the prairies, the growing traffic between St. Paul, Minnesota and Fort Garry, and the American purchase of Alaska in 1867. It looked as though influential groups in the United States might be engineering a "flanking movement" intended to block Canadian westward expansion. With understandable alarm the Dominion government prepared to take positive action.

While initial steps for the acquisition of the North-West had been begun as early as 1865 by the Province of Canada (with the sympathetic approval of the British government), it was not until December of 1867 that serious negotiations began. In July of 1868 the Imperial Parliament passed the Rupert's Land Act, authorizing the Crown to take over the Hudson's Bay Company lands and transfer them to the government of Canada. By the final terms of settlement it was agreed that the Company would cede Rupert's Land to Canada in exchange for £300,000 and the right to retain its posts and one-twentieth of all fertile land. At the same time the British government transferred the North-West Territories to Canada as well.

Alarm in Assiniboia. Unfortunately, the Métis of Assiniboia were not consulted as to the transfer or, for that matter, informed of Ottawa's plans for the North-West. The Métis were alarmed that they might lose their way of life, their culture (including the Roman Catholic faith) and their freedom to hunt buffalo on the open prairie to an invasion of English-speaking, Protestant farmers. When Canadian surveyors began surveying land in Assiniboia into quarter sections, which in some cases crossed the old river front strips of the Métis, open hostility resulted. The proud, independent Métis found among their own people a natural leader—the eloquent, hot-tempered, Louis Riel, who had at one time been a candidate for the priesthood.

The Red River Insurrection. In the fall of 1869, under the leadership of Riel, the Métis seized Fort Garry and established a "provisional government." When the new lieutenant-governor of the North-West, William McDougall, came via the United States to take up his position at Red River, he was stopped at the border

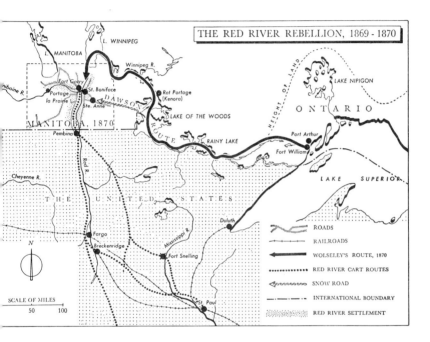

THE RED RIVER REBELLION, 1869 - 1870

ROADS
RAILROADS
WOLSELEY'S ROUTE, 1870
RED RIVER CART ROUTES
SNOW ROAD
INTERNATIONAL BOUNDARY
RED RIVER SETTLEMENT

SCALE OF MILES
50   100

near Pembina by armed Métis guards. The intention of the Métis in all these illegal acts was to delay the transfer until their terms of union could be discussed with the government in Ottawa.

Macdonald at last allowed the Métis to voice their opinions in the belief that through discussion some agreement could be reached. However, the issue was soon complicated by the execution at Fort Garry (on debatable charges) of an Ontario Orangeman, Thomas Scott. He had been one of a number of settlers from the East who had been imprisoned by Riel for "antagonism" towards the provisional government. There is no question that the hot-headed Scott had provoked and insulted Riel, but the Métis leader apparently seized upon a minor provocation to demonstrate his determination to Ottawa. The Red River revolt now became a national issue in Canada that re-opened the split between English Protestant Ontario and French Roman Catholic Quebec. Ontario demanded Riel's execution for "murder" while Quebec loudly defended a French-Canadian "hero."

Through the patience and skill of Bishop Taché, of Red River, the rebellion was finally resolved. Riel was persuaded to release the other prisoners arrested at the same time as Scott, to restore the property of the Hudson's Bay Company, and to accept the principle of union with Canada. The federal government agreed to negotiate with delegates from the Red River on terms of entry into Confederation; the Manitoba Act was the result of these discussions.

The Manitoba Act.   Most of the Métis demands were included in the *Manitoba Act.* The Canadian government made the fur-trading district of Assiniboia into the Province of Manitoba on July 15, 1870. The French and English languages were to be officially equal, there was to be provision for separate schools and land was to be set aside for the Métis population. However, natural resources were to be transferred to the Dominion, and plans were to be made for a railway to be built across the prairies in order to encourage extensive settlement. After the *Manitoba Act* had been approved by the British government, Manitoba and the North-West Territories (now provided with a lieutenant-governor and council appointed by Ottawa) were incorporated officially into the Dominion.

While negotiations were underway, Macdonald tried to appease Ontario by sending Colonel Wolseley on a difficult ninety-five day journey from Toronto to Manitoba with several hundred troops. This show of force was designed to impress the Métis, the provinces and the United States with Canadian intentions in the North-West.

Riel, learning of their approach, fled to the United States. The Red River Rebellion was over, although within two decades Métis living farther west were once again to resist the advance of settlement.

The North-West Mounted Police.   In 1873, the Dominion government decided that a civil police force would be more effective than a military garrison in maintaining order in the North-West. As a result the North-West Mounted Police came into being. The first 300 men were well-educated men "of birth and breeding and social advantage." During the summer of 1874, after an initial training period, they were stationed at posts throughout the West.

By December, 1874, the Mounted Police were able to report that they had brought a complete stoppage to the illegal whisky trade with the Indians carried on mostly by American smugglers. From then on the police played an important part in the organization of the North-West, helping new settlers and patrolling isolated areas. Above all, they earned the respect of the Plains Indians by helping them adapt to a more restricted way of life and by helping to bring about treaties between the tribes and the Dominion government. In 1904, the force became the Royal North-West Mounted Police. In 1920 it absorbed the Dominion police and became the Royal Canadian Mounted Police.

British Columbia.   With the ending of the Cariboo gold rush, the Crown Colony of British Columbia had slipped into a period of depression. In 1866 Vancouver Island was reunited with the mainland, and the colony's capital was permanently established at Victoria. The union reduced the colony's administrative costs somewhat but did nothing to lessen its heavy debt. The continued bad times resulted in a strong movement for annexation with the United States, especially among those Americans who had come north during the gold rush period. This movement, combined with the American purchase of Alaska, alarmed many persons in the colony.

Under the leadership of Amor de Cosmos, a strong pro-federation group successfully countered the annexationists and persuaded the province to unite with Canada if acceptable terms could be obtained. Supported by John A. Macdonald, who had dreams of a transcontinental dominion, and encouraged by the British government, talks began in 1870. It was finally agreed that British Columbia should enter Confederation. The Dominion government pledged to take over the colony's debt and make an annual grant based on population. It also promised a railway connecting British Columbia with the East. The railway was to be started within two years and finished within ten years. Thus, on July 20, 1871, British Columbia became Canada's sixth province.

Prince Edward Island.   In 1873, Prince Edward Island also agreed to join the Dominion. This was done after the federal government promised a grant to buy out absentee landlords, to establish communication with the mainland, to assume its crippling railway debts and to grant a generous subsidy. Macdonald's policy of "buying love and purchasing peace" had proved successful in every area except Newfoundland.

THE TREATY OF WASHINGTON

Between March and May of 1871, an Anglo-American commission deliberated in Washington in an attempt to settle a number of problems aggravating relations between Canada and the United States. These included: (1) American claims for damages from Great Britain arising out of the activities of the *Alabama* and other Confederate ships built in British ports; (2) the free navigation of the St. Lawrence River by American ships; (3) the San Juan boundary dispute (involving the boundary in the gulf southeast of Vancouver Island); (4) American fishing rights in Canadian inshore Atlantic waters; and (5) Canadian claims resulting from the Fenian raids. Macdonald was appointed one of the five British commissioners, the first colonial statesman to be included in an Imperial delegation. Canadians hoped that the negotiations would bring a renewal of the Reciprocity Treaty (that had expired in 1866) with the United States, or at least a favourable trade agreement in exchange for fishing rights. American bargaining, and a lack of support of Canadian aims from the British commissioners, largely frustrated Macdonald's attempts to secure provisions more favourable to Canada.

The major clauses of the Treaty of Washington, signed on May 8, 1871, provided for free navigation of the St. Lawrence River and Lake Michigan (no mention being made of the Canadian canals). It allowed bonding privileges to and from New York City, Boston and Portland, and it granted the free entry of Canadian fish to American markets and the entry of Americans into Canada's Atlantic fisheries for ten years. (The compensation for this last concession was established by a subsequent international commission at $5,500,000 in Canada's favour.) By the Treaty, the *Alabama* claims were referred to an international tribunal. The San Juan dispute was referred for arbitration to the German Emperor, whose award in 1872 favoured the United States. The Treaty completely ignored Canadian claims for the Fenian raids. Faced with bitter dissatisfaction at home, Macdonald used ratification of the Treaty as a bribe to wrest from Britain a promise to compensate Canada for the Fenian damages. With this slight sweetener for an otherwise bitter pill, Parliament ratified the Treaty of Washington in 1873. Despite the blow to Canada's national pride, Macdonald was probably correct in summarizing the benefits of the Treaty as peace for the Empire and markets for the Maritime fisheries.

MACDONALD'S GOVERNMENT

The year 1872 was an election year in Canada. It was the first occasion on which Macdonald and his government were required to give the Canadian electorate an account of their work in the past and to announce their plans for the future. Except for some comparatively densely populated areas in the East, the nation they served contained only four million people thinly spread between the Atlantic and Pacific Oceans. Although an urge toward nationality was discernible, national objectives were vague and national policies were generally undetermined. The divisive forces of religion, language, cultural heritage and economic regionalism were never more than just below the surface of national affairs and constantly threatened to destroy the whole Confederation experiment.

In his party and in his cabinet Macdonald had managed to reconcile and even mute the voices of disunity. His policies and programmes of the first term had effectively expressed all the national aspirations of the new nation and had left the opposition with little to oppose. The territorial expansion of the Dominion was almost complete, with only Newfoundland, the distant and unexplored Arctic Islands, and Prince Edward Island left to be brought into the Confederation. (The latter's entry was known at that time to be imminent.) Immediately after Confederation the Intercolonial Railway linking Halifax and Quebec had been started with the help of a loan from Britain.

For the future, Macdonald's policy involved three phases: the settlement and agricultural development of the West, the industrial development of the East, and the construction of a transcontinental railway to link the two. Initial steps had been taken on all three. Specifically, the *Dominion Lands Act* of 1872 offered a settler a quarter section of western farming land and the right to an adjoining quarter at low cost after three years of settlement; the *Trade Unions Act* encouraged organized labour in the cities of the East by granting unions the right to strike. Negotiations were started and preliminary plans were laid for the construction of the railway. There were two groups bidding for the charter to build the transcontinental route; the first was headed by Sir Hugh Allan, a Montreal shipping magnate, while the second was a Toronto company called Inter-oceanic Railway Company. Early in 1873, following the election, the government awarded the charter for a railway from Montreal to British Columbia to Allan's Canadian Pacific Railroad Company.

"The Pacific Scandal." Macdonald was not able to enjoy success for long. Within a few weeks railway politics threatened to destroy his government. It was disclosed that members of Macdonald's party had accepted campaign funds in the recent election from Sir Hugh Allan, and that George Cartier, Macdonald's Quebec lieutenant and the most important recipient of these funds, had even promised Allan the charter in return. No personal guilt was ever attached to Macdonald, but when Parliament met in the fall of 1873 he saw his support wither quickly and he was forced to resign. The Liberal leader, Alexander Mackenzie, became prime minister, and in a subsequent election the public reacted to "the Pacific Scandal" by giving the Liberals (as the Reformers were now being called) a clear majority of sixty seats in the Commons.

BIBLIOGRAPHY

CARELESS, J. M. S. *Brown of the Globe.* Vol. II. Macmillan, 1964.

CREIGHTON, D. G. *John A. Macdonald.* 2 vols. Macmillan, 1952-55.

HARDY, W. G. *From Sea to Sea.* Doubleday, 1960.

MCDOUGALL, J. LORNE. *Canadian Pacific.* McGill University Press, 1968.

ROBERTSON, R. W. *The Execution of Thomas Scott.* Burns and MacEachern, 1968.

SAYWELL, J. T. *Nation Making.* Burns and MacEachern, 1967.

SHELTON, W. G. *B.C. and Confederation.* Morris Printing Co., 1967.

STANLEY, G. F. G. *The Birth of Western Canada.* University of Toronto, 1963.

STANLEY, G. F. G. *Louis Riel.* Ryerson, 1968.

WILD, ROLAND. *Amor de Cosmos.* Ryerson, 1958.

9

Early National Development, 1873-1896

With the resignation of Sir John A. Macdonald in the autumn of 1873, Alexander Mackenzie, an immigrant Scots stonemason, was sworn in as prime minister of Canada's first Liberal government. An election was called for January of 1874, and when the votes had been counted the Canadian people had unmistakably demonstrated that they wanted a new government. Unfortunately, the victorious Liberals were not equally prepared for office. The party was overwhelmingly based in Ontario and lacked any strong central organization. Quebec in particular proved to be an especially weak area. The *Parti Rouge*, the Liberals' Quebec wing, came under strong attack from ultramontanist forces. These were reactionary Catholic groups who followed the lead of the *Syllabus of Errors* of 1864, a papal condemnation of liberalism. In the other provinces the Liberal party was forced to depend on its weak provincial Liberal organizations.

The Liberals in Office.   Mackenzie lacked the qualities of leadership necessary to pull the party together and even found difficulty in controlling dissenters in Ontario, such as the strong-willed Edward Blake. Instead of clear policy statements, there was more often a discordant chorus of voices in both cabinet and Commons.

The Liberals, however, cannot in any way be blamed for all the problems of their term. By late 1873 Canada was feeling the full effect of a world-wide depression, with its falling prices, business failures, chronic unemployment and declining world trade. As has so often been the case, Canada was at the mercy of forces over which her government had relatively little control. Three measures were tried by the government—a reduction in government expenditures, the promotion of exports, and an increase in tariffs for revenue. Not surprisingly, and certainly not entirely to the Liberals' discredit, all three failed.

The most important programme to be scrapped in the course of the government's economy drive was the transcontinental railway. Liberal railway policy attempted to ignore Macdonald's commitments to British Columbia and substitute a scheme for completion on a pay-as-you-go basis. This satisfied neither British Columbia nor the Senate, and the Liberals were so continually plagued with the problem that little progress was made.

In an attempt to expand trade, George Brown was sent to Washington to negotiate a new reciprocity treaty, a traditional Liberal policy. At first his mission seemed successful, but the new treaty was rejected by the United States' Senate.

Higher tariffs proved to be even more disastrous for the Liberals. Reversing their long and loudly proclaimed belief in free trade, the Liberals raised tariffs in 1874 in the hope that domestic production would thereby be stimulated. Even so, their support for protection was only skin-deep. As the depression deepened during 1876 the Conservatives demanded a thorough-going policy of protection and blamed the Liberals' half-hearted tariff measures for the country's economic crisis.

By 1878 the Liberal government was in serious trouble, although surprisingly enough its members themselves seemed confident of their ability to win the approaching election. Nevertheless, their railway policy had accomplished little except to anger British Columbia, where secession was being loudly threatened. Only a visit to the western province by the Governor-General, Lord Dufferin, combined with the efforts of the Colonial Secretary, Lord Carnarvon, resulted in a compromise by which British Columbia accepted an extension of the time limit. The failure of reciprocity negotiations had left new markets unopened while, ironically, Liberal talk of reciprocity had aroused fear of competition in Canada's infant industrial circles. The tariff question divided the party and the country—the Maritimes favoured free trade, and Ontario and Quebec, the centres of industry, supported protection.

The Liberals did have several accomplishments to their credit. They had established the Supreme Court of Canada as a court of appeal and had introduced the secret ballot in elections. The Royal Military College at Kingston, Ontario, had been founded and all survey work on the Pacific railway had been completed. Liberal accomplishments, however, were not sufficient to offset the government's poor public image or the general dissatisfaction and feeling of unease arising from the depression.

By comparison, the Conservatives were promoting an election platform cleverly formulated by Macdonald while in opposition. Their programme under the appealing slogan, *The National Policy,* put before the disillusioned electorate no less than three major policies. In its broadest sense the National Policy promised country-wide development through a combination of higher tariffs (the key item intended to encourage the growth of Eastern industry), a vigorous immigration policy (to populate the West and thus promote its great agricultural potential), and the prompt completion of the Pacific railway (to link together East and West, the factory and the farm, the consumer and the producer, and to take the settler to his homestead).

Beside the golden and prophetic vision implied in the National Policy, the Liberal election slogan in 1878, "Honesty, Integrity and Economy" seemed sincere but weak. This was precisely the impression the Liberals had presented over the last four years. The Liberals rested on their record and warned of the "demon protection." However, the electorate listened to the promises of leadership and prosperity that would result from the return of Macdonald. The results of the September election took even the confident Conservatives by surprise. They found themselves back in power with a majority of sixty-eight, a most satisfactory endorsement of the National Policy. Largely as a result of this defeat, Alexander Mackenzie retired in 1880 and was succeeded as leader by Edward Blake.

The Conservatives Return to Power.   It is possible the Conservatives had been relieved to be out of power during the black depression of the last four years. Once back in power they soon realized that a politician's oratory and nationalistic slogans are of little help when the problems themselves have to be confronted. Macdonald may have had a majority but he still had the depression, plus a situation where more people left the country than arrived, plus a massive gap in communications between East and West.

In 1879, Macdonald's government raised tariffs as they had promised. The general tariff rose from seventeen and one half to twenty per cent. Tariffs on semi-finished products ranged from ten to twenty per cent and on fully manufactured goods from an average of twenty-five to a high of thirty per cent. In an important gesture to the Maritimes a duty of fifty cents a ton was placed on coal. To keep the farmers happy a rather useless tariff was placed on agricultural products.

Perhaps the most stubborn problem faced by Macdonald was the completion of the Pacific railway. Convinced that it must be carried out by a private company with government backing and assistance where necessary, Macdonald listened to two major proposals. The Grand Trunk Railway of Toronto showed interest, but their offer was definitely unacceptable, for they wanted the route to pass through Chicago and around the south shore of Lake Superior. The second proposal was made by a Montreal syndicate headed by James J. Hill (a Canadian veteran of American railroad building) and George Stephen, president of the Bank of Montreal. This syndicate agreed to the overriding principle of an all-Canadian route.

Late in 1880 negotiations established the terms of the charter, and in February, 1881 the Canadian Pacific Railway Company was awarded a charter under the Canadian Pacific Railway Act. By the official terms, the Company received 700 miles of line already completed or under construction. It was allowed a full tax and tariff exemption on all materials and equipment, a subsidy of 25 million dollars, and 25 million acres of fertile prairie land (tax-free for twenty years) in alternate mile-square sections on both sides of the right of way to a depth of twenty-four miles. The Company was granted a monopoly guaranteeing the prohibition for twenty years of any rivals between the United States border

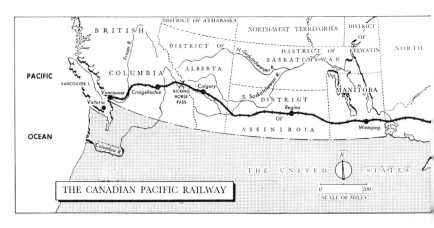

THE CANADIAN PACIFIC RAILWAY

and the C.P.R. line. For its part, the Company promised to complete the line by 1891.

For the first year, construction on the C.P.R. was slow, but by 1882 the irrepressible William Cornelius Van Horne, a famous American railroad engineer had been hired. Under his astute direction and fired by his tremendous energy and enthusiasm, track mileage rapidly increased across the prairie section. From the west coast, track was laid more slowly because of the mountainous terrain. Other sections of the line, in British Columbia and along the north shore of Lake Superior, were also built, so that by 1884 the directors of the Company were confidently predicting completion well in advance of the 1891 deadline.

In spite of this spectacular construction success, the C.P.R. was plagued with constant and sometimes almost fatal financial problems. One historian has said: "To detail the intricacies of C.P.R. financing would be to write a textbook in arithmetic." By the winter of 1883 the Company's funds, derived mainly from the government subsidy and the fortunes of the original investors in the syndicate, had been exhausted. As yet the Company's land was yielding little return, since a completed railway was necessary to open up the West to settlement. Moreover, the year 1883 witnessed crop failures in the East and the return of the depression. In an already depressed stock market the C.P.R. was an unattractive investment indeed. At first the Macdonald government sought to improve the desirability of C.P.R. stock by guaranteeing a three per cent dividend which, combined with two per cent from the Company, would offer an attractive annual dividend of five per cent. This measure failed to reverse the lack of enthusiasm

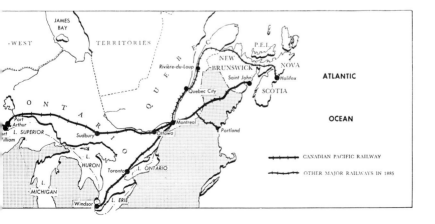

in the New York and European investment markets, and the Company had to attempt to borrow $22,500,000. Again they found apathy in the money markets.

Stephen, the president of C.P.R., turned to Macdonald for a government loan. Macdonald knew that his party and his cabinet were sharply divided on the issue since the government had already been generous in the extreme. He was also convinced, however, that both the party and the country might collapse if the C.P.R. were not completed. After much hesitation he arranged a government loan of five million dollars in return for a mortgage on the railway's main line. This was enough to tide the Company over until 1885, when the east and west lines met at Craigellachie, near Revelstoke, British Columbia. That same year the C.P.R. was able to suggest its worth and to justify the North Shore route in particular by transporting troops to the West to put down Louis Riel's second rebellion. British investors were suddenly impressed, and a bond issue of $35 millions was bought out at ninety-one per cent of face value by Barings of London. With this boost the C.P.R. was saved. In the summer of 1886 the complete line was in operation, five years ahead of schedule, and the first transcontinental train reached the west coast.

Throughout almost the entire construction period of the C.P.R., Macdonald and the Conservatives had been bitterly disappointed to find that neither the British government nor the British people shared their own great enthusiasm for the future of the West. This same lack of interest was a constant brake on the Conservatives' immigration policy. Despite a lavish propaganda campaign in Britain and repeated promotion efforts by Galt, Canada's first High Commissioner in London, the number of immigrants did not live up to the high hopes of the government.

Despite the desperately slow rate of growth, a tide of settlement was slowly moving across the Canadian prairies, bringing in its wake serious problems. While Canada never had an Indian problem in the West as great as that of the United States, she did in 1885 have one more uprising against the western press of civilization.

The North-West Rebellion.   In 1884 Louis Riel returned to Canada. Since 1870, when he had fled from Fort Garry, Riel had led a turbulent, transient life. After remaining in rather careless hiding in the Red River area for some months he had finally gone to the United States in 1872. The following year he returned to contest and win a by-election and subsequent election (1874) in the Manitoba riding of Provencher. Despite a bold trip to Ottawa (where he was subject to an Ontario warrant for his arrest), he was formally expelled by a resolution of the House before he even took his seat. In 1875 he was exiled for ten years. Within a short time his sanity gave way and for almost two years he was secretly confined in various mental institutions in Quebec. Riel was obsessed with the notion that he had a divine mission to found

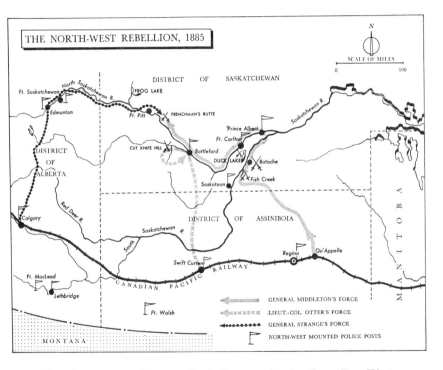

THE NORTH-WEST REBELLION, 1885

and to head a new Roman Catholic state in the Canadian West. After being released from hospital in 1878, Riel went to Montana where he worked as an interpreter and trader. In 1884 he was invited by the Métis to return to Canada and to lead them once more against a slow but steady Anglo-Saxon advance across the West. Convinced of his destiny, Riel could not refuse.

The centre of Métis life had moved to the Saskatchewan region. The spread of settlement was becoming more and more of a threat to the traditional freedom of these half-breeds; the buffalo were now almost completely gone from the prairie, as were many of the fur-bearing animals. Following the Red River Rebellion, the Métis had been given land and scrip but they had sold these to speculators for the sake of short-term gains. The Métis' traditional allies, the Indians, were also discontented with their new, limited life on government reservations.

Late in 1884, under Riel's leadership, a petition was sent to Ottawa making a variety of demands for the Indians, Métis and whites of the North-West. The government ignored the petition and Riel proceeded to duplicate his actions of 1869—he established a "provisional government" and began to organize the Métis into armed bands. A Mounted Police force was ambushed and attacks on outlying white settlements took place. As most of these raids were committed by roving bands of Indians, the English half-breeds and many Métis were reluctant to take part in what looked more and more like an Indian uprising.

Ottawa now acted by dispatching a militia force to put down the insurrection. Perhaps as significant as the ensuing military operation was the fact that the expeditionary force was transported to Winnipeg via the new C.P.R. line in eight days. After gathering reinforcements, the force was split into three columns. One was to attack Batoche, a second to rescue the town of Battleford from Chief Poundmaker's besieging Indians and a third to capture Chief Big Bear's band of Cree Indians. Batoche, Riel's headquarters, was taken, and Riel himself surrendered soon after. The Indian bands were either captured or scattered and their leaders, Chiefs Poundmaker and Big Bear, taken. The North-West Rebellion (or Saskatchewan Rebellion), which had cost two hundred lives and six million dollars was the last significant resistance to the settlement of the Canadian West.

Riel continued to be the focal point around which racial and religious animosities raged, particularly in Ontario and Quebec. Macdonald's government, much as it might have wished to do otherwise, was forced by Ontario opinion to bring Riel to trial in 1885. Refusing to plead insanity in his own defence, he was found guilty of treason and hanged. Even today he remains a controversial figure in Canadian history. In the harsh practical world of politics his career and fate have continued to have repercussions. His execution under the auspices of a Conservative government marked that party as a prime subject of suspicion and even hostility in Quebec where Riel was considered a martyr in the French-Canadian cause. In fact, for over sixty years Quebec turned its back on the Conservatives and voted against them.

Dominion-Provincial Affairs.   Although Riel's execution intensified the underlying racial animosity in the Canadian federation, it
did have a curious result. It brought, for the moment, a measure
of unity to other forces almost as old as Confederation itself—the
forces of provincial dissatisfaction.

For every province except Ontario, finances had been a constant
problem, especially during the years of depression. Usually Macdonald was able to soften the voices of dissent by an adjustment
of the federal grant to the provinces. But this could never be more
than a temporary solution. It did nothing to satisfy the two basic
demands for a revision of Dominion-provincial fiscal arrangements
and the grant of greater provincial autonomy. While the arguments
for "provincial rights" had only a weak foundation, they did
serve as an effective base from which provincial governments and
premiers could bargain for additional concessions and advantages.

One of the most powerful weapons that Macdonald used in
his attempts to create a strong central government was the federal
power under the BNA Act to disallow provincial legislation. He
looked upon this as a protection for the federal government against
any possible encroachment upon its powers by the provinces. In
the first twenty years of Confederation sixty-eight provincial laws
were disallowed. However, the provinces, most of which were
controlled by Liberal premiers, were determined to have "exclusive powers" in their own affairs.

The first dispute over provincial rights arose over the Ontario-
Manitoba boundary, both provinces claiming the territory between
the Lake-of-the-Woods and Port Arthur. Macdonald tried to
arrange a settlement favourable to a Conservative-led Manitoba.
He lost face, however, when Ontario's aggressive Liberal premier,
Oliver Mowat, forced the issue to arbitration by the Judicial Committee of the Privy Council, which upheld Ontario's claim.

Three other judgments by the Judicial Committee of the Privy
Council were of even greater future significance in Dominion-
provincial relations. These were made in disputes between the
Ontario government and Ottawa—the Rivers and Streams Act,
1884, and two decisions regarding the control of liquor sales in
1883 and 1896. In these decisions, their lordships, for all practical purposes, restricted the federal government to those powers
explicitly set out in Section 91 of the BNA Act. It was these decisions that began the long trend away from the basic intent of
Confederation to make the provinces subordinate to the central
government. Hereafter, the residual power, that is the power to

legislate upon matters *not* specifically enumerated in the BNA Act, were to be given to the provinces.

Religion was another source of conflict. In an episode in which the usual loyalties became curiously mixed, Macdonald found himself beset by the Equal Rights Association, an Orange-supported organization founded by a leading Ontario Conservative, D'Alton McCarthy. The issue was Macdonald's refusal to disallow the Quebec Jesuit Estates Act, which McCarthy and his supporters believed dealt unjustly with the Protestant schools of Quebec. (Following the suppression of the Jesuit Order in 1773, the income from its property in Quebec had been directed to education. When the Order was rehabilitated in the 1840's, this settlement was questioned. The Jesuit Estates Act, passed by the provincial government of Quebec, sought to settle the conflicting claims by giving $400,000 to the Jesuits and the Quebec bishops and $60,000 to the Protestant schools of Quebec.) Macdonald, however, refused in this case to interfere with provincial rights.

McCarthy thereupon became interested in the Manitoba "Schools Question." By the Manitoba Act, that province had been given a school system guaranteeing the rights of the French-speaking Roman Catholic minority, although no legal system of separate schools was actually established. In 1880, a Liberal Manitoba government, spurred on by McCarthy and firmly backed by a large Anglo-Saxon majority in the province, changed the educational system to conform with that of Ontario, but *without* any provision for separate schools. Macdonald hesitated to employ disallowance again but the Conservatives were pledged to guard French educational rights in Manitoba. The Ottawa Liberals defended their Manitoba colleagues and urged conciliation. The Conservatives, although they promised remedial legislation to establish separate schools in Manitoba, temporized.

The Decline of the Conservatives.   In 1891 a general election was called, and the Conservatives rallied to the cry: "The old flag, the old man, the old policy." The Conservatives indeed could take some satisfaction from the results of their policies. The National Policy tariff increases had not been the solution for depression that had been expected but they had encouraged industrial development and that was an important achievement. Likewise, the C.P.R. continued to be beset by problems and was not the instant success that had been the original dream; but the railway was constantly proving its value to the vast Dominion, and even those who had been its most vociferous critics before 1885 were now openly voicing their admiration. It had become a source of national pride.

Macdonald himself had become something of a national institution. In 1891 he conducted an exhausting campaign, attacking the Liberal policy of unrestricted reciprocity as the prelude to annexation and loudly proclaiming his own loyalty to Britain: "A British subject I was born and a British subject I will die!" The pace of the campaign, however, caught up with him and he was forced to curtail his trip before the March 5 polling day. Nevertheless, the results brought victory with only some losses in Ontario and Quebec.

The next few months for Macdonald brought failing health, then a seeming recovery, and finally a last shattering plunge. In early June he died.

Without Macdonald the Conservatives drifted. There was no heir-apparent, and the first successor was the aged J. J. C. Abbott, who resigned after eighteen months. His successor, John S. Thompson, who generally followed Macdonald's policies, was just beginning to establish himself when he died suddenly in 1894. The mantle of leadership then passed to Senator Mackenzie Bowell, the senior cabinet member. His colleagues had little confidence in him. With his inability to act on the Manitoba schools question he lost their confidence completely, and Sir Charles Tupper assumed the party leadership in the House. Tupper was unlucky enough to have been called to save the party just before an election which the Conservatives had little chance of winning. The main issue was a remedial bill to settle the Manitoba schools question. The withdrawal of this bill because of party dissension and Liberal opposition only served to divide the Conservative party even further. Tupper lost to the Liberals. The new prime minister was Wilfrid Laurier, the first French Canadian to hold that office.

BIBLIOGRAPHY

ANDERSON, F. W. *1885—The Riel Rebellion*. Frontier Books. Frontiers Unlimited, 1962.

COULTER, J. *The Trial of Louis Riel*. Oberon Press, 1968.

CREIGHTON, D. G. *John A. Macdonald*. 2 vols. Macmillan, 1952-55.

DAFOE, JOHN W. *Laurier*. McClelland and Stewart, 1963.

GUILLET, E. C. *You'll Never Die, John A.* Macmillan, 1967.

HILL, DOUGLAS. *The Opening of the Canadian West*. Heinemann, 1967.

JEFFERYS, C. W. *Picture Gallery of Canadian History, Vol. III.* Ryerson, 1968.

MCKEE, S. L. *Gabriel Dumont-Indian Fighter.* Frontier Books. Frontiers Unlimited, 1967.

SLUMAN, NORMA. *Poundmaker.* Ryerson, 1967.

STANLEY, G. F. G. *The Birth of Western Canada.* University of Toronto, 1963.

TANGHI, R. *Laurier.* Harvest House, 1966.

THOMSON, D. C. *Alexander Mackenzie, Clear Grit.* Macmillan, 1960.

10

The Age of Laurier, 1896-1911

The election of 1896 brought a new age to Canada. The once vital era of Macdonald, which had sputtered to a dreary conclusion after the death of its guiding spirit, was replaced by the bright and confident administration of Wilfrid Laurier.

It is perhaps too easy to draw a contrast between the Scots-born, Protestant, John A. Macdonald and the French-Canadian, Roman Catholic, Laurier. There is no question that where Macdonald was perhaps jovial, homely, and casual, Laurier was dignified, handsome, and elegant. Where Macdonald spoke with wit and folksy appeal, Laurier cast a different spell with his eloquent, polished oratory. These obvious differences aside, both men made a striking personal impact on Canadians, and both were superb politicians, interested far more in broad lines of policy than in the details of administration. Both eras contained the same problems of nationhood—economic development, race and religion. Above all, the policies that the Liberal Laurier consciously followed were very much those of his predecessor.

Laurier's new cabinet proved to be a body equal to the prestige of its leader. Among its members were W. S. Fielding (Finance), Sir Richard Cartwright (Trade and Commerce), A. G. Blair (Railways), Sir Oliver Mowat (Justice), and from Manitoba, Clifford Sifton (Department of the Interior).

The Manitoba Schools Question. The new ministry was, of course, immediately faced with one problem left behind by the former Conservative government—the Manitoba schools question.

Emphasizing the need for co-operation and compromise, Laurier arranged for discussions between the federal and Manitoba governments. It was finally agreed (1) that the non-denominational nature of the Manitoba schools would remain unimpaired; (2) that *any* religion could be taught by any denomination at the end of the day and under certain conditions; and (3) that where a certain specified number of pupils spoke French a bilingual teacher could be employed. This compromise did not satisfy the Roman Catholic bishops; but their protests were eventually silenced by a Papal legate, and the Manitoba schools question lost its immediate political importance.

The Liberal Tariff Policy. The skill demonstrated by the Laurier government in handling the racial and religious trouble caused by the Manitoba schools problem was also used in dealing with the tariff question. The Liberals had, of course, been traditionally anti-tariff, or at least advocates of freer trade. Laurier, however, was an avowed disciple of Macdonald's policies and had even publicly supported tariffs before his election. Once in office, the Liberals did little more than tinker with the National Policy tariff schedules and relied on the claim that tariffs were for revenue purposes, thus hoping that they could avoid being labelled as protectionists. In particular, some nuisance tariffs were eliminated and the principle of *ad valorem* duties (duties based on the value of the goods concerned) was introduced. Of greater importance was a new principle of preferential tariffs designed to favour those countries, particularly Britain, that gave Canada favourable rates. Some industries, though, were happy to find that they were given even more protection by the Liberals than they had received under the Conservatives. The government also gave bounties on some of the few products that suffered from the revisions. For these reasons the Liberal tariff policy remained remarkably close in spirit and effect to the Macdonald National Policy and provoked little complaint from Canada's industrial community.

A Flood of Immigrants. While observing the precedent of the National Policy tariff structure, the Laurier government also maintained, and with considerably more success, the Macdonald policy on immigration. The Conservative campaign for immigrants to settle Canada's vast and fertile Western prairies had suffered constant frustration because of the seemingly endless depression of the last two to three decades. Laurier's accession to office, however, roughly corresponded with the ending of the depression, a

factor which helped the new Liberal government in its development of the West. The Liberals encouraged the construction of
grain elevators, ships and railways and waged a magnificent campaign promoting the Canadian West as a new goal for Europe's
restless and crowded millions. Laurier's policies were aided by
a reviving national economy, the development of faster-maturing
and hardier wheat strains, and advances in farm and allied
machinery.

It was Clifford Sifton, from Manitoba, who, with his own great
faith in and knowledge of the West, spearheaded the new immigration programme. Under his leadership the Canadian government
sent out tens of thousands of posters, pamphlets and advertise-
ments to Europe and the United States telling of the opportunities,
the free homesteads and assisted passages. Agents were sent to
important European centres, and European and American journal-
ists were given expense-paid trips to Canada to see for themselves
"the last, best West" and to tell their countrymen of its great
promise.

The ultimate result of this programme was a vast influx of
immigrants from Britain, Germany, Scandinavia, the Balkans, the
Ukraine, Russia and the United States. In all, two million persons
arrived in Canada during the fifteen years of Liberal rule. This
was the coming of age of the Canadian prairies. Where a few
years before there had been only a scattering of settlers, a few
small towns and lonely Mounted Police posts, there was, by 1911,
a growing population, great expanses of wheat and other grains,
prosperous and energetic farming towns, and throughout the West
there was an air of buoyant confidence and anticipation. In 1905
the development of the West was far enough advanced that the
provinces of Alberta and Saskatchewan were created out of the
southern portion of the North-West Territories.

The spectacular development of the prairies was accompanied
by a similar surge in growth and prosperity throughout the entire
country. Lumbering, mining and fishing expanded in British
Columbia; in the Yukon gold-mining dominated the scene; Ontario
and Quebec began to tap their mineral wealth, particularly copper
and silver, and the pulp and paper industry flourished; from the
Maritimes came processed steel for new railways. Manufacturing
industries, centred along the St. Lawrence and lower Great Lakes
in Quebec and Ontario, grew out of their infancy and provided a
large variety of products from furniture and clothing to heavy
agricultural machinery and tools. All these developments were

naturally followed by a great increase in the number of commercial and financial institutions. Montreal and Toronto, favourably situated in the industrial heartland, became increasingly important as their populations soared with the influx of industrial workers (both immigrants and former farm workers) and as they strengthened their positions as the focal points of commerce, transportation and finance.

With this tremendous increase in productivity it was natural that Canada should begin to emerge as a major trading nation. Wheat and flour headed the list of exports, of course, but there was a wide variety of other items as well—all types of grains, vegetables, dairy products, livestock, lumber, fish, minerals (particularly silver) and even some manufactured goods. Montreal, as the meeting place of rail and lake traffic with ocean traffic, re-established its historic position as Canada's major ocean port.

The Railway Boom.   From the beginning of Canada's history communications had been a major problem. Macdonald's railway policy had raised communications to the level of prime instruments of nationalism and national development. Laurier, the leader of Canada when Macdonald's dream of national development actually began to take place, was forced to follow in an already established pattern. By 1901, the quantities of wheat being hauled out of the prairies had become too great for the C.P.R. to handle on its line between Winnipeg and the Lakehead. As Van Horne said, "the hopper was too big for the spout." Moreover, if prairie settlement was to expand beyond the immediate vicinity of the C.P.R.'s main line, more railways were needed.

In answer to both needs the Grand Trunk Railway in 1902 proposed to build a second transcontinental line from North Bay to the Pacific—if Laurier's government would provide a subsidy of up to 75 per cent of construction costs. Almost at the same time the Canadian Northern Railway, operated by William Mackenzie and Donald Mann, which had been building and accumulating short lines in Manitoba, announced its desire to expand its operations to include still another transcontinental line from the Atlantic to the Pacific. Laurier feared that three lines would be too much, and the government tried to arrange a combined venture. Both companies, however, were blinded by their anticipation of future profits and refused to accept the government's warnings. With what one historian has termed "irresolution and possibly irresponsibility," Laurier's government gave in to regional and provincial pressures and agreed to charter both companies.

To assist them the government followed a policy similar to Macdonald's policy of combining public and private enterprise. The government agreed to build a line, to be known as the National Transcontinental, from Moncton to Winnipeg. From Winnipeg the Grand Trunk Pacific, a new railway company, was to take over and complete a line to the Pacific coast, the government agreeing to be the principal backer of the necessary bonds. The Grand Trunk Pacific Company was to rent the National Transcontinental line, in order that the two lines together might form a complete ocean-to-ocean railway. Despite bitter opposition and even the resignation of A. G. Blair, the Minister of Railways, the National Transcontinental Railway Bill was passed by Parliament in 1903, and construction started soon after.

Curiously, the Canadian Northern received much less publicity and opposition than the Grand Trunk Pacific. A bill was passed by Parliament guaranteeing the company's bonds to the extent of $13,000 per mile on the Manitoba to Edmonton section. The company was also permitted to build and to acquire lines in Ontario so as to connect its existing operations in the province, thereby forming a third transcontinental line.

With two parallel transcontinental systems under construction it is an understatement to claim that Canada was rapidly becoming overendowed with railways. This was most acutely obvious in Northern Ontario where three lines would pass through the virtually untracked, unsettled, undeveloped wilderness of the Canadian Shield. Indeed, the transcontinental Canadian railway policy established by Macdonald, had now been taken to a most illogical, inefficient and wasteful extreme.

The C.P.R. was at this time also riding the crest of the railway boom, adding thousands of miles to its existing lines, building hotels and entering into the steamship business. Many other new railways were being built as well, notably the Timiskaming and Northern Ontario constructed by the Ontario government and the Pacific Great Eastern guaranteed by the British Columbia government. The result of this unprecedented railway expansion that had all been started by prairie wheat was a tremendous injection of vitality and prosperity into the entire Canadian economy. Thousands of new jobs were created from the pick and shovel gangs at the "head of steel" of a railway under construction to the factory workers constructing rolling stock to the lumberjack cutting timber to be made into ties. It is estimated that between 1904 and 1914 railway construction added $775,000,000 to the economy in wages and $825,000,000 in the purchase of materials and equipment (both amounts stemming largely from British capital investment). Thus, in spite of the waste and lack of foresight that characterized the boom, it did serve as a powerful stimulus to Canada's growth between 1900 and 1914.

CANADA IN THE WORLD

The great burst of economic expansion and vitality that transformed parts of Canada as the nation moved into the twentieth century had a parallel in the development of national awareness. It was inevitable that as Canada became more involved in international trade and in the growth of her own economy she should become more concerned in the affairs of the world as a whole and in identifying her position in it. In line with past tradition, the two poles of Canadian concern were (1) Great Britain and the Empire and (2) the United States.

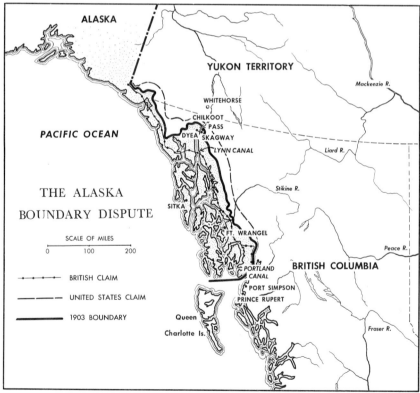

The Alaska Boundary Dispute.   By 1890 the only boundary question with the United States still unsettled was that between Alaska and the Yukon in the area known as the Alaska "Panhandle." In the Anglo-Russian Treaty of 1825 the exact location had been only vaguely described. It became a practical issue in 1896 when gold-seekers moving into the Yukon Territory from the Pacific coast passed through the disputed area. The American government claimed that when the treaty spoke of the boundary following "the summit of the mountains situated parallel to the coast" it was to be interpreted to mean a line that generally followed the configuration of the coast, thereby giving an unbroken strip of land to the United States. The Canadian government interpreted the phrase as referring to the mountains nearest the ocean, which would have given to Canada direct access to the Pacific across the "Panhandle" by way of several deep inlets, the most important at the time being the Stikine River and the Lynn Canal.

A Joint High Commission failed to resolve the dispute. President Theodore Roosevelt, waving his "big stick" at Canada, sent troops close to the Yukon in 1903 to emphasize his demand for arbitration. An arbitration tribunal, composed of three Americans, two Canadians and the British Chief Justice, Lord Alverstone, was established in 1903. With the Canadians and Americans being stout defenders of their countries' positions, Alverstone was the key to the tribunal, and much to the disgust and indignation of Canadians, he did not press Canada's claim. The final boundary line was in part a compromise between the two claims but it did have the important effect of cutting off all Canadian access to the Pacific across the "Panhandle."

The South African War.   In 1899 Canada's attention was drawn to South Africa where friction between British colonists and the Boer farmers of the Orange Free State and the Transvaal broke into open hostility. The situation in South Africa aroused contrasting emotions in Canada. Most English Canadians, notably in Ontario, were anxious to go to the aid of Britain and the empire, while in Quebec the war was denounced as another British imperialist adventure that Canada should ignore. Once again racial passions placed the government in a serious quandary. Laurier was finally overwhelmed by pressure from Ontario, and the government authorized the dispatch of a Canadian contingent of volunteers to South Africa. Other Canadians were recruited directly by the British War Office, and Lord Strathcona organized at his

150

THE DOMINION OF CANADA IN 1900

own expense Strathcona's Horse, a mounted unit, for service in the British army in South Africa.

Altogether, Canada contributed over 8,000 men to the South African War (1899-1902). Extremists in Canada, however, denounced the government's policy as either too little, too late, or as meddling in an unjustifiable affair that was of no concern to Canada. The cabinet itself was shaken by the controversy, and Laurier's hot-tempered protégé, Henri Bourassa, resigned his seat in Parliament to found the *League Nationaliste*, an organization dedicated to defending the rights of French Canada.

Canada and the Empire. The South African War controversy also called attention to the problem of Canada's relation to the British Empire. The question was not new; at the first Colonial Conference in 1887 there had been discussion of a political, military and commercial union of the Empire, but Canada had remained non-committal on the issue. In 1897 at the third Colonial Conference the original proposal was made more forcefully. It was suggested by Joseph Chamberlain, the British Colonial Secretary, that an Imperial Council be established with certain executive powers. To the colonial representatives the idea suggested imperial federation and was clearly a threat to the measure of autonomy they had struggled to achieve. They therefore passed a resolution affirming confidence in their existing political relations with Britain.

A defence union was similarly blocked. Canada in particular refused to contribute to an imperial army or navy for fear that she could be committed to military action without her own approval. Commercial union was also abandoned; again it was Canada that put up the strongest objection by refusing to forego her protective tariffs. On all three matters Laurier was obviously attempting to guard Canada's freedom to chart her own destiny, free from the weaknesses of other parts of the Empire and problems encountered by the mother country.

The question of colonial unity was raised once again in 1902 at the fourth Colonial Conference. Once again Canada and her sister colonies refused to accept further British overtures of closer Imperial union. Indeed, far from accepting the idea of free trade within the empire, the delegates endorsed the general idea of tariffs by passing a resolution in favour of imperial tariff preference. The delegates also informed the British government that they were quite uninterested in sharing the costs of imperial defence.

At the fifth Colonial Conference in 1907 (the first Imperial Conference) the attitude of the colonial prime ministers remained as before. But within a year the news of Germany's growing navy brought second thoughts. At a special Imperial Defence Conference in 1909 the Dominions were asked by the British government to begin planning "Dominion navies to be maintained in different parts of the Empire." Although the request represented a victory for the Dominions, since it acknowledged their right to have national navies, Laurier was at first unwilling to make any commitments.

The "Tin-pot" Navy.   When the Canadian parliament met in 1910, Laurier presented his Naval Service Bill, which proposed to establish, in easy stages, a small Canadian navy that could be placed at the disposal of the British Admiralty. Despite bitter Opposition criticism of a "tin-pot" navy and demands that Canada immediately contribute directly to British naval expansion, Laurier stood behind his bill until it was passed. (In the fierce debates over naval policy, other defence measures already passed by Laurier's government—substantial increases in the defence budget, a larger militia force, the acquisition of new weapons and material—were largely ignored.)

Reciprocity.   Throughout Laurier's term as prime minister tariff policy had remained a burning issue. While manufacturers supported "Laurier's National Policy" and even urged higher tariffs, the idea of protection was basically foreign to Liberal thinking and weighed uneasily on the consciences of many members of the party. For that matter, the high tariffs weighed heavily on the pocket-books of almost all Canadians, who had to pay higher prices for both domestic and foreign goods. The Western farmers, in particular, felt hard-pressed. Stiffly opposing the policy of protective tariffs, a delegation of prairie farmers marched into the House of Commons in 1910 and demanded a return to the traditional Liberal policy of reciprocity with the United States, specifically in farm products.

With the opposition to tariffs becoming more vocal and organized, it is not surprising that in 1911 Laurier's government responded to American overtures to negotiate a reciprocity agreement. The resulting agreement called for both governments to pass parallel legislation that would establish reciprocity in a number of primary products and reduce tariff rates on certain manufactured products.

In Ottawa the immediate Opposition reaction to the agreement was confused and divided. But since the government delayed passage of legislation until the United States' Senate took the first step, Laurier and his cabinet gave the Conservatives time to rouse a storm of protest. Critics across the country prophesied great damage to the country's growing but hard-won industrial strength and emphasized that reciprocity would surely be followed by political union with the United States. It soon became clear that British industrialists feared the loss of their Canadian market, that railway financiers in Britain and in Eastern Canada feared American competition, and that the manufacturers of Ontario and Quebec feared an influx of United States' goods. As the storm grew, all the major newspapers spoke out against reciprocity, public emotion was whipped into a frenzy of anti-Americanism, and finally eighteen prominent Toronto Liberal businessmen openly broke with the party. In Parliament the Conservatives dug in to obstruct the bill. On September 21, after facing more than thirty days of Conservative filibustering, Laurier decided to call a surprise election.

The Liberal Defeat, 1911.   The Liberal intention was to fight the election on reciprocity. But inevitably other issues of other years were raised. Thus, while the Liberals were faced by imperialistic, anti-reciprocity forces in Ontario, in Quebec they were opposed by Bourassa and the *Nationalistes*. These Quebec opponents were still denouncing the Naval Service Bill of 1910 as a preliminary to conscription and Canadian involvement in British imperialist adventures. When the election was over, the Liberals had suffered serious losses in Ontario and their defeat in Quebec was just short of a complete rout. In British Columbia they had failed to get a single seat, while in the Maritimes they had lost ground. Only in the wheat-growing prairies had they managed to strengthen their hold. The age of Laurier had come to an abrupt end.

BIBLIOGRAPHY

HARDY, W. F. *From Sea to Sea.* Doubleday, 1960.

SCHULL, J. J. *Laurier, the First Canadian.* Macmillan, 1965.

SKELTON, O. D. *The Life and Letters of Sir Wilfrid Laurier.* McClelland and Stewart, 1965.

11

The Test
of War,
1914-1918

In retrospect the election campaign of 1911 which resulted in a change of government was a significant landmark in Canada's twentieth-century history. This was so not because of any radical policy differences between a defeated Liberal party and a victorious Conservative party, for in most important respects their programmes differed more in detail than in principle. It was significant, however, because by 1911 the crucial problems of national unity, national autonomy, and economic development were coming more clearly into focus. The days had passed when a statement of National Policy was sufficient to inspire wide popular confidence, or when a token distribution of cabinet seats between French and English was sufficient to ensure a spirit of co-operation between the founding races. Gestures, words, and uncomplicated solutions were no longer acceptable because both Canada and the world had entered a new era of highly complex and often frightening problems. Canada's new leader, Robert Borden, a Nova Scotian lawyer, was destined to lead the nation through a time of testing more severe than any yet encountered.

Robert Borden.   In contrast to the elegant and suave Laurier, Borden was stocky in appearance, with heavy eyebrows and moustache, silver-grey hair and a ruggedly handsome face. During the personally frustrating years since his accession to the Conservative leadership in 1901, he had proved himself as a party leader. He possessed a penetrating mind, strong debating skill and considerable political insight. But in spite of these qualities it was only after several years in office that Borden was able to forge a real unity within his party and cabinet. Indeed, there is reason to believe that Borden privately thought that his party had gained power before it was ready.

Naval Policy.   Borden had won the election principally because of *Nationaliste* support in Quebec, where Laurier's naval policy had disenchanted most of his old followers. Unfortunately for Borden though, the *Nationalistes* proved to be difficult allies for they were to oppose Conservative naval proposals as often and as loudly as they had those of the Liberals. As a result the government appeared to be paralyzed on the issue.

Despite continuous criticism of Laurier's "tin-pot" navy from the government benches, Borden's first legislative proposals made no mention of a navy, and so failed to produce any alternative to the Liberal policy. In essence Borden was afraid of rousing the opposition of the Quebec *Nationalistes* who had supported his "cash contribution" proposal of 1909. At that time he had proposed a direct cash contribution to the British Royal Navy. However, in the summer of 1912 Borden visited London where he learned from Britain's youthfully arrogant but perceptive First Lord of the Admiralty, Winston Churchill, of the alarming growth of German naval power. Borden returned to Ottawa convinced that further delay was impossible and introduced into Parliament a Naval Aid Bill by which Canada was to contribute $35,000,000 to the building of three battleships for the Royal Navy. In an attempt to appease Quebec, it was provided in the bill that Canadian sailors could train on these ships and that in the future these ships could become a Canadian unit within the Royal Navy. F. D. Monk, the *Nationalistes'* representative in the Cabinet, resigned in protest against the Naval Aid Bill. After a very stormy passage through the Commons, the bill was scuttled by a Liberal-dominated Senate. The Senators refused to acknowledge the existence of any emergency that would require Canada to make such an important concession to Britain. As a result, Canada made no pre-war contribution to imperial defence.

Autonomy.   The Liberals, posing as defenders of Canadian autonomy, were trying to make Borden appear to be an imperialist. Whereas in fact Borden was almost as far from being an imperialist as was Laurier. Laurier viewed nationalism in isolationist terms, as the freedom to remain aloof from Europe's constant internal quarrelling. Borden's nationalism conceived of Canada as a partner in the Empire, exercising her autonomy by accepting shared responsibility in such matters as defence. The Naval Aid Bill was an expression of this view.

Another expression of Borden's theory of shared responsibility was his constant assertion to British statesmen of Canada's right to share in the making of imperial foreign policy, which was legally binding upon the Empire. The increasing danger of war in Europe by 1912 was the occasion for his most forceful statement of this view. But as on previous occasions, he was frustrated by the failure of British leaders to agree with his theory.

The Outbreak of War.   When the First World War did break out in August of 1914, Borden quickly assured the British government that Canada as a loyal member of the Empire would cooperate as fully as possible. The Canadian people in 1914 were overwhelmingly behind Borden in this commitment. A hastily summoned Parliament unanimously passed a War Measures Act giving the government extraordinary powers to carry out the war effort, and men flocked to recruiting stations. Under the direction of the tireless Minister of Militia, Sam Hughes, the recruits were assembled, trained and dispatched overseas. By February of 1915 the First Canadian Division had entered trenches in France. Eventually four divisions were formed, composing the Canadian Corps. In all, Canada provided just over 600,000 soldiers in the course of the war. In addition, over 9,000 Canadian sailors enlisted in the Canadian navy, and another body of Canadians made up almost a quarter of the British air services, the Royal Flying Corps and the Royal Naval Air Service. Of these latter, many became outstanding "aces." Major W. A. ("Billy") Bishop, with seventy-two "kills," was the third ranking air ace in the war.

Industry and War.   Probably as important as her contribution in men was the nation's contribution in equipment and supplies. Great quantities of munitions, aeroplanes, merchant ships and naval vessels poured from Canada's industrial plants. The products of mine and forest found greatly expanded markets. Canadian farm production supplied Britain and the Allied armies with most of their foodstuffs. The result was a tremendous boost to the economy. During the war Canada's industrial output surpassed agricultural production for the first time: the nation's economy was transformed into an industrial one.

Men in Arms.   In numerical terms the force of Canadian soldiers in Europe was one of the smallest of the Allied side. Nevertheless, it quickly became known as one of the best fighting formations in the war, feared by the Germans and admired by its allies. Frequently it was assigned the most difficult objectives and brought into the bloodiest battles, with the result that the Canadian casualty rate was particularly high (60,661 men killed, one of every 10 men who enlisted). For example, in their first action of the war, the desperate battle of Ypres, during which the Germans used gas, the complement of the Canadian Division was depleted by almost a third. Several weeks later, in the fighting around Festubert, the cost of a mere 600 yard advance was 2,500 casualties in five days fighting. During eleven weeks of the Battle of the Somme in 1916 Canadians covered themselves with glory—but at the appalling cost of 24,000 casualties.

The final two years of the conflict saw Canadians engaged in some of the bloodiest and most important battles of the war. At Vimy Ridge, the prelude to the crucial Flanders campaign of 1917, the four Canadian divisions and a British brigade took the Ridge in ten hours in what has been described as the "most perfectly organized and the most successful battle of the whole war." Following Vimy Ridge, the Canadian Corps fought in such bloody encounters as Arleux, Hill 70, and Passchendaele. In 1918 the Canadians particularly distinguished themselves at Amiens and then, in the last hours of the war (November 11), drove a retreating German army from Mons, avenging the first British defeat that had taken place there in 1914.

The Home Front.   On the home front the war had several important effects. The emotional drain on Canadians cannot be underestimated. At first a pleasant patriotic glow had followed the early reports of Canadian heroism at Ypres, but it soon gave way to a grim sense of shock and tragedy as the casualty lists were published. As the months and years went by, there was hardly a family that did not mourn a father or a son or suffered the haunting fear that such a loss was only a matter of time.

Economically, the war brought greatly increased profits to farmers and to the producers of war supplies of all kinds, from mess tins to bully beef (the front-line soldiers' staple diet). Canada's mineral wealth, in particular, was much in demand for munitions. By 1916, 800,000 shells a month were being shipped from Canada. Industrial expansion of all kinds was at a record level. Whereas previous to the war, Canada had usually been content to export much of her raw materials, particularly to the

United States, she was now developing her own secondary industries.

The cost of the war in financial terms was immense. To meet this extra demand on the treasury, the government sought to raise money by increasing taxes, imposing new taxes and issuing bonds. Customs duties were raised and new taxes were placed on such items as coffee, sugar, liquor, tobacco, and railway tickets. Stamps were required on cheques and postal rates were increased. To raise further revenue and in an attempt to curb wartime profiteering, a business profits tax was introduced in 1916, and a personal income tax in 1917. Both these latter taxes were purposely mild and so failed, for the most part, in their two intentions. The government's biggest success in raising money was in the issuing of bonds. Five series of Victory Loan drives were launched and together covered 85 per cent of the total cost of the war. Unfortunately, they also constituted the largest element in the massive increase in the national debt.

Inflation became an increasingly serious problem as the war progressed, and during the period prices doubled. In some measure government policies must be blamed for this. To promote the Victory Loans, the government encouraged high profits in business and industry, the major purchasers of the bonds. Coupled with a natural scarcity of supplies, this policy drove prices up. Since business and income taxes were kept low the industrialists and farmers, riding the crest of the boom, were able to cope with the higher prices. However, many wage earners with lower incomes were forced to bear more than their share of the costs of the war effort.

The Railway Fiasco. Adding to the financial burden on the government during the war and to the national debt, which was carried into the post-war period, was one problem not directly connected with the war—the bankruptcy of the Canadian Northern and Grand Trunk Pacific railway systems. These two enterprises had been in almost continual financial trouble since the beginning of their ill-advised and overly-optimistic expansion programmes. Now faced by the decline of anticipated immigration, shortages of steel, inability to replace worn-out rolling stock, lack of manpower and higher costs, they were in critical condition. In 1917 the government was forced to begin taking over both ventures. By 1922, when the take-over was completed, the taxpayers had spent $700,000,000 in bailing out the promoters and shareholders. In 1923 these two railway systems, with the Grand

Trunk (parent of the Grand Trunk Pacific), the Inter-colonial and National Transcontinental, became the core of the state-owned Canadian National Railways.

Unity Strained. The beginning of the war brought a patriotic fervour that united the country. "Ready, aye, ready" was heard from the lips of French Canadians as often as from those of English Canadians, and the dispute between Liberals and Conservatives over imperial defence was forgotten in the united effort to aid the Allies. The shock of war overshadowed domestic issues, and it appeared that national unity had never been stronger. But as the war, contrary to early optimism, dragged on from 1914 to 1915 and into 1916, new strains brought a gradual return of old dissensions.

The Borden government had made two important policy decisions early in the war: (1) that Canadian troops in Europe would be kept together as a Canadian Corps, and (2) that the Corps (a large one in proportion to population) would be maintained at top strength. Ironically, this second policy, (unique among the allies) earned for the Corps a reputation of being strong and suited to offensive assaults, the very type of battle in which casualties were likely to be high. During the later years of the war, as the other Allied armies lost strength because of the toll of casualties and the difficulty of replacing all of them, Canada's force remained at a fairly constant strength. But by the end of 1916 the rate of voluntary recruitment became insufficient to offset the steep casualty rate, and the government was forced to consider conscription.

Conscription and Quebec. The immediate reaction in Quebec was strong opposition. By temperament the French Canadians were traditionally opposed to Canada's involvement in European conflicts; that Britain and France were allied on this occasion made little difference. But the fact is that the French reacted to conscription in much the same fashion as did most Canadians in similar social and economic brackets. The differences arose because Quebec society was still overwhelmingly agrarian and naturally farmers are loathe to be taken away from their fields or to have their sons taken. Moreover, no Canadian father, English- or French-speaking, was anxious to leave his family, and in Quebec social convention dictated early marriage and large families. Thus, those of French origin who were in the most desirable age range militarily were married with families, while those of British origin were more likely to be single and thus more willing (and possibly anxious) to participate in a supposed adventure that had overtones of glory and patriotism. In spite of these reasons, English Canadians criticized the French-Canadian attitude and accused French Canadians of not pulling their fair share of the load. With the introduction of a Military Service Bill in June 1917, racial tension rose sharply and the nation came close to outbreaks of violence. The Bill was passed in August, a large body of English-speaking Liberals breaking party lines to vote with Borden's government.

The value of the conscription policy is still an issue of debate—some persons regarding it a success and others a failure. In the remaining year of war, it produced little more than 60,000 recruits. Quebec might be overwhelmingly opposed to it, but in English Canada too, almost one-third of the people were against conscription. Throughout the country there were many defaulters, and there was a high rate of applications for exemption. But the worst fault of conscription was the way in which it created deep dissension among the people; city folk opposed farmers; English Canadians opposed French Canadians; soldiers opposed civilians. Indeed almost all class, racial and economic distinctions were exaggerated to a dangerously high level, seriously weakening the unity of Canada that had at first been so significantly strengthened by the war.

The 1917 Election.   While the conscription controversy raged, the Borden government, already in office more than the statutory five years, made preparations for an election in December 1917. Knowing that their political position had been weakened by scandals, profiteering, and the Canadian Northern Railway deal, the Conservatives passed two measures through Parliament designed to bolster their strength. These were: (1) the Wartime Elections Act, by which the female next-of-kin of soldiers were given the vote; and (2) the Military Voters Act, by which soldiers were allowed to vote in a riding other than their own home riding. The Conservatives correctly judged that these two groups would favour a government that had introduced conscription and that the soldiers would be willing to vote in ridings where the government was weak.

In addition, negotiations between Conservatives and a group of important English-speaking Liberals resulted in the formation of a Union government. Borden hoped that Laurier and his Quebec followers would join the coalition in order to prevent a complete racial split. But the Liberal leader, harassed by the angry protests of his former protégé, Henri Bourassa, found that he no longer held undisputed control of the Quebec wing of the Liberal party. At most he could act as a moderating influence.

Even without the support of Laurier and his followers, not all of whom were in Quebec, the result of the election was a sad but foregone conclusion. The Union government swept English Canada; Laurier's Liberal remnant swept Quebec. Although the Union victory in many ridings outside Ontario rested on the military vote, the racial split had reached a tragic limit with not one French Canadian of any political significance in the government.

Commonwealth Relations. While the war brought grave new strains to the old problem of national unity within Canada, it also strained relations between Canada and Great Britain. Canadians, their national pride stimulated by the war, were acutely aware that, despite their important contribution, they were almost completely left outside the councils in which important decisions were made affecting the lives of their fighting men. Borden persistently called for more information and for an opportunity to share in the making of important policy decisions. Finally, the Dominion prime ministers were invited in 1916 to join the five-man British War Cabinet to form the Imperial War Cabinet. In the meetings of this body in 1917 and 1918 an important precedent was laid, helping to stress the autonomy of the Dominions.

The Treaty of Versailles. With the convening of the Peace Conference on January 18, 1919, delegates to the Imperial War Cabinet moved to Paris to form the British Empire delegation. Led by Borden, the Dominion representatives demanded and received recognition as individual national delegations as well. When the Treaty of Versailles was signed, each Dominion signed for itself. Following from this important recognition of Dominion autonomy, each Dominion was given a seat in the League of Nations, which was originally established by the Treaty of Versailles.

With the ending of the war, Canada reached the end of one of the most significant periods of her history. National unity had been strained to the very limit of endurance. But the nation had been preserved, despite its grievous wounds, giving Canadians a chance to redevelop a new political and cultural order. Happier consequences of the war were the growth in industrial power and the recognition of a greater degree of Dominion autonomy. Buoyed up by a new spirit of pride arising from the successful war effort, Canadians entered the post-war period with expectant confidence.

BIBLIOGRAPHY

ALLEN, RALPH. *Ordeal by Fire*. Doubleday, 1961.

DAWSON, R. M. *William Lyon Mackenzie King*. University of Toronto, 1958.

FERNS, H. S. and OSTRY, B. *The Age of Mackenzie King*. Heinemann, 1955.

MCGREGOR, F. A. *The Fall and Rise of Mackenzie King, 1911-1919*. Macmillan, 1962.

MACGREGOR, R. *William L. Mackenzie King, 1874-1923*. University of Toronto, 1959.

NICHOLSON, G. W. L. *The Canadian Expeditionary Force*. Queen's Printer, 1962.

SWETTENHAM, J. A. *To Seize the Victory*. Ryerson, 1965.

12

The Post-War Years, 1919-1929

The end of the Great War brought a natural wave of relief to Canadians. It had been a bitter experience, with its heart-breaking toll of casualties and the strains it had imposed on national unity. But at the same time, Canada had emerged as a nation and Canadians began to look forward to the benefits of their new strength and status. In the decade following World War I new political leaders arose and the nation embarked on a period of confident optimism and expansion as its people strove to increase their material prosperity.

THE POLITICS OF THE TWENTIES

W. L. Mackenzie King. Early in 1919, Sir Wilfrid Laurier died, leaving the Liberal party leaderless and divided. Later that same year a party convention chose a new leader, an energetic man with an historic Canadian name, William Lyon Mackenzie King. A grandson of the "firebrand" of the Upper Canada rebellion of 1837, King had already distinguished himself with a brilliant academic record and a successful career in industrial and labour relations in both Canada and the United States. Although his political career had not been quite so successful, King had been a loyal supporter of Laurier for over two decades. Being called to Ottawa, first as a civil servant, he entered the House of Commons in 1908 and became Canada's first Minister of Labour shortly thereafter. However, he was defeated in both the 1911 and 1917 elections. During this period outside parliament, King pursued his interests in industrial problems in the United States, but his figure remained a familiar sight in Liberal backroom circles. At the 1919 convention, even before his election as leader, it was obvious that, particularly in the labour field, King was quietly but effectively guiding Liberal policy. Moreover, the Liberal party's future looked promising due to King's wide support in Quebec.

While the Liberals were becoming accustomed to a new leader, the Conservatives' Sir Robert Borden still led the Union government. But within less than a year Borden was forced to retire, his energy and health exhausted by the immense strain of his duties as wartime prime minister. Thus within a year both of Canada's political parties had passed under new leadership.

Arthur Meighen.   Borden was succeeded by Arthur Meighen who had been a successful trial lawyer before entering politics. In 1908 Meighen was elected to parliament and thereafter advanced rapidly. In 1913 he entered Borden's government as Solicitor General, and two years later became a cabinet member. He was forceful and sharp in debate, clear and effective in his writings, hard-working and determined to be constructively involved in the affairs of his country. Yet Meighen was an extremely reserved man who never went out of his way to seek friends and who lacked the techniques of compromise which are essential to political leadership. He was respected but never loved by those around him and has been called an "upright figure of ice."

King and Meighen had been contemporaries at the University of Toronto. That, however, was probably the only point of common ground between them. King's speeches were so long and rambling that it was often difficult to determine what he was saying, whereas Meighen was a superb debater. King was plagued by self-doubts and insecurity but Meighen gave an air of self-confidence. King's success lay in his ability to organize men, to delegate authority, to plan political strategy, and to deal ruthlessly with opposition when necessary. While no one probably ever understood his complex character or personality and although he had never gained popular affection in the way that Macdonald and Laurier had, he became a living legend—seemingly almost indispensable to the Canadian political scene.

Labour Unrest.   Following the war, social and political ideas were in a ferment. During the conflict inflation had driven prices up, placing a strain on the purchasing power of the lower income groups. At the same time there had been obvious examples of profiteering. In the years immediately following 1918, dissatisfaction in labour circles increased when the transition to a peacetime economy and demobilization of the armed forces resulted in unemployment. Labour leaders across the nation, but particularly in Western Canada, sought ways to redress the gross inequalities that had developed. Some of them even announced that Canadian workers should follow the example of the Russian revolutionaries of 1917. In March, 1919, at a labour conference held in Calgary, it was suggested that the workers unite to organize "One Big Union." Exhilarated by violent vocal attacks on capitalism and democracy, the delegates, most of whom were from the West, drew up a constitution for the O.B.U. and passed various resolutions that owed much to the influence of Marx and communism.

The leaders of the O.B.U. now turned to direct action. Convinced of the total corruption of the owners of industry, they planned to organize general strikes in cities across Canada. In the summer of 1919 many Canadians became uneasy when a general strike developed in Winnipeg. Thirty thousand workers left their jobs and alarmists thought they could see a "red" plot to establish a Bolshevist state. After six tense weeks, the strike had failed to achieve shorter hours, higher wages and a strong political union of workers. As working men drifted back to their jobs, the federal government stepped in to arrest the strike leaders. After the failure of the Winnipeg strike, the influence of radicalism declined rapidly and labour leaders began to turn to more moderate, political action to promote their cause.

Farm Protest. Labour was not the only restive social group in Canada. The farmers of Ontario and the West, who with their families composed close to one-third of the population, believed that government policies were weighted too much in favour of eastern big business. They claimed that high tariffs and railway freight rates raised the farmers' operating costs and that mild taxes on business profits allowed the capitalists to increase their wealth at a much faster rate than the farmer could ever seriously expect to enjoy. Spurred by this feeling of injustice, the national farmers' organization, the Canadian Council of Agriculture, sought to bring political pressure to bear on Ottawa by issuing a statement of aims called the "New National Policy" in 1918. Going one step further, Ontario farmers founded a new political party, the United Farmers of Ontario, which won the provincial election of 1919. Encouraged by this success, a national convention of farmers in Winnipeg in 1920 established the National Progressive Party under the leadership of T. A. Crerar, a Manitoban who had briefly held the agriculture portfolio in Borden's Union government. The New National Policy became the party's platform and included lower tariffs, aid to the farmers, higher taxes on profits and income, public ownership of utilities, co-operative methods of marketing and more direct control of the government by such measures as the more frequent use of the referendum. Its aim was to gain both the farm and the labour vote across Canada.

Thus, as the nation prepared for a federal election in 1921, the political scene was complicated by the presence of two new, relatively untried leaders in the old parties and a new third party attempting to unite the farm and labour groups in protest against the traditional parties. The results of the election showed a country divided along regional, racial and economic lines. The Liberals with 117 seats formed a minority government; the Conservatives retained only 50 and the Progressives showed surprising strength by taking 65 seats. The division of the seats regionally, however, was even more significant. The Liberals, having swept Quebec's 65 seats, were centred in that province with the additional support of 52 seats mainly in Ontario and the Maritimes. The Progressives found their greatest support in the West, where they took no less than 41 seats, but also showed strength in Ontario where they won 24 seats. The Conservatives dropped down to 50 seats, mostly in Ontario, New Brunswick and British Columbia.

The two important factors in the politics of the twenties were the rivalry between King and Meighen and the presence in Parliament of the Progressives. Although numerically stronger than the Conservatives, the Progressives were not aggressive in Opposition. In fact their sympathies generally lay in the direction of the Liberals, and Prime Minister King actively sought their support in order to maintain his minority government in power. Two measures that won Progressive support during these years were the lowering of tariffs and a national old age pension. Within two years of the election, however, prosperity returned and the Progressives began to show signs of disintegration. Crerar resigned, and other Progressives drifted into the Liberal party.

With the Progressives unwilling to take a strong position against the Liberal party, the burden of opposition fell to the Conservatives. Meighen was only too eager to take up this task since it provided the opportunity to vent his dislike of King. In the election of 1925 the Liberals campaigned on their record and only retained 101 seats in the Commons. The Conservatives on the other hand called for a return to high tariffs and gained 66 to take a total of 116 seats. The Progressives, whose depleted ranks stood at 25, held the balance of power once more. With their support, King contrived to remain in power.

The Byng-King Crisis. In 1926 the Liberal government was shaken by Conservative charges of scandal in the Customs Department. Knowing that a motion of censure against the government (which the Progressives would probably support) was imminent, King requested the Governor General, Lord Byng, to dissolve Parliament so that an election could be held. Byng refused and instead asked Meighen to form a government.* The new Conservative government was defeated three days after taking office.

The election campaign of 1926 demonstrated King's outstanding political skill. Ignoring the dangerous disclosures of graft in the Customs Department, he made a prime issue of what he maintained had been the constitutional injustice of a governor general refusing a prime minister's request for dissolution. King implied complicity by Meighen in the matter and compared the affair with his grandfather's struggle of almost a hundred years before against an irresponsible governor.

Despite Meighen's indignant protests to the contrary, King succeeded in convincing a substantial number of voters that the Governor General's decision seriously threatened to reduce Canada to colonial status. When the ballots had been counted the Liberals had gained wide support across the country and had won 116 seats. The Conservatives had been reduced to 91 members and Progressive representation had dwindled to 13. For twenty-five of the next thirty years, Canada was to be ruled by the Liberal party, and the nation passed the greater part of that era under the personal leadership of Mackenzie King.

---

*Some authorities believe that on constitutional grounds Byng acted within his authority. Byng's reasoning was based on three points: the previous election had been held only eight months before; the Conservatives were the largest party in the Commons; and the Liberals had resigned without having been defeated in the Commons on a vote of confidence. Believing it to be his prerogative to either grant or refuse a dissolution of Parliament, Byng decided that the wisest and fairest course under the circumstances was to give Meighen an opportunity to form a government. Debate continues today as to the constitutionality of this action, and what is more important, whether a governor general today could follow a similar course.

FOREIGN POLICY

The 1920's were important years for Canada in the field of foreign policy. Having won an important measure of autonomy at the Peace Conference and through membership in the League of Nations, Canada's foreign policy was the first step in her continuing drive for wider autonomy. Indeed, this was the dominant motive in her relations with other countries. Canada demonstrated little desire to formulate any marked foreign policy of her own, but rather a desire to avoid responsibility in the outside world. For five years Canadians had been involved in total war. After such a bitter world experience domestic problems naturally became more absorbing and many Canadians wished to avoid further international disasters. Moreover, the twenties witnessed a new boom in Canada's economy. But above all was the need to restore national unity, and especially a unity between French and English Canadians. In that context foreign policy was potentially one of the most divisive issues. Prime Minister King recognized this and intentionally followed policies that would least divide the nation. Two of these policies were to achieve the widening of autonomy and to avoid overseas commitments.

Anglo-Japanese Alliance.   The first important international issue affecting Canada after the war arose in 1919 when Great Britain began to move towards a renewal of the pre-war Anglo-Japanese Alliance. Alarm in the United States spread to Canada, where American fears of Japan were shared. More important, though, Canada, faced by the perennial problem of her close links with both the United Kingdom and the United States, was concerned to maintain cordial relations between Britain and the United States. At the 1921 Imperial Conference, Meighen (who had succeeded Borden as prime minister the previous year) persuaded Britain to set aside the treaty with Japan in favour of a nine-nation conference on the Pacific and the Far East. At the Conference in Washington in 1921, Canada was represented by Sir Robert Borden, but he was only a member of the British delegation. While this was scarcely even an advance on Macdonald's participation at the earlier Washington conference, the fact that the 1921 conference took place at all was directly due to Canadian influence.

The Chanak Crisis.   In 1922 the basic issues of Canada's ill-defined autonomy were brought sharply into focus when Turkish troops invaded a neutral zone created along the Straits of the

Dardanelles. This zone had been created out of Turkish territory under the terms of the Allied peace treaty of 1920 with Turkey, and a force of British troops centred at the town of Chanak was all that remained of an international force that had garrisoned the zone. Amidst rumours of war, Britain asked the Canadian government if it would pledge troops to help reinforce the British garrison if war broke out. In Quebec, Bourassa reflected French-Canadian opinion when he asked, "Who in Canada has ever heard of Chanak until this moment?" Even in English Canada, where there was considerable vocal support for the request, public opinion was by no means unanimous. Moreover, while Bourassa's question might reflect Quebec's traditional dislike of Canadian participation in imperial affairs, it also pointed to the failure of the theory advocating a common imperial foreign policy. The fact was that although Canada had not been consulted on the policy that had led to the so-called "Chanak crisis," she was now being asked to accept that policy without question. Once again Britain appeared to be taking Canada's support for granted, and though many Canadians were inclined to offer help, they were also angry that Britain should automatically assume that there would be help from Canada.

Admittedly in a world of fast moving events, consultation between Britain and the Dominions might often be impossible. On the other hand, Canadians were beginning to object to being taken for granted and were starting to realize that their own interests, both domestic and external, could best be served by an independent foreign policy. King sensed this national feeling and, while not closing the door, insisted that the whole matter of Chanak would have to be discussed by the Canadian Parliament. Since Canada at this time was legally still a British colony, she was probably committed to granting the British request for troops, but fortunately the issue never became a serious one because Britain and Turkey resolved their differences by discussion and treaty. The crisis, however, had highlighted the problems of Canadian foreign policy more strongly than ever before.

The Halibut Treaty. Two of the basic necessities for the pursuance of an independent Canadian foreign policy were the power to negotiate and sign treaties and the power to appoint diplomatic representatives to foreign countries. The first step was taken in 1923 when Canada negotiated with the United States the Halibut Fisheries Treaty governing Pacific coast fisheries. On Mackenzie

King's insistence, the sole signatory for Canada was her Minister of Fisheries, Ernest Lapointe. The treaty was subsequently approved by the Canadian Parliament and ratified by King George V, solely on the request of Canada's Parliament. Thus Canada had concluded, for the first time in her history, an independent treaty. (As it happened, the right of each Dominion to pursue an independent foreign policy where no Imperial interests were involved was ratified at the Imperial Conference of 1923.)

In 1927, the second practical step towards an independent foreign policy was taken when Canada appointed Vincent Massey as her first permanent minister in Washington. Similar appointments were soon made to other important countries.

Commonwealth Evolution.   The appointment of Canadian ministers abroad grew out of decisions taken at the Imperial Conference at 1926. Mackenzie King, supported by the Irish and South African leaders, made strong demands for a definition of the nature of imperial relationships. What were the powers of the Dominions and their relationship to each other and to Great Britain? The views of the conference were embodied in the Balfour Report, which spoke of a commonwealth of nations, "in no way subordinate one to another in any aspect of their domestic or external affairs, though united by a common allegiance to the Crown." The principles of the modern Commonwealth had been enunciated.

It remained only to conclude several details. These were disposed of at the Conference of 1930, thus allowing the new principles to be translated into law in the Statute of Westminister of 1931. This important statute of the British Parliament repealed the Colonial Laws Validity Act, thereby allowing the Dominions to enact any legislation they wished, whether repugnant to English law or not. Among other things it also allowed the Dominions full extra-territorial rights and responsibilities over their citizens. At the request of Canada, amendments to the British North America Act were to continue to be made by the British Parliament until a more satisfactory method could be agreed upon. In addition, certain legal appeals were to be allowed from the Supreme Court of Canada to the Judicial Committee of the Privy Council. It was understood, though, that both these legal arrangements would be terminated whenever Canada wished. Thus, in all but two minor legal details Canada had achieved full autonomy.

ECONOMIC EXPANSION

The most spectacular aspect of Canada's history during the 1920's was her economic expansion. The war had already given great impetus to Canadian industrial growth, and it is from this decade on that Canada ceased to be a predominantly agricultural nation. The figures of the 1921 census amply prove this point: rural population—4,436,041, urban population—4,352,442; agricultural production — $1,403,686,000, industrial production — $2,747,926,675.

Primary Industries. Economic development in the twenties was characterized by great expansion in several major industries. Reflecting Canada's continued heavy dependence on primary industries, pulp and paper was the largest single industry in the country, being three times larger than its nearest rival. By 1929 Canada enjoyed 64 per cent of the world's trade in pulp and paper. Frequently allied with pulp and paper but also a major industry in its own right was the production of hydro-electric power. The development of hydro-electric power, particularly in British Columbia, Ontario and Quebec, provided cheap power for the expansion of other industries. During this one decade $600,000,000 were spent in the expansion of hydro facilities. By 1930 seven out of every ten Canadian homes had been electrified, a significant achievement in a country of such sparse settlement. Mining also underwent great expansion. The fortunes gained in the pre-war mineral boom were now turned to the exploration and development of base metal mines, particularly in Manitoba, northern Ontario and Quebec.

Although Canada was less dependent after the war on farming, agriculture was still a major factor in the economy. With Europe ravaged by war, Canadian farmers found a large and ready market in which prices were high. Once again wheat was the major crop. On the prairies the population increased by over 300,000, and new acreage, especially in northern Alberta was brought under cultivation. As in the period 1900-1913, railways and other related industries were stimulated by the wheat boom.

Manufacturing and Investment. Primary industries may have dominated the scene but manufacturing also grew during the decade. Automobiles became a major concern that stimulated other industries such as petroleum production. Consumer goods in ever-increasing quantity and variety poured from Canada's factories. Manufacturing employed thousands and was an important link in the total expansion of industries and services.

One prime feature of the economic expansion of the 1920's was the immense capital investment it stimulated. Much of this investment was in durable goods and equipment—highways, mills, factories, railways, hydro plants—all of which contributed to further expansion in productivity. It is estimated that during the decade $6 billion were put into such investment, much of it coming from Canadians themselves.

Regionalism. A less fortunate feature of the 1920's was the regional aspect of the economic development, which contributed to the increase in sectionalism. British Columbia development was centred on hydro and industries of the sea, the mine and the forest. The prairies were, of course, preoccupied with farming in general and wheat in particular. Ontario and Quebec, like British Columbia, found wealth in the mines and forests, but were also the scene of manufacturing expansion. The Maritime provinces, lagging behind the other regions, were not as fortunate in industrial expansion, and were forced to rely on fishing and lumbering.

As the decade of the twenties passed into its second half, the pace of development and expansion continued to increase. A number of Canadians were generally pleased with their political achievements and contented with their material lot. They looked to the future with optimism, firm in the belief that, so far as international affairs were concerned, they lived in a "fire-proof house" and that their domestic well-being would continue indefinitely. If they thought of the future at all, it was probably to dream of their wealth after the harvests of next year or the year after; or they might calculate their profits from that next foray into the buoyant "bull market" on the stock exchanges of Bay and St. James Streets.

In many ways the decade of the twenties was the beginning of our modern way of living. Women were becoming more independent and entering into business and politics. Moving pictures could be seen in large ornate theatres, automobiles were becoming a necessity, areoplanes were no longer a curiosity, and simple radio sets were being introduced into many homes. Never before had the future apparently promised such variety and luxury.

Approaching Calamity. Few, if any, Canadians saw the signs of impending calamity. Canada's prosperity rested on a mere handful of great industries, for example, pulp and paper, wheat, and mining. These, in turn, were dependent upon exports and were therefore subject to pressures and conditions outside Canada. In particular Canada's economy was closely linked to that of the United States and to the recovery of Europe. If this export trade to either Europe or the U.S. were ever to be cut off, or even reduced, many large Canadian corporations would simply crumble, crushing at the same time the many allied industries that had grown up alongside them.

There were other features that complicated this general picture. Regional specialization, over-production, the low average income of many Canadians and a high cost of living were only some of the indicators that are now known to have been important warnings of the shaky foundation upon which Canada's prosperity rested in the late twenties. In the last years of the decade economic nationalism spread across Europe and the United States. It took the form of rising protective tariffs and created a potentially dangerous international situation, especially for trading nations such as Canada. Finally, Europe was recovering from the dislocation of the war years and was less ready to pay the high prices that Canadian producers of foodstuffs and raw materials had grown accustomed to receiving.

The climax came in 1929 when, on the heels of unprecedented activity, the New York stock market crashed, precipitating the financial destruction of thousands of corporations and individuals. The Great Depression had begun. Those Canadians who had such a short time before been unshakably confident in the future now feared the unknown miseries that the future would bring.

BIBLIOGRAPHY

ANDERSON, F. W. *The Rum Runners*. Frontier Book. Frontiers Unlimited, 1966.

BALAWYDER, A. *The Winnipeg General Strike*. Problems of Canadian History Series. Copp Clark, 1967.

GRAHAM, ROGER. *Arthur Meighen, A Biography*. 3 vols. I. *The Door of Opportunity* (1960); II. *And Fortune Fled* (1963); III. *No Surrender* (1965). Clarke, Irwin.

NEATBY, H. BLAIR. *William Lyon Mackenzie King*. University of Toronto, 1963.

13

Through the Great Depression, 1929-1939

The optimism of the twenties was shattered by the crash of 1929 and by the economic chaos and disintegration that soon spread across North America and Europe. Yet Canadians did not at first realize the full extent of the disaster that had befallen them. For months many assured themselves that it was only an economic phase that would soon pass and that the country's former prosperity would return. As a result only stop-gap measures were taken to alleviate the worst hardships of the Depression. Further complicating the crisis was the intensification once more of the disruptive forces of regionalism, race and religion that always lie beneath the surface of Canadian federation. Thus Canada struggled through the Depression until the Second World War brought renewed economic growth and a new focus for national unity.

THE EFFECTS OF THE DEPRESSION IN CANADA

The Individual. The catastrophic effects of the Depression on Canada were most clearly observed by the ordinary citizen in terms of his own life and experience. He might be lucky enough to keep his job but day after day he could not fail to see the growing lines of unemployed workers queueing up for food "handouts." He could hear of the tens of thousands at government-run depots, of individuals and families who depended on government relief and private charity in order to subsist. Even those who were lucky enough to remain employed almost invariably found their incomes reduced. Parents found it increasingly difficult to keep their children at school and many promising students were forced to leave school early or to forget their dreams of university. Even university

175

graduates were sometimes happy to obtain unskilled work. Often wives had to find at least part-time work so that the family could "make ends meet." Indeed "making ends meet" became the daily concern of almost every Canadian.

Industry.   Of less immediate concern to the average individual but of fundamental importance was the dislocation of both primary and secondary industries. The formerly swelled values of stocks and bonds dropped sharply. Many business firms simply ceased to exist as the demand for their goods or services shrank. Other firms, including such giants as Canada Steamship Lines and Algoma Steel, were forced to retrench and to reorganize, while still others, such as Massey-Harris, managed to stagger along, in some cases with no yearly profits at all. Even the C.P.R., long considered one of the world's most stable investments, was unable to declare a dividend in 1932. The prairie farmers suffered terrible financial hardship. The bottom fell out of the world wheat market, the price per bushel tumbling from a 1929 high of $1.60 to a 1932 low of 38 cents. Other primary industries also lost their markets, notably fishing and newsprint (which was part of what had been Canada's largest industry, pulp and paper).

While mounting unemployment soon helped to accelerate the downward slide of industry by reducing purchasing power, the initial and most important cause was the loss of export markets. Canada's industries were capable of producing far more than could be consumed by the domestic market and had developed an extensive and vital export trade. But the spirit of economic nationalism that had originally been a contributing factor to the Depression was intensified as the crisis deepened and as nations attempted to insulate their own domestic industries by raising still higher protective tariff walls. Between 1929 and 1933 Canada's income from exports dropped a ruinous 67 per cent. It is not surprising, therefore, that so many industries, which had been over-capitalized, should collapse when their earning power disappeared. Tragically, they brought down at the same time the secondary industries, notably the construction industry, which had been so closely allied with them in the days of prosperity and expansion. By the winter of 1932-33 the Depression was at its worst and the national income had fallen to less than $3,500,000,000, a drop of almost 50 per cent in just over three years.

Regional Dislocation.   A significant feature of the Depression in Canada was the unequal dislocation evident in different regions of the country. Worst hit by far were the prairie provinces, where incomes were almost totally dependent on wheat. With the export trade at a disastrously low level, the price of wheat often did not cover the costs of production, let alone farm taxes, depreciation, and interest on debts. As if this blow was not great enough, the period of the Depression, more particularly that of 1933 to 1937, saw the southern regions of the prairie provinces devastated by severe drought. Where previously the yield per acre had been 27 bushels, the return dropped to as little as 3 bushels, and total prairie wheat production dropped from over 350,000,000 bushels to 182,000,000 in 1937. Even the prairie cities were seriously affected by the collapse of the wheat market. A measure of the disaster caused by the Depression on the prairies can be seen in the fact that a quarter of a million people migrated from the prairies in the decade 1931-1941, some to other parts of Canada, especially the cities, and others to the United States.

Although the prairies were the most seriously disabled region of Canada, other areas that depended on the export of primary products were seriously affected. British Columbia found the markets for her fish, lumber and fruit seriously depleted, and the northern sections of Ontario and Quebec, which depended on the export of the products of mine and forest, were also hard hit. In Newfoundland (at that time a self-governing Dominion), the effects of the Depression were so ruinous that the island had to surrender responsible government in 1934 as a condition of financial aid from Britain. The Maritime provinces, in spite of their heavy dependence on primary products, were not as seriously affected as most other parts of the country. With a greater diversity of occupations and a lower economic level to begin with, the Maritime economy dropped proportionately less.

The industrialized regions of Ontario and Quebec were affected least by the Depression. Because they produced goods for a protected domestic market in which price levels were more stable, and engaged predominantly in mixed farming for domestic consumption, these regions were able to withstand the crisis. Nevertheless, the urban centres were the scenes of the bread lines and soup kitchens. Moreover, it was to the cities that bankrupt farmers and unemployed miners and forest workers gravitated, swelling the already large ranks of unemployed industrial labour. For this reason some of the more spectacularly depressing memories of the era are associated with the large cities of the East.

FEDERAL GOVERNMENT DURING THE DEPRESSION

The Depression found Canada's political leadership unable to deal with a crisis of such magnitude. Prime Minister King was either unaware of, or refused to acknowledge, the severity of the crisis. He predicted an early return to prosperity, and insisted that the federal government did not possess the constitutional power to assist the victims of the Depression. Constitutionally he was correct, but the provinces were hamstrung by greatly reduced revenue, and some were unable to meet even normal responsibilities adequately. King finally did move to provide the prairie provinces with relief grants. But he compromised his poltical position when, in reply to the observation that (Conservative) Ontario had not been so favoured, he injudiciously retorted that he would not give "a five-cent piece" to "any Tory government."

R. B. Bennett. The "five-cent piece" remark was exactly what the Conservatives, under their new leader, Richard B. Bennett, needed to weaken King's position. Bennett, an abrupt, headstrong, millionaire lawyer from Calgary, dramatized King's slip as one example of the tired cynicism that he claimed pervaded the Liberal government's attitude and recent record. Accusing the Liberals of being unwilling and incapable of dealing with the Depression, Bennett promised to work energetically to promote the strengthening of Canadian industry behind tariff walls and to "blast (Canada's) way into the markets of the world." Canadians generally were inspired by Bennett's confidence and energy and in the election of 1930 demonstrated this by returning 137 Conservatives to Parliament. Liberal representation was reduced to 88, the remaining 20 seats being taken by an assortment of farmers' groups and independents.

True to the principles of his party, Bennett's first plan to turn the tide of Depression was to raise tariffs on the theory that this would protect the manufacturers. He also believed that this action would in some way convince other nations to lower their tariffs on Canadian goods. The side-effects of the higher tariffs were, however, enough to produce more damage than good. Higher tariffs did nothing to increase exports and, in some cases, increased exporters' costs, thereby reducing their business. Moreover, while high tariffs might protect the domestic market, that market was not sufficiently large enough to consume enough manufactured goods to give any significant life to the economy.

Ottawa Conference of 1932.   At an Imperial Economic Conference in Ottawa in 1932, Bennett attempted with some success to increase Canada's export trade.   But the Conference's intention of establishing a broad system of Commonwealth preferential tariffs was defeated.   Bennett's often voiced support of co-operation fell before his determined economic nationalism.   In the end, separate trade treaties were negotiated between the nine participating countries.   In this way Canada gained preference for the sale of a number of primary products in Britain in return for minor concessions to British manufacturers.   But the Ottawa agreements were totally inadequate to offset Canada's almost complete lack of trade with the United States and Europe.

Bennett's trade and tariff measures emphasized business expansion as a means of reducing unemployment.   They were typical both of the party and of a man who had made his fortune as a corporation lawyer in the days of business prosperity.   These policies, however, did not recognize the full extent and complexity of the crisis.   Neither the Maritimes nor the prairies were satisfied and both pointed out that Ontario and Quebec received most of the benefits of the early Conservative policies.   In 1932, though, Bennett summoned an emergency session of Parliament to pass increased grants to the provinces for unemployment relief and to establish a public works programme to create employment. Special grants were also made to the prairie provinces.

The CBC and the Bank of Canada.   Not all the Bennett government's achievements were directly concerned with resisting the Depression.   In 1932 the Canadian Radio Broadcasting Commission was created to establish a publicly owned radio network broadcasting in French and English.   After several years of slow development the Commission was reorganized as the Canadian Broadcasting Corporation, with the power both to operate its own stations and to regulate all private broadcasting in Canada.

In 1934 the government also created the Bank of Canada.   The Depression had demonstrated the federal government's inability to effectively regulate the nation's monetary system, and the new national bank was given the necessary powers to perform this function.   Among its duties, it was to regulate currency and credit, serve as a private bankers' bank, and advise the government on financial matters.   Both these new institutions proved in succeeding decades to be of considerable value.

Bennett's "New Deal." The nation was astounded (not to say sceptical) when in 1935 Bennett, the conservative capitalist, suddenly proposed a sweeping programme of economic and social measures to deal with the Depression. This programme resembled the "New Deal" offered to the American people by President Franklin D. Roosevelt in 1933. Bennett's about-face was probably brought about by a number of factors. A Royal Commission on Price Spreads in the retail trade had disclosed that many large business concerns were buying their supplies cheaply but overpricing their products. There was a growing realization that something drastic had to be done to offset the Depression, and there was genuine admiration for the imagination and energy of the Roosevelt administration. Bennett's programme included a wages and hours act to improve labour conditions, a comprehensive unemployment insurance scheme, government control of prices, marketing, anti-monopolies, measures against unfair business practices and rehabilitation schemes for the prairie provinces.

Whatever the motivation behind Bennett's "New Deal," it was less than successful. The Conservatives, shaken by Bennett's newfound distrust of capitalism, were badly split over the party's new programme. At the other end of the spectrum, Canadian socialists insisted that Bennett had not gone far enough. In the centre, the Liberals took advantage of widespread discontent and frustration and the growing public distrust of Bennett. Campaigning under the slogan, "King or Chaos," they claimed that the Bennett New Deal was largely unconstitutional and that his tariffs were hurting the Canadian economy. While calling for social reform and effective measures against the Depression, the Liberals avoided making anything but vague suggestions of their own. In the election of 1935 the Conservatives were decisively defeated, winning only 39 seats. The Liberals took 171 seats, and the rest were divided between two new parties, the Social Credit and the Co-operative Commonwealth Federation (C.C.F.).

PROTEST AND REGIONALISM

As the Depression dragged on year after year, with the federal government apparently unwilling or unable to move effectively to improve economic conditions, a mood of despair and frustration seized Canadians, particularly those in the hardest hit regions of the country. As a result, new political movements arose in protest against the two traditional parties and people turned away from the federal government looking instead to their own provinces for a solution to the crisis.

The C.C.F. Party.   Since 1921 J. S. Woodsworth, a politically idealistic Methodist minister from Western Canada, had led a very small labour group in the House of Commons. Although Woodsworth was strongly anti-communist, Canadians were generally unsympathetic (or simply apathetic) to his criticisms of the capitalist system and to his calls for social reform. The Depression, however, was viewed by many as the collapse of capitalism. Thus Woodsworth's formerly unheeded views now seemed to ring with the authority of truth. As a result, in 1932 a representative group of farmers, labour leaders, and intellectuals met in Calgary to found a genuine socialist party, the Co-operative Commonwealth Federation or C.C.F. party. At the party's national convention in Regina in 1933, Woodsworth and others drew up the party's platform, the Regina Manifesto, which called for the replacement of capitalism, the elimination of class exploitation, and the widespread introduction of government economic planning, including the nationalization of such key industries as railways and banks. As short-term objectives the new party advocated rural electrification, slum clearance, and public works programmes.

In general the C.C.F. was a conscious attempt to adapt to Canadian needs evolutionary socialism of the type expressed by the British Labour party. While the party's support was firmly agrarian, it did attempt, with moderate success, to attract labour support. However, it never received widespread backing from organized labour. Its greatest strength remained in the West. Quebec and the Maritimes showed little interest in the C.C.F., and in Ontario its appeal proved to be limited. Nonetheless, in the 1935 election, the C.C.F. sent 7 members to Ottawa. One of them was M. J. Coldwell, a future party leader.

Social Credit.   The Canadian West was the major region of discontent in the Depression and was also the birthplace of a second radical political protest movement known as Social Credit. Organized by William "Bible Bill" Aberhart, a Calgary teacher and radio evangelist, the Social Credit party was founded on the unorthodox monetary theories of one Major Douglas, a Scots engineer. Douglas maintained that a fundamental weakness existed in the capitalist system in that consumer purchasing power was never sufficient to equal potential production. To offset this disparity, he proposed that government should issue a "social dividend" or cash payment to all citizens.

At political rallies, often with strong revivalist undertones, Aberhart denounced the country's financial system and expounded Social Credit theory. In spite of the taunts of the orthodox economists who called this theory a "funny money" policy, Aberhart struck a responsive chord among Alberta farmers, many of whom were impoverished by debts and their inability to secure credit. Riding a crest of enthusiasm, Social Credit won control of the Alberta provincial government in 1935. In the federal election a few weeks later, 17 Social Credit members were returned to Parliament.

Once in office, however, Aberhart discovered that his provincial policies conflicted with federal power. After the federal government had rejected a number of items of provincial legislation aimed at controlling banking, credit, and finance, Aberhart contented himself with a more conventional administration of the province. At the same time, the dream of putting Social Credit theories into practice on a national scale remained with the party's adherents as they tried, without success, to gain power in federal politics.

Union Nationale. Quebec was the scene of the emergence of a third distinct protest movement. In that province the growth of finance and industry during the 1920's, tightly organized and controlled by an English-speaking minority of Britons and Canadians, had encouraged a corresponding growth of Quebec nationalism. The industrial dislocation and unemployment of the Depression caused French-Canadian resentment and anger against "foreign" employers. This situation quickly became a focus of Quebec politics and was a prime factor in the rise of Maurice Duplessis, and his *Union Nationale* party, a coalition of dissident Liberal radicals and the tiny Conservative party.

The new party was authoritarian in nature and originally stood on a platform of social reform and the defence of "the rights of Quebec." Drawing support from many former Conservatives and gaining stature from comparison with the corruption of the Liberal administration then in power, the *Union Nationale* swept to power in 1936, winning 76 of the legislature's 90 seats. However, the party's early promises of social reform were never heard of again, and under the overwhelming personal dominance of Duplessis the *Union Nationale* was greatly changed. It came to stand for close association with the Roman Catholic Church, and with the business community in the province. It also supported the suppression of radical opinions and movements, state control of labour unions, the protection at all costs of Quebec's unique culture, and an extreme doctrine of provincial autonomy. With this philosophy the *Union Nationale* remained in power for over two decades, except for a brief interlude during the Second World War.

Mitchell Hepburn. A less extreme but still radical doctrine of provincial rights became the rallying cry in Ontario. Mitchell Hepburn, a successful onion farmer turned politician, carried the Liberal party into power in 1934 after almost three decades in Opposition. Beginning with considerable reformist zeal that resulted in legislation to raise farm prices and to provide legal protection for labour unions, Hepburn eventually lost interest in reform and in 1937 even attempted to bar the United Automobile Workers from organizing the Oshawa employees of General Motors. Hepburn's career was also marked by an extreme personal dislike of Mackenzie King that coloured Ontario relations with the federal government. Although Liberal in name, Hepburn represented sectional interests. He resigned in 1942 shortly before the Liberal administration was defeated at the polls.

T. D. Pattullo. Another Provincial Liberal who quarreled with the federal government was British Columbia's premier, T. D. Pattullo. His government spent large sums on programmes to offset the Depression. The provincial debt sky-rocketed. Because of the influx of unemployed people from other parts of the country Pattullo continued to press the federal government for larger grants. However, he insisted that these be given with no strings attached, demanding that the province keep complete control of its financial affairs. Both R. B. Bennett and Mackenzie King disagreed with this, claiming that Ottawa should have some voice in the expenditure of federal funds. Thus, in spite of their apparent common allegiance to the Liberal party, Pattullo and Mackenzie King failed to co-operate.

THE ROWELL-SIROIS ROYAL COMMISSION

Some Canadians had been conscious since Confederation of the built-in strains imposed upon national unity by the nature of the federation. However, it was probably not until the Depression that many Canadians began to realize the complexity of Canadian federalism and, moreover, the important and subtle changes that had taken place since 1867. The necessity for a concerted attack on Depression problems in general and on Bennett's "New Deal," so much of which was of questionable constitutionality, made the matter of Canadian federalism an issue of immediate concern. On returning to power in 1935, Mackenzie King referred the Bennett legislation to the courts. When it was settled that much of it was *ultra vires* (beyond the jurisdiction of the federal government), King in 1937, established a Royal Commission on Dominion-Provincial Relations, the now historic Rowell-Sirois Commission, to investigate Canadian fiscal and constitutional problems.

The Report. The Commission worked for three years to produce a report that immediately became one of the most important collections of documents in Canadian history. This report highlighted two developments of great importance.

(1) Since Confederation the effect of a series of decisions by the British justices of the Judicial Committee of the Privy Council* had been to reverse the original intention of the Fathers of Confederation—in spite of a specific clause in the BNA Act to the contrary. In effect, residual powers of government, that is those powers unspecified in the BNA Act, had been given to the provinces (except in such times of "national emergency" as war), for example the regulation of wage levels, hours of labour, trade union legislation, public health measures, etc.

(2) The specified areas of authority of the provinces had grown far beyond the limits anticipated by the Fathers in such areas as education, social services, and highways, thereby giving the provinces very costly responsibilities to fulfil on strictly limited sources of income, the major powers of taxation still resting with the federal government.

The commissioners in their report made two further important observations: that as Canada's economy had expanded and grown in complexity, there had been regional disparity in that growth and an increasing need for proper central machinery to control and guide the economy.

Recommendations. Having analysed the state of the Canadian federation, the Rowell-Sirois Report made several significant recommendations. These were designed to eliminate the inequalities among the provinces and to allow Canadians to pursue the economic and social goals of a modern industrialized state. At the same time it wanted to maintain what the commissioners believed to be the original and proper distribution of powers between the provincial and federal levels of government. To ensure

---

*The highest court of appeal for Canada until 1949.

a more equitable distribution of wealth among the provinces, the Report recommended that:

(1) the federal government assume provincial debts;

(2) the statutory subsidies to the provinces be replaced with a system of "adjustment grants" intended to provide each province with the funds necessary to provide adequate administration and social services;

(3) The provinces agree to allow the federal government full powers in the collection of direct taxes—personal income, corporation, and succession duties;

(4) the federal government assume full responsibility for unemployment relief, thereby assuring a uniform standard in administration and in social services across the nation.

Dominion-Provincial Conference of 1941. The Rowell-Sirois Report was brought before a Dominion-Provincial conference in January, 1941, where it met immovable opposition from Alberta, British Columbia and Ontario. These three delegations, unofficially led by Ontario's Premier Hepburn, refused even to discuss the Report, which they felt would destroy the balance of Dominion-Provincial power and lead to increased centralization. But although the Report was substantially laid aside, it had not been without effect. Already, in 1940, after an amendment to the BNA Act, a national unemployment insurance scheme was established. Furthermore, the pressure of war resulted in tax rental agreements between the federal and provincial governments that recognized federal domination in taxation. Finally, the Report had given influential expression to the belief that the state had a responsibility to act positively for the social and economic welfare of the people. This belief, arising from the Depression and strengthened by the war effort, was to have a profound effect on Canadian politics.

Even before the Rowell-Sirois Commission had submitted its Report, Canada had begun to recover from the Depression. The cost of complete recovery, however, was great; it was brought about by the beginning of World War II. While Canadians had struggled through the Depression years at home, events abroad had been leading with increasing rapidity towards the outbreak of war in Europe in 1939. When Canada went to the aid of Great Britain, new demands were made upon all major industries. Within a few short months Canada's manpower and industrial capacities were being strained to the limit. The Great Depression was over at last.

BIBLIOGRAPHY

ALLEN, F. L. *Since Yesterday, 1929-39*. Bantam Books of Canada, 1961.

PRATT, V. W. *Famous Doctors*. Canadian Portrait Series. Clarke, Irwin, 1956.

SANDERS, B. H. *Famous Women*. Canadian Portrait Series. Clarke, Irwin, 1958.

THORBURN, HUGH G. *Party Politics in Canada*. Prentice-Hall, 1967.

YOUNG, W. D. *Democracy and Discontent*. Ryerson, 1969.

14

The Second World War, 1939-1945

During the Great Depression of the 1930's, the attention of Canadians had inevitably been drawn inward to the economic and social dislocation that seemed to tear at the very heart of the nation and its people. When world problems did intrude they aroused little genuine concern. Most Canadians remained secure in the belief that they lived isolated and insulated from the affairs of the wider world of Europe and Asia. This tragic misconception of reality was, however, soon to be dispelled once again by the holocaust of world war and the accompanying problems of national survival and national unity.

THE YEARS THAT LED TO WAR

Three important assumptions lay behind Canada's attitude towards international affairs during the years before World War II:

1. National autonomy, achieved so recently, had to be preserved at all costs, and any domination or interference, be it by Great Britain or an international body, was to be avoided.

2. As a trading nation, Canada's interests would best be served by avoiding any international commitments that could antagonize customers or in any way restrict freedom of trade.

3. The nation's destiny lay in North America and could only be adversely affected by entanglements outside that sphere.

Canada and the League of Nations. It might have been expected that Canada would be reluctant to become involved in international agreements with Great Britain, but the broader implications of Canada's isolationist position were clearly evident in her reaction to the League of Nations. Canada welcomed membership in the world body as a sign of her autonomous status. Even before the Covenant had been signed, however, she had tried to mute the effect of Article X. This article sought to establish a system of collective security under which League members would undertake to enforce mutual respect and peace among the nations of the world. Having failed to secure amendment of Article X, the Mackenzie King government collaborated with other League members in rendering the collective security system virtually void by simply failing to invoke its power when an occasion arose.

The Spread of Aggression. The first critical test of the collective security principle came in 1931 when Japan invaded the Chinese province of Manchuria. Canada, together with other League members, declined to agree to any aid in defence of China and Japanese aggression went unchallenged.

In 1935 the League was given a second chance to assert its peace-keeping authority when the Italian Fascist dictator, Benito Mussolini, made open preparations to invade the ancient African kingdom of Abyssinia, or Ethiopia. Influenced more by Italy's clear intent of war than by the moving, personal plea for help by Ethiopia's diminutive Emperor Hailé Selassié, the League compromised. Italy was publicly condemned and economic sanctions were voted against her (that is, League members were forbidden to export a list of certain products to Italy). However, not included among the sanctions were iron, coal, and in particular, oil, the one item without which Italy's Ethiopian invasion would have collapsed. Canada's representative, Dr. W. A. Riddell, realized the critical issue involved in this omission and courageously proposed that oil be added to the list. Unfortunately, Riddell had not consulted Ottawa before acting. As a result, after a few days of indecision, Prime Minister King repudiated Riddell's plan with the remark that it was not Canada's job to "regulate a European war." Having rejected the opportunity to take a bold step on the world stage, Canada's government remained consciously uncommitted in international affairs.

In defence of the government's policy it must be said that Mackenzie King realized that foreign affairs had in the past been a divisive force in Canadian affairs. It is also true that many Canadian politicians shared with many world leaders the belief that through appeasement and stalling war could be avoided. (Perhaps hindsight alone allows us today to see that it was this very policy that thrust Canada into even more frighteningly divisive circumstances—a world war.) Prime Minister King, along with many Canadians fatally misjudged the character and intentions of Adolf Hitler, the German Nazi leader. Although Hitler's insatiable appetite brought about the re-occupation of the Rhineland, the downfall of Austria, and the invasion of Czechoslovakia, Canada refused to foresee the coming of war. She maintained neutrality, refusing to take practical action or even to display disapproval. Even in the area of self-defence Canada was unprepared. In 1937 the military budget was increased but remained far below what it should have been until after the out-break of war in 1939.

The Beginning of War.   Any remaining illusions Canadians might have had about the peaceful intentions of Adolf Hitler were shattered in September, 1939. At that time Nazi Germany invaded Poland in defiance of British and French warnings that they would defend Poland against aggression.

Seven days after Britain had declared war on Nazi Germany, Prime Minister King summoned the Canadian Parliament into session.   Unlike the constitutional situation in 1914, in 1939 Canada possessed the right to declare war herself.   With only three dissenting voices, Parliament approved a declaration of war and on September 10, King George VI, as King of Canada, proclaimed a state of war between Canada and Nazi Germany.

Within a short time steps were taken to organize the country for war. The War Measures Act of 1914 was proclaimed to be in force again. By this the cabinet was granted extensive powers through order-in-council. Steps were taken to increase the armed forces, to suppress subversive organizations, to establish censorship, and to lay the foundations of a war-time economy. A number of government committees were established: The Wartime Prices and Trade Board to control civilian prices and to prevent hoarding; a Foreign Exchange Board to control the flow of money; a War Supply Board (later replaced by the Department of Munitions and Supply) to supervise production; and a Defence Purchasing Board to place orders for war materials.

THE STRUGGLE FOR EUROPE,
JUNE 1944-MAY 1945

Kiel Canal

Kiel

Wismar

Hamburg

Bremen

Elbe R.

4 May 45

Stettin

POLAND

Berlin

Munster

Torgau

25 April 45

Oder R.

essen

Dortmund

Kassel

Leipzig

Dusseldorf

Dresden

logne

GERMANY

Remagen

Frankfort

Prague

CZECHOSLOVAKIA

Rhine R.

Karlsruhe

R.

Danube

Vienna

R.

Munich

AUSTRIA

SWITZ.

Milan

Venice

YUGOSLAVIA

Po R.

ITALY

Florence

15 Aug 44

THE FIGHTING FRONT

The Royal Canadian Navy.   When war began Canada's military establishment was very small and unprepared for the magnitude of the task ahead. Taking advantage, however, of the relatively inactive early months of the war, the so-called phoney war, Canada's military forces began the process of building up their strength. In 1939, the Royal Canadian Navy, the smallest of the three services had less than 2,000 men and only fifteen vessels; by 1945, the Navy was composed of almost 100,000 men and women, and almost 1,000 vessels. From the opening of hostilities the Navy assumed the task of escorting convoys carrying supplies and men across the North Atlantic from North America. In addition it contributed men and ships to the vital Normandy invasion of 1944.

The Royal Canadian Air Force.   The Royal Canadian Air Force also underwent a spectacular expansion from a peace-time force of 4,500 men to more than 200,000 men, an organization that contributed 45 squadrons to the European theatre of war and became the fourth largest Allied air force. Canadian aircrews and ground crews also saw action in North Africa, Sicily, Italy, India and Burma. One of Canada's most important contributions to the war was the maintenance and management of the Commonwealth Air Training Plan, a scheme which brought over 130,000 airmen from all parts of the Commonwealth to train in Canadian skies.

The Army.   The largest of Canada's military services, the army, grew from one division (hastily dispatched to Britain late in 1939) to a complement of 650,000. At first, Canadian military policy was to keep troops together rather than to have them distributed and divided throughout Allied comands. As a result, by 1942 Canada had a full-fledged military strength of three infantry divisions and two armoured divisions in Britain. In the words of their Commander, General A. G. L. McNaughton, the Canadian troops, trained to a peak of efficiency and skill, were to be "a dagger pointed at the heart of Berlin" ready to lead the invasion of Germany. The original plan, however, was abandoned in July of 1943 when the Canadian army was broken up and the 1st Canadian Infantry Division became part of the British forces invading Sicily. Subsequently it was joined by the 5th Armoured Division in the hard, bitter struggle for the liberation of Italy.

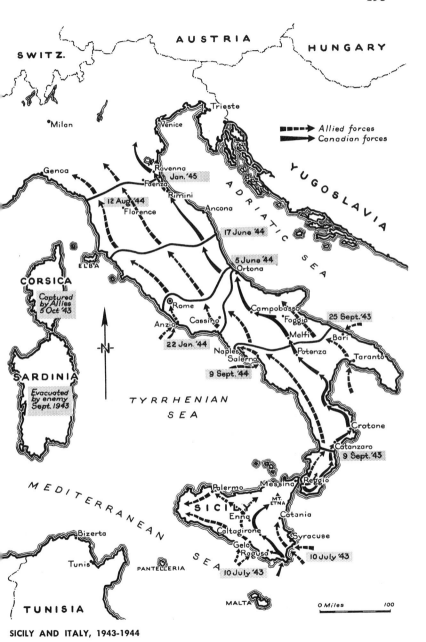

SWITZ.

AUSTRIA   HUNGARY

•Milan

Trieste

Venice

Genoa

Ravenna
Jan. '45

•Faenza
Rimini

A D R I A T I C

S E A

Y U G O S L A V I A

Allied forces
Canadian forces

12 Aug '44
•Florence

Ancona

17 June '44

ELBA

5 June '44
Ortona

CORSICA

Captured
by Allies
5 Oct '43

•Rome

Cassino

Campobasso
•Foggia

25 Sept. '43

Anzio

Melfi
Potenza

Bari

22 Jan. '44

Naples
Salerno

Taranto

—N—

9 Sept. 44

SARDINIA

Evacuated
by enemy
Sept. 1943

T Y R R H E N I A N
S E A

Crotone

Catanzaro
9 Sept. '43

M E D I T E R R A N E A N

Palermo

Messina
Reggio

MT.
ETNA

Catania

S I C I L Y

Enna

Bizerta

Caltagirone

Syracuse

S E A

Gela
Ragusa

Tunis

PANTELLERIA

10 July '43

10 July '43

TUNISIA

MALTA

0 Miles   100

SICILY AND ITALY, 1943-1944

Dieppe. The first action seen by Canadian troops was when 5,000 of them formed the bulk of the ill-fated 6,100-member striking force that landed at Dieppe in 1942. Controversy still rages as to the advisability of this raid, which was intended to be a test of men, equipment, and tactics in preparation for the full-scale invasion of Europe. Errors of judgment and bad luck resulted in a terrible toll of over 3,000 casualties.

Canadian Military Engagements. Canadians had an important, though less spectacular role in the invasion of Normandy and in the succeeding rout of the Nazi armies in Europe in 1944 and 1945. The invasion force itself included 14,000 Canadian troops. With the beachhead firmly established, the First Canadian Army was given the difficult task of liberating the Channel ports, including Dieppe. A particularly bloody campaign was the one to secure the great Belgian port of Antwerp, desperately needed by both sides. The British had taken the city itself but it fell to the Canadians to clear the islands in the estuary of the Scheldt River thereby opening the port to Allied shipping. From Belgium, Canadians moved into Holland and crossed the Rhine River pushing Nazi forces before them into Germany.

THE POLITICS OF WAR

In the pre-war years Prime Minister King had based his foreign policy not so much on international considerations as on domestic necessities. His intent had been to avoid any action that would delay the restoration of national unity following the crisis of the First World War. When the advent of the Second World War finally forced Canada to involve herself in world affairs, King continued to do all in his power to prevent any fissures opening in the growing structure of Canadian unity. In the same speech in which he told the special session of Parliament that a declaration of war would be forthcoming, he repeated his pre-war promises that his government would never introduce conscription for overseas duty. Despite these assurances, repeated many times by King and his chief Quebec lieutenant, Ernest Lapointe, the question remained, would King be able to avoid the highly emotional issue of conscription?

Challenge from Quebec. The first serious challenge to King's leadership came not in federal politics but from Quebec's premier, Maurice Duplessis, who sought to strengthen his government's hold on Quebec and also to weaken the federal powers in Canada. Calling a snap election in October of 1939, Duplessis campaigned on a highly emotional anti-federal government platform, claiming that Ottawa was using the war as an excuse to promote centralization and to undermine the autonomy of Quebec. Lapointe realized that Duplessis' campaign was more serious than the usual cry of Quebec nationalism, and that, if it were successful, it could seriously hamper the war effort and cause untold bitterness between Canada's two major races. Thus, with three other cabinet ministers from Quebec, Lapointe personally entered the fray, repeating the promise of no conscription. He also made it clear that he and his colleagues would consider a Duplessis victory a demand from the people of Quebec that the four ministers resign from the King administration, thereby withdrawing Quebec representation from the federal cabinet. This dramatic appeal paid off; Duplessis was defeated, and the Quebec Liberal party held office for the next five years.

Challenge from Ontario. Quebec was, however, not the only provincial source of opposition. Ontario's Liberal premier, Mitchell Hepburn, a bitter political foe of Mackenzie King, joined the provincial Conservative leader, George Drew, in strongly condemning King's conduct of the war effort. If Quebec thought Ottawa was doing too much, Ontario, a very British province, thought too little was being done. The federal Conservative party held the same opinion and kept calling for an all-party national government (similar to Borden's Union Government of 1917-1918) committed to "a more vigorous" prosecution of the war.

Election of 1940. King, as sensitive as ever to the divisive forces within Confederation and the issues that could aggravate those forces, refused to accept Conservative demands. Instead he caught his critics unawares by calling an election in March, 1940, and requesting a mandate from the nation for himself and his government. Again King's administration boldly gambled in the face of challenge and again it won. The Liberals secured 178 seats in the House of Commons, the largest majority since Confederation.

THE CONSCRIPTION CRISIS

Though King had won the election of 1940 handily, complaints of his government's conduct of the war did not disappear. In fact, criticism increased rather than diminished and steadily focused around the dangerous issue of conscription, the issue that had almost rent Canada in two in 1917. In an attempt to gloss over the issue, King introduced in 1940, the National Resources Mobilization Act which gave the government wide control over persons and property and the right to conscript men for training and service within Canada. However, it explicitly forbade the conscription of men for overseas duty. This Act was followed by national registration which forced all men over sixteen years of age to carry registration cards.

The problem, however, remained contentious, particularly in English Canada, and in 1942 King was forced to act once more. While still determined not to introduce conscription for overseas service, he called for a plebiscite asking the people to release him and the government from the pledge repeatedly made that full conscription would not be introduced. The result, as might have been expected, was overwhelming approval in English Canada but less than one-third support in the province of Quebec. With the proof of the danger involved in the issue so dramatically revealed, King tried to obscure the government's attitude to military "call-up" still further by ambiguously describing future policy as "Not necessarily conscription but conscription if necessary." Having thus provided himself with an apparently comforting reply, he sought thereafter to avoid taking any action to introduce conscription.

It is now known that the cabinet was as seriously divided over conscription as the nation. The anti-conscriptionists were led by the Prime Minister and Louis St. Laurent, King's new Quebec lieutenant replacing the late Ernest Lapointe. The conscriptionists followed the lead of Colonel J. L. Ralston, the Minister of National Defence. The chief arguments in favour of conscription during the early years of the war were ones of sentiment and principle; since the other major allies were conscripting men for overseas service, Canada was being less than wholeheartedly enthusiastic in her support of Britain and the Allied cause by not doing so as well. But during these early years the anti-conscriptionists could, with justification, claim that Canada was living up to her military commitments overseas without conscription and that to have adopted such a policy would have been to pay too high a price to "rally 'round the flag."

The Manpower Crisis. By 1944 the background of the debate was noticeably changing. Following the Normandy invasion casualties mounted, and Canada appeared to be falling behind in replacing lost manpower. Ralston returned from a visit to Europe, emphatically declaring that 15,000 men were needed immediately. King still refused to accept conscription for overseas duty and in his search for an alternative discovered that General A. G. L. McNaughton (retired from active duty) agreed with him. McNaughton, a well-known, if perhaps controversial figure, believed that he could successfully produce volunteers for overseas service to overcome the manpower shortage. King, without warning Ralston, dismissed him from office and appointed McNaughton Minister of National Defence.

McNaughton failed both in his attempt to gain a seat in the House of Commons and in his campaign for overseas volunteers. King was forced to act. With St. Laurent's reluctant concurrence, an order-in-council was approved authorizing the dispatch of 16,000 home-service conscripts to Europe. Opinion in Quebec was naturally aroused, but St. Laurent was successful in heading off a major anti-conscription motion of no confidence by the Quebec members of the House of Commons. French-Canadians did not approve this conscription move but the government's agonized attempts to forestall what had probably always been inevitable was enough to prove to much of Quebec that its opinion was not being dismissed lightly. The fateful step was thus taken, as little strain as possible being placed upon the unity of the nation. Actually, a lessening of casualties and the end of the war resulted in very few conscripts being sent overseas.

THE WARTIME ECONOMY

The First World War had supplied the needed stimulus to begin to change Canada from being a predominantly agricultural nation to an industrial one. The Second World War, coming after an uneasy period of adjustment, firmly consolidated and strengthened Canadian industrial and commercial power.

Industrial Development. Canada's primary industries met the heavy demands of wartime needs. Agricultural production increased by thirty per cent, thus servicing not only domestic consumers but also a British market that had been cut off from many of its normal supply points. Other products required in increased quantities for wartime consumption were lumber, copper, lead, nickel, zinc and uranium. Above all, the war brought increased demands upon manufacturers of secondary goods, such as pulp and paper, iron and steel products, electrical equipment, airplanes, trucks, cars and high-octane gasoline. New techniques and products were introduced to Canada during the war (electronic equipment, synthetic rubber), most of them becoming integral parts of the national economy after 1945.

It has been estimated that Canada herself used only thirty per cent of her wartime production, the rest going to her Allies. Britain in particular was an important consumer of Canadian products. Further aid was given to Britain through low-interest loans and an outright gift of one billion dollars for the purchase of Canadian goods.

Co-operation with the United States.   The war also stimulated the already important trade between Canada and the United States. Inevitably under the circumstances this trade was decidedly lop-sided, with Canada purchasing far more than she sold, thus creating a trade deficit in which Canadian supplies of U.S. currency became dangerously low. To offset this condition, Prime Minister King and President Roosevelt in 1941 concluded the Hyde Park Agreement whereby the two nations undertook to complement each other's war production, buying certain goods from their neighbour and selling others in return. It was also arranged that goods bought by Canada for products eventually to be sent to Britain could be charged against British "Lend-Lease" accounts. The result of these measures was to ease the demand on Canadian reserves of American currency and to relieve the potentially disastrous downward pressure on the Canadian dollar.

The Cost of War.   The financing of the Canadian war effort required heavy taxation. It also brought about the need for further centralized economic direction. This was achieved by new federal-provincial tax-rental arrangements by which the provinces vacated the field of corporation and income taxes to the federal government in return for direct subsidies, thus enhancing the power of the federal government in relation to the provincial governments. This federal predominance was to be a major factor in post-war domestic politics for over two decades. Other methods of raising money were found in excess profit taxes, compulsory savings, and war saving stamps, the latter being sold even to school children. Over twelve billion dollars was borrowed by the government during the war, mostly by means of "Victory loan" war bonds. Since much of the war debt remained within the country among its citizens, the strain of repayment was kept to a minimum, although it represented a steady demand on government revenue for many years after 1945.

The tremendous drain of the war effort resulted in shortages in both manpower and consumer goods. Legislation was passed attempting to encourage essential industries, to protect workers, and to prevent inflation.

The National Selective Service Act, 1942, limited labour in non-essential industries and, in many cases, "froze" workers to their employment.

Amendments to the Industrial Disputes Investigation Act and the formation of a Wartime Labour Relations Board discouraged labour strife by encouraging collective bargaining and arbitration. The manufacture of unnecessary consumer goods, such as automobiles, was discouraged. Ceilings were set on wages and prices. Rationing was introduced for such goods as tires, butter, sugar, tea and gasoline. By these methods Canada was one of the most successful war powers in stemming the threat of inflation.

INTERNATIONAL RELATIONS

The Second World War inevitably enhanced Canada's stature in world affairs. Following the defeat of France, Canada was Britain's major ally until Germany invaded Russia in June of 1941 and Japan attacked the American naval base at Pearl Harbour in December, 1941. But, as before, Canada was self-consciously concerned about avoiding being taken for granted by her more powerful and more important friends, the United Kingdom and the United States. British attempts to establish a centralized direction of Commonwealth participation in the war were met with the same coolness bordering on hostility that had been demonstrated over twenty years before towards the proposals for an Imperial war cabinet and integrated Commonwealth defence and foreign policies. Prime Minister King emphasized the advantages of Commonwealth co-operation but took great pains to avoid any broad form of commitment that could limit Canadian independence. He was even reluctant to attend the 1944 Prime Ministers' Conference in London.

The Bridge Between Britain and the United States. Canada has frequently considered herself a bridge between Britain and the United States. While this concept has often been overemphasized at other times, during the Second World War it was an important fact. Symbolizing this relationship was the meeting of President Roosevelt and Prime Minister Churchill with Prime Minister King as host at the Citadel in Quebec City, in 1943. The three leaders discussed the prosecution of the war and preliminary plans for bringing order and peace to the post-war world.

Canada's relations with the United States during the war were very close. In 1938 President Roosevelt had stated that the United States would not stand idly by and see its neighbour, Canada attacked. A short time later Prime Minister Mackenzie King had responded by promising "reciprocity in defence." Beginning with the early informal measures to get needed supplies from the United States to Great Britain, Canadian-American co-operation became more formal and more binding with the Ogdensburg agreement of August, 1940, which provided for the establishment of a Permanent Joint Board on Defence to ensure co-ordination of North American defence. Growing out of the work of this advisory body were such important projects as measures for the defence of Newfoundland and Labrador, the construction of the Alaska Highway, the Canol pipeline from Norman Wells to the Pacific Coast, the establishment of Arctic air routes to Britain, and the construction of air bases in both countries. The Hyde Park Declaration of 1941 (already mentioned) was another important example of Canadian-American co-operation.

The United Nations. As the conclusion of the war approached, attention began to focus on post-war problems. Canada was not present at the Dumbarton Oaks Conference of 1944, where initial plans were laid for world peace, but she was present at the San Francisco Conference of 1945, the founding conference of the United Nations Organization. Canada's role at San Francisco was small, but the Prime Minister reminded the conference of the potential importance of the smaller world powers in the maintenance of world peace. This was to be a recurring Canadian theme in the future and foretold the enthusiastic support Canada was to give the U.N. in future years.

THE CONFLICT ENDS

When the Second World War ended in 1945, Canada was a considerably different nation from that of 1939. Once again she had faced the strains of an international conflict. This time, however, she was stronger and more united. While she might harbour apprehensions about the future, she was now more committed than ever before to active participation in the establishment and maintenance of a secure peace throughout the world. This principle was to be a major factor in her foreign affairs.

Domestically, Canada in 1945 was on the brink of an era of unprecedented expansion. Her people looked forward to the fruits of peace and were ready to use fully the new industrial and manufacturing power and also the skills and newly developed resources that war had given them.

BIBLIOGRAPHY

ALLEN, RALPH. *Ordeal by Fire*. Doubleday, 1961.

DAWSON, R. M. *The Conscription Crisis of 1944*. University of Toronto, 1961.

GRANATSTEIN, J. L. *Conscription in the Second World War, 1939-1945*. Ryerson, 1968.

Official History of the Canadian Army in the Second World War. I. STACEY, C. P. *Six Years of War: The Army in Canada, Britain and the Pacific* (1955); II. NICHOLSON, G. W. L. *The Canadians in Italy, 1943-1945* (1956); III. STACEY, C. P. *The Victory Campaign: The Operations in North-West Europe, 1944-1945* (1960). Queen's Printer.

PICKERSGILL, J. W. *The Mackenzie King Record, Vol. I, 1939-1944*. University of Toronto Press, 1960.

PICKERSGILL, J. W. *The Mackenzie King Record, Vol. II, 1944-1945*. University of Toronto Press, 1968.

15

Canada
After the War

Although Canadians born since the war have come to expect economic prosperity and social security as a matter of course, Canadians of the previous generation were not so optimistic. In 1945, the memory of the Depression was still fresh enough in the minds of most people to arouse anxiety about the possibility of a repetition. The government was fully aware of this threat to prosperity and took steps to allay the fears. Thus, a White Paper issued in 1945 stated that the "extension of opportunity, welfare and security among the Canadian people . . . (was) a major aim of government policy." The extent to which these aims were achieved is reflected in the optimistic attitudes of Canadians in the present day.

FEDERAL POLITICS IN THE POST-WAR ERA

Canada's war-time Liberal government under Prime Minister Mackenzie King was re-elected with a much reduced, but clear, majority in 1945. King, however, was aging and worn out; in 1948 he retired. Two years later he died.

Mackenzie King. Mackenzie King had held the office of prime minister longer than any other man in British Commonwealth history. For this achievement alone he deserves a place in history. His service to the nation entitles him to be ranked among Canada's great prime ministers. A Canadian patriot above all, King fought consistently throughout his career for national autonomy. During pre-war years he followed a policy of isolation and pacifism; and yet he also guided the nation through the greatest war in its history. In the post-war years his government effectively guided the country through the period of transition and onto a peace-time footing.

This enigmatic figure had dominated the affairs of his day and deftly guided his people through some of their most dangerous times. Often criticized for his apparent lack of positive leadership, he nevertheless held Canada united and guided her growth. Few people really knew him personally, and even today critics vary widely in their assessments of him. At the time of his death, few mourned his passing. For his achievements he had earned respect but seldom affection.

Louis St. Laurent. Mackenzie King's successor was Louis St. Laurent, a prominent Quebec corporation lawyer who had been introduced to politics late in life when he was made King's chief lieutenant from Quebec, first as Minister of Justice, then as Secretary of State for External Affairs. St. Laurent's personality stood in marked contrast to that of his former mentor. His sound administrative ability and warm Gallic charm quickly earned him both respect and affection in English and French Canada alike. Politically the St. Laurent administration was the direct heir of the King government; neither the personnel nor the policies underwent basic change.

Following the traditional Liberal policy of extending and defining Canada's sovereignty, the St. Laurent government made several significant achievements. The words "Dominion" and "British," long a source of annoyance to French Canadians, were dropped from Commonwealth terminology. In 1947, the Governor General had been given full right to all the prerogatives of the Crown in Canada. In 1952, Vincent Massey became the first Canadian-born Governor General. In 1949, appeals to the Judicial Committee of the Privy Council were abolished and the Supreme Court of Canada became the final court of appeal in all matters, including constitutional issues. Attempts were also made to devise a formula that would allow Canadians to alter the British North America Act themselves, thereby ending the embarrassing need to petition the British Parliament for every amendment. The problem of provincial rights blocked complete "repatriation" of the BNA Act, but in 1949 provision was made for the federal government to amend those sections in which it had exclusive interest.

Newfoundland Becomes a Province. In 1949, Newfoundland was admitted to Confederation, the first new province to be created in almost half a century. The oldest of Britain's colonies, Newfoundland had remained aloof from Confederation in 1867, proud of her history and hopeful that she could maintain her unique status. She had been granted responsible government in 1855, but her economy was too restricted and too vulnerable to withstand the great Depression of the 1930's. In 1934, she was forced to surrender her self-government in order to gain British assistance. During World War II, Canada and Newfoundland were drawn closer together in the face of common dangers. After the war a measure of prosperity and economic stability returned to the island. Thus, following 1945, three possible courses lay open to Newfoundland: she could remain under British administration; she could seek independence once again; or she could join Canada. After considerable debate and two referendums, those in favour of union with Canada, led by J. (Joey) R. Smallwood, gained a narrow popular majority. With the admission of Newfoundland in 1949, Canada gained a province that was at the time relatively undeveloped but one that had great potential for the future in her forest and mineral resources and which had an important strategic position at the mouth of the St. Lawrence River.

The Liberal Demise. The. St. Laurent government continued secure in office until the mid 1950's. But it had become complacent and arrogant, having held power continuously for over twenty years. Symptomatic of the attitude was the so-called "pipeline debate." In the summer of 1956, C. D. Howe, the Minister of Trade and Commerce, introduced a measure into the House of Commons providing for government assistance to an American-backed company that was building a natural gas pipeline from Alberta to eastern Canada by way of the north shore of Lake Superior. Preoccupied with their desire for speed and efficiency, the government forced closure on debate in the Commons in order to meet a self-imposed deadline. The opposition, led by an aggressive new Conservative leader, John Diefenbaker, capitalized on this use of closure. The public was also indignant about the government's action, particularly since it appeared to have been a special favour to American interests. Diefenbaker posed as the defender of parliamentary rights and subtly appealed to the latent anti-Americanism of the Canadian electorate. To many Canadians he appeared to be a refreshing change from the Liberals who seemed to be more interested in "running a tight ship" than in providing imaginative and aggressive leadership. In the general election of 1957, Diefenbaker led his party to victory. The Conservatives, however, did not win an outright majority in the Commons. Their 112 members could be outvoted by a possible combination of the Liberals with their 105 members, the C.C.F. with 25, and the Social Credit with 19. Thus the years of Liberal government had come to an end.

THE POST-WAR ECONOMY

As World War II drew to a close, there was some concern that post-war conditions would be a repetition of those that had followed World War I—a period of rising inflation followed by a disastrous depression. To ensure the orderly adjustment to a peace-time economy, the Canadian government hesitated about removing the elaborate system of price controls that had been applied during the war. Some controls were lifted during the first year of peace but others, such as those on rents, transportation, meat and butter, were retained until the end of the decade. But these cautious steps were little more than incidental to the establishment of post-war stability and prosperity. It quickly became apparent that Canadians were about to enter an extended period of economic expansion and national vitality.

Secondary Industry. Since Canada had not been in the front line of battle herself, her industries were undamaged and at the peak of their efficiency. The late forties saw a period of uninterrupted economic growth. Only the relatively simple process of retooling was necessary to convert machinery to the production of the many consumer goods that Canadians had been denied for over five years. Cars, electrical appliances, clothing and many other products poured onto the market. Factories were stretched to capacity to meet the apparently unlimited demand. At the same time, the construction industry prospered as it met the demand for new housing, schools, roads, and industrial buildings which had been postponed during the war years. The development of well-established industries was paralleled by the rapid expansion in fields such as aviation and shipbuilding which prior to the war had been relatively undeveloped.

By 1950, as the boom seemed to be losing some of its vigour, there was a short revival created by the needs of the Korean War.

This was followed in the mid 1950's by a brief period of stagnation. However, the 1960's were years of steady growth and expansion primarily due to the increase in population, a resultant increase in the domestic market, advanced manufacturing techniques, aggressive marketing, and the development of new products.

Primary Industry. Although secondary industry grew at a rapid pace following the war, the Canadian economy continued to derive its greatest strength from primary industry. As in earlier years, agricultural products were a major source of income. Europe, her agricultural capacity depleted by the ravages of war, turned to Canada, particularly for grain. After a strong post-war demand from western Europe, agricultural production fluctuated sharply from year to year. However, the general picture was one of growth, and several times during the 1960's Canadian annual wheat exports exceeded one billion dollars. The principle reason for this increase was the large shipments of wheat to the U.S.S.R., mainland China, India and western Europe. On the other hand, Britain, which before the war had taken 62 per cent of Canada's wheat, took only 24 per cent in 1965. The percentage of wheat bought by the United States also declined from 21 to 16 per cent in the same period of time. By the late 1960's the situation had once again changed. World production had outstripped demand. The major wheat producing countries, including Canada, reaped a succession of bumper harvests. Despite international agreements, prices in the world market-place were declining. The result for Canadian farmers was falling sales and mountains of unsold wheat stored in grain elevators and on farms throughout the west. In 1970 the government took drastic measures to reduce this surplus by paying farmers up to $10,000 if they did not plant wheat but instead left the land fallow or planted forage crops.

Another important pre-war industry, the production of pulp and paper, continued as Canada's leading industry. By the mid 1960's Canadian newsprint, which found its largest market in the United States, accounted for over half of the total world production.

Natural Resources. The traditional staple natural resources were joined and even surpassed after the war by new ones that had scarcely been tapped before. In 1947, after many years of intensive exploration, the Leduc oil field south of Edmonton was discovered. Though important in itself, Leduc was only the forerunner. Further immense reserves of oil were discovered in Alberta and the Northwest Territories near Great Bear Lake. At the close of the sixties, large-scale exploration was underway in the Arctic which promised further rich yields of oil. (This exploration also raised the question of Canadian ownership and control of Arctic waters.) The development of new technology permitted the extraction of oil from the Athabasca tar sands. It has been estimated that these tar sands will produce between 300 and 400 billion barrels of crude oil, an amount equal to the entire world supply of known oil reserves. Even these deposits are believed to be only a fraction of the oil still to be discovered in Canada.

The importance of oil in the post-war Canadian economy was as great as that of wheat a generation before. In particular, Alberta, formerly a relatively poor province, troubled by debt and plagued by the unpredictable forces of nature and the vagaries of the world wheat market, supplied two-thirds of the country's petroleum and became one of the richest provinces. The Alberta government claimed a royalty on all crude oil produced in the province and used these funds for reducing the once large provincial debt as well as for the financing of a variety of social, cultural, medical and other projects.

With the discovery of oil came new sources of natural gas. Production of this resource increased from 48 billion cubic feet in 1946 to 1,400 billion cubic feet in 1965. Together oil and gas stimulated many sectors of the Canadian economy. Pipelines crossed the country from the Pacific Ocean to the St. Lawrence Valley. New or enlarged refineries were built at strategic points. These new sources of fuel and power stimulated established industries and opened up many new industrial regions, thereby creating new opportunities for employment, new demands for a wide variety of equipment and stimulating the construction of allied industries. Cheap and abundant supplies of fuel also aided in maintaining reasonable transportation costs in a country that depended heavily on efficient means of communication and distribution. Petroleum products also stimulated the expansion of Canada's petro-chemical industry. Finally, oil and natural gas transported through pipelines to the United States helped to increase Canada's exports.

Of equal importance to the discovery of oil was the discovery of large deposits of high grade iron ore. With United States' supplies quickly dwindling after the war, Canada's new mines found a ready market. The first important iron ore discovery was in 1938 at Steep Rock, a lake west of Lake Superior and north of the great Mesabi range in Minnesota. Even greater iron ore deposits were

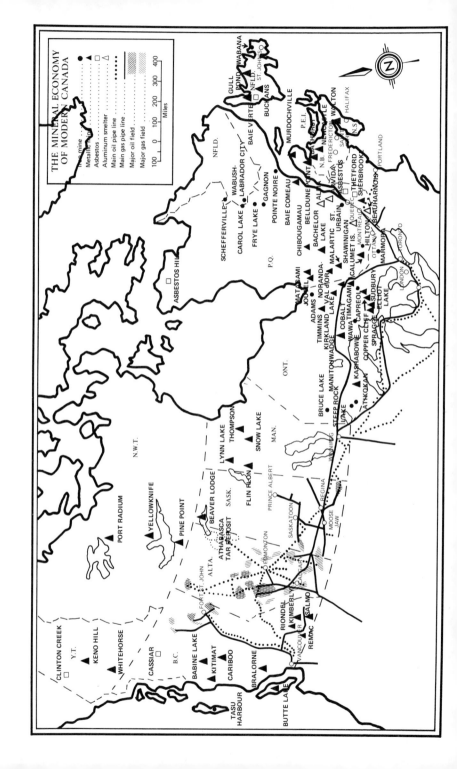

THE MINERAL ECONOMY
OF MODERN CANADA

Coal mine ●
Metallic mine ▲
Asbestos □
Aluminum smelter △
Main oil pipe line
Main gas pipe line
Major oil field
Major gas field

Miles
100   0   100   200   300   400

later discovered on the Belcher Islands in Hudson Bay, in Labrador, northern Quebec, the Yukon and on Baffin Island. The first development in Quebec took place at Knob Lake in the early 1950's. From this mine near Schefferville, the ore was taken 350 miles by a rail line constructed for the purpose to Sept Îles on the St. Lawrence River. Here a new harbour was built to accommodate the ore carriers that transported the iron to the great steel manufacturing complexes of central North America. In the 1960's several more iron and coal mines in British Columbia were opened, and others were expanded, to supply the Japanese market.

Iron ore was not the only mineral to increase its importance to the Canadian economy. World War II had given an impetus to mineral production, and scientific developments of the post-war world accelerated the search not only for basic minerals but also for others that had formerly been considered of little use or value. Extensive post-war exploration proved that Canada had rich resources of many of the minerals required by modern science and industry. New sources of nickel, lead, zinc, and asbestos were discovered. One of the world's largest potash fields was opened in Saskatchewan. Newly important minerals such as titanium, bismuth and molybdenum were extracted and marketed. In the twenty-two years following the war the value of mineral production in Canada increased eight-fold.

One of the most publicized and glamorous minerals that acquired value in the post-war world was uranium. (The first mine in Canada had opened at Great Bear Lake before the war.) Explorations uncovered deposits in Saskatchewan and in two Ontario areas— near Bancroft and west of Sudbury. At the latter site a planned community, Elliot Lake, sprang up adjacent to the mines. Being important in the new field of nuclear energy, uranium quickly became the centre of a boom. But the uranium producers over-estimated the demand for their product and by the late fifties the boom began to lose impetus. By 1965 the production of uranium was almost at a standstill. However, 1966 was a significant year for the industry because of an increased demand for nuclear-generated power plants which resulted in the completion of the first large contracts for the sale of uranium for peaceful purposes. Exports to other countries indicated a resurgence of uranium demand extending into the 1970's.

Water Resources. Among the most fundamental of Canada's natural assets are her water resources, which have been developed both for transportation and for industry. The outstanding example of water being used for transportation is the St. Lawrence Seaway.

The expansion of the canals of the St. Lawrence River to accommodate all but the very largest ocean-going vessels had long been a Canadian dream. The development of the international waterway promised to open the Great Lakes to international shipping. Canadians saw great benefits from the project and for their cities and industries. Pre-war attempts to gain the co-operation of the United States had been unsuccessful. But after the war, when it became known that Canada was ready to proceed without the

United States, the American authorities finally agreed to participate.

By 1954, agreements were finalized providing for the construction of two new locks on the American side of the river to bypass part of the International Rapids section, and for the co-operation of the Ontario Hydro Commission and the New York State Power Authority for the construction of a massive power generating system between Cornwall, Ontario and Massena, New York. Construction on this huge programme began in 1954 and the Seaway was formally opened by Queen Elizabeth and President Eisenhower in 1959. Lake ports in both Canada and the United States became important ports of call for the shipping of the world. Traffic in the Great Lakes increased so rapidly that by 1966 major improvements

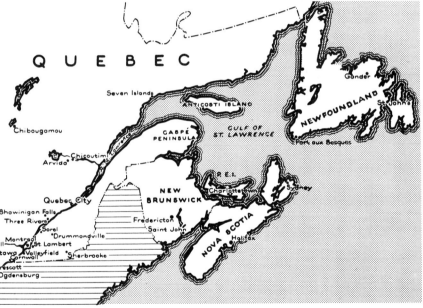

THE ST. LAWRENCE SEAWAY

had been made to the Welland Canal between Lake Ontario and Lake Erie. This work included canal widening and straightening, the "twinning" of all single locks so that they could be used for two-way traffic simultaneously, and the installation of closed circuit television to direct vessels through the canal and thus reduce time. Plans were laid for an all-Canadian canal at the International Rapids section of the St. Lawrence River that would increase the Seaway's capacity. Further improvements to the Welland Canal system were also being carried forward. The success of the Seaway was a striking symbol of Canada's economic progress during this period.

A second benefit to Canada of the St. Lawrence Seaway was as a source of hydro-electric power for the homes and factories of the industrial east. The power of this mighty river was harnessed near Cornwall, Ontario where the river drops 90 feet in 44 miles along the International Rapids section. The Moses-Saunders generating station adds 1,824,000 kilowatts of hydro-electric power for the industries of Ontario and New York State.

The harnessing of the St. Lawrence River was just the first of many enormous projects designed to supply Canada's growing population and manufacturing complex. In New Brunswick, the power of the picturesque St. John River was harnessed in 1969 by the Mactaquac dam and generating station. Quebec was tapping her northern rivers with huge projects such as the Daniel Johnson installation on the Manicouagan River. In Saskatchewan, the first important hydro development in the Saskatchewan River was opened at Squaw Rapids in 1963. Two of the largest construction projects ever undertaken anywhere were started in Labrador and in British Columbia. The mighty Churchill Falls on the Churchill River would add millions of kilowatts for the insatiable needs of cities on the eastern seaboard and St. Lawrence Valley. An international agreement (The Columbia River Treaty), signed by Canada and the United States in 1961 and modified in 1964, allowed work to begin on the Peace and Columbia rivers in British Columbia. The power from these ambitious projects would be used throughout the Pacific Northwest. Two further mammoth projects were in their initial stages; the harnessing of Nelson River in Manitoba and perhaps the most ambitious of all, the tapping of the mighty Bay of Fundy tides.

Foreign Trade.   The opening of the St. Lawrence Seaway reflected the increasing importance of foreign trade to the Canadian economy. By 1960, revenue from trade represented one-fifth of the national income and Canada ranked fifth among the world's trading nations, behind the United States, West Germany, Britain, and France. The chief exports had been agricultural products, especially grain, but after the war such products as automobiles and accessories, pulp and paper, base metals, petroleum, and other goods valuable to industry assumed an increasing importance.

The direction of Canadian trade also changed significantly in the post-war years. Previously Britain had been the chief customer, but after 1945 the United States, whose prosperous industrial society was a ready market for Canadian products, occupied that role. Britain, on the other hand, was short of dollars after the war and was also attempting to rebuild her own industrial strength behind import restrictions. By 1966 almost three-fifths of all Canadian exports went to the United States; in addition, almost two-thirds of Canada's imports came from the United States. Britain occupied second place, taking one-eighth of Canada's exports and supplying one-fifteenth of her imports.

Canada strongly supported the General Agreement of Tariffs and Trade (GATT) which came into force in 1948. Its purpose was to expand world trade by reducing tariff barriers over a period of years. This policy was accentuated in 1967 when Canada cooperated in the Kennedy Round of negotiations for the easing of restrictions on international trade.

American Economic Domination. The increasingly close connection between the Canadian and American economies was a mixed blessing. It brought prosperity and a high standard of living to Canadians but a number of problems as well. The balance of trade between the two countries was in favour of the United States. This imbalance, or trade deficit as it is sometimes called, caused a heavy drain on Canadian reserves of American dollars. The normal effect of this would eventually have been to place a severe strain on the value of the Canadian dollar followed by growing economic dislocation. Fortunately, during most of the post-war period the trade deficit with the United States was offset by a large inflow of American investment capital. In 1962, however, there was a brief monetary crisis during which the government devalued the Canadian dollar and "pegged" its value in terms of American dollars. This policy proved to be successful and the uneasy balance was restored.

The inflow of American capital following the war, while helping to maintain economic stability and giving great impetus to industrial expansion, created problems as well. Canadians realized that many of their major industrial concerns, particularly oil, minerals and paper, were subject to varying degrees of American domination. This point was brought into sharp focus in 1958 when it was widely reported that a Canadian automobile manufacturer was prevented by its American parent company from trading with mainland China. The general picture was less dramatic but some informed Canadians warned that American domination was a serious threat to Canada's national development and possibly even to Canadian political autonomy.

Successive governments since 1945 have sought to tackle the problem of American influence in the economy. The Gordon Royal Commission on Canada's economic prospects (1957) suggested that Canadians be given more opportunity to participate in managerial and executive capacities in American-controlled companies and that Canadian investors be given more opportunity and encouragement to own voting stock in these companies. The commission also warned that Canadian financial institutions should not be allowed to pass into foreign hands. Some legislation was enacted in an attempt to control American domination; in particular, restrictions were placed on the ownership of Canadian banks and advertising in American magazines was discouraged.

Despite these measures, however, American domination of the economy continued to grow. Between 1955 and 1965, total foreign investment in Canada almost doubled to $34 billion, of which 73 per cent came from the United States. American ownership at this date accounted for 70 per cent of the petroleum and natural gas industry, 50 per cent of mining and smelting, 40 per cent of manufacturing in general and 95 per cent of automobile manufacturing. In 1968 the controversial *Foreign Ownership and the Structure of Canadian Industry,* commonly known as the Watkins' Report, sounded a strong warning that if government action were not taken to control this trend, even our *political* sovereignty might be threatened. A great deal of controversy was aroused over the conclusions drawn in the Report. The basic problem, however, still remained: how could Canadian control be kept without discouraging the foreign investment which is still essential for expansion? Unquestionably, the role of the United States in the economy poses one of the most difficult dilemmas for Canada's future.

SOCIAL AND CULTURAL CHANGES

The expansion of Canada's economy in the post-war years would not have been possible without a corresponding increase in the population. With this increase, however, new social patterns began to emerge deeply affecting the social and cultural life of Canada.

Population Growth. Between 1945 and 1970 the population rose by 75 per cent (from 12 million to over 21 million). The immediate post-war growth was primarily the result of natural increase. The Canadian birth rate began to rise during the war and continued at a very high level until 1959. The peak year was 1947 when the rate was 28.9 live births per 1,000 of population—one of the highest in the industrialized world. By 1966, the rate had declined to 19.4 per 1,000 of population where it seemed to stabilize.

Although second to natural increase in importance, immigration was a major factor in the post-war population increase. Between 1945 and 1965 over 2,500,000 immigrants representing sixty ethnic groups arrived. The flow of immigrants reached a peak in 1957 when 282,000 arrived. This was followed by a period of decline which reached its lowest level of 71,600 in 1961. In 1962 the economy revived. A change in regulations permitting people with "technical or other needed skills" to enter the country, opened the door to immigrants from countries which previously had few eligible citizens. By 1966, the rate of immigration had reached nearly 200,000.

Urban Growth. The majority of post-war immigrants (unlike those of previous periods) made their new homes in the cities, particularly in the large urban areas of central Canada and British Columbia. This fact is indicative of a much wider population change that was taking place in the country—the shift to the cities from rural areas. This movement had been noticeable since Confederation but after 1945 it was greatly accelerated. In 1951, 57 per cent of the population lived in urban areas; only five years later, in 1956, 67 per cent lived in urban areas. (The previous increase of 10 per cent in relative urban size had required almost forty years.) By 1961 the percentage had risen to 70 and by 1966 to 73.6. The result of this increase in urban population was the transformation of Canadian cities. The need for housing created vast suburbs radiating from the central core. The inner cities were rejuvenated as new commercial, apartment and office develop-

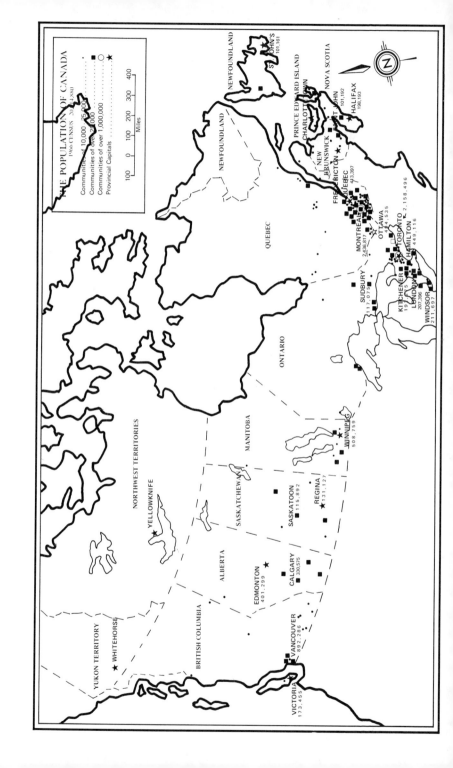

THE POPULATION OF CANADA
1966 CENSUS 20,014,880

Communities of 10,000 - 25,000 · · ·
Communities of over 25,000 · · · ■
Communities of over 1,000,000 · · · ○
Provincial Capitals · · · ★

Miles
100 0 100 200 300 400

YUKON TERRITORY

★ WHITEHORSE

NORTHWEST TERRITORIES

★ YELLOWKNIFE

BRITISH COLUMBIA

VICTORIA
173,455
VANCOUVER
892,286

ALBERTA

EDMONTON ★
401,299
CALGARY
330,575

SASKATCHEWAN

SASKATOON
115,892
REGINA ★
131,127

MANITOBA

WINNIPEG ★
508,759

ONTARIO

QUEBEC

NEWFOUNDLAND

NEWFOUNDLAND

ST. JOHN'S
101,161

PRINCE EDWARD ISLAND
CHARLOTTETOWN
NOVA SCOTIA
NEW BRUNSWICK
SAINT JOHN
101,192
FREDERICTON ★
HALIFAX ★
198,193

QUEBEC
413,397
MONTREAL
2,436,817
OTTAWA
494,535
TORONTO
2,158,496
HAMILTON
449,116
KITCHENER
192,275
LONDON
207,396
WINDSOR
211,697
SUDBURY
117,075

ments replaced older and less attractive buildings. Paradoxically, Canadian cities were at the same time, experiencing serious problems of urban blight and slums. Other problems included the need for expanded utilities, new schools, and educational and recreational facilities of all kinds. There was also a seemingly insatiable demand for new and improved methods of transportation, including expressways and subways. Great social problems arose from such factors as automation and the consequent fear of unemployment, the adjustment and assimilation of immigrants, increases in the proportion of children and old people, and the generally increasing pace and complexity of urban life. All these problems placed great strains on the social and economic resources of the community, particularly at the municipal and provincial levels of government where the responsibility for action frequently fell.

Another problem arising as a by-product of urban and industrial expansion has been the threat of pollution. As the 1970's began, it became ever more apparent that there were insufficient safeguards against the depletion and pollution of resources. Industrial cities were covered by a noxious blanket of exhausts spewed from factories and automobiles. Rivers and lakes had become the dumping ground of industrial waste. (Wildlife and fish were also being exterminated by the indiscriminate use of insecticides.) The dimensions of this problem were only beginning to be realized and the first efforts were being made to undo the mistakes of the expansion years.

The Welfare State.   One important effect of post-war social problems was the growth of the "welfare state"—that is the system whereby the state provides various forms of social assistance and social security. Because the responsibility for health and welfare is constitutionally divided between federal and provincial governments, Canada's social welfare system has had rather a haphazard development. The total expenditures on health and social welfare are constantly rising, but it is interesting to note how the percentage contribution of each level of government varies. In 1926, out of a total expenditure of $89 million, the federal share amounted to about $49 million, or 55 per cent. This share rose to a high of 70.4 per cent in 1961 but then declined to 60.7 per cent in 1967. This was caused, to a large degree, by the increased hospital expenditures by provincial governments and by the effect of the "opting out" arrangements made available to the provinces. The provincial share was 26.4 per cent in 1961 but rose to 36.9

per cent in 1967, while the municipal outlays declined in the same period from 3.2 per cent to 2.4 per cent.

In 1940 the federal government passed an unemployment insurance act which was extended and expanded from time to time. A family allowance ("baby bonus") payment was begun' in 1945 for every child under sixteen and in 1964 this was expanded to include sixteen- and seventeen-year-olds who attended educational institutions. In 1951, Old Age Security legislation instituted a flat rate payment for persons seventy years of age. This was amended in 1965 to provide an annual lowering of the age limit so that by 1970 pensions were being paid to all persons at the age of sixty-five. In 1967 a minimum level of income was established for all persons on old age security. A federal-provincial hospital programme (1957) resulted in the federal government paying 50 per cent of specified hospital services. The Medical Care Act (Medicare), which became effective in 1968, provided for a portable scheme by which the federal government would pay one-half of the overall costs. (Saskatchewan had been the first to introduce a compulsory medical insurance' scheme in 1962.)

A further step in the co-ordination of provincial and federal government welfare came with the establishment of the National Council of Welfare, which held its first meeting in April 1965. Another government agency, the Department of Manpower and Immigration, was established in 1966. It administers immigration policies and is responsible for counselling and effective placement of workers, occupational training of adults, manpower mobility, stabilizing employment created by seasonal demands, and rehabilitation of the handicapped. Paralleling the federal involvement in social welfare measures, the provinces produced complementary plans of social assistance including minimum hourly wages, medicare and pension benefits.

Cultural Developments. The culture of a nation includes all phases of its "way of life" but common usage identifies the word "culture" with the arts. In Canada, a unique national culture had developed slowly and sporadically inhibited by the strong influence of British, French and American culture. The early fifties, however, saw a vigorous and original growth of the arts which was marked by the Royal Commission on Arts, Letters and Sciences (The Massey Report) in 1951. Largely as a result of this report the Canada Council was established in 1957 by the federal government. Its purpose is to assist the arts, humanities and social sciences. Such world-renowned artistic companies as the Royal Winnipeg Ballet, the Stratford Festival, and the Canadian Opera Company could not survive without the Council's help. Funds are provided from the income of an endowment fund, federal grants and private bequests. Over $21 million annually are being distributed by the committee to individuals and organizations. The Council also shares the responsibilities of Canada's cultural relations with other countries. The federal government also promotes the arts through the CBC and the National Film Board.

Complementing the federal government's contributions to the arts is the assistance of provincial governments, some of which have established their own councils. Most municipalities also contribute, in varying degrees, to the arts. The Centennial celebrations of 1967 created a surge of artistic endeavours across the country. A permanent National Library and Archives building was opened in that year in Ottawa, and two years later the National Arts Centre was also opened, "to nurture and encourage growth and excellence in the performing arts both in the national capital and throughout Canada."

BIBLIOGRAPHY

FOX, PAUL (ed.). *Politics: Canada.* McGraw-Hill, 1962.

FRASER, BLAIR. *The Search for Identity.* Doubleday, 1967.

GWYN, R. *Smallwood—The Unlikely Revolutionary.* McClelland and Stewart, 1968.

KING, A. R. *The School at Mopass.* Holt, Rinehart and Winston, 1967.

LONN, GEORGE. *Canadian Profiles.* Pitt Publishing, 1965.

MASSEY, VINCENT. *On Being Canadian.* Dent, 1948.

THOMAS, J. and VAN ES, P. (eds.). *Mid-Canada Development Corridor, A Concept.* Acres Research and Planning Ltd., 1967.

THOMSON, D. C. *Louis St. Laurent: Canadian.* Macmillan, 1967.

16

Politics in
the 1960's

The 1960's were years of steady growth and expansion in
Canada. The population passed the 21 million mark. Greater
interest was taken in the northern regions and the Arctic Islands.
The economy expanded at a rapid rate. The trend towards a welfare state continued. Nevertheless, the decade ended with serious
unsolved problems, some old and some new. The division of
powers and finances between the provincial and federal governments, a serious inflationary threat, continuing federal budgetary
deficits, numerous clashes between labour and management, which
were handicapping the economy, and Canada's position in international affairs were all questions challenging both the government
and the people of the country.

FEDERAL POLITICS

L. B. Pearson. With the Liberal party defeated, St. Laurent
retired from the leadership. He was succeeded by Lester B.
Pearson, an outstanding Canadian diplomat. After a short period
as a university professor, he began what proved to be a brilliant
career in the Department of External Affairs, rising to be Minister
in September 1948. In 1952-53 he served as President of the U.N.
General Assembly, and in 1957 he was instrumental in the formation of the United Nations Emergency Force (UNEF), which
brought the Suez crisis under control. For his contributions to
world peace, Pearson received the Nobel Peace Prize for 1957.
To Canadians at large he symbolized the country's new status as a

responsible leader among the world's so-called middle powers. It was, therefore, not unnatural that the Liberal party should choose him as their leader. Pearson, however, had never been closely involved in Canada's domestic affairs and indeed had shown little interest in these issues. Moreover, he was not a politician and was unused to the rough and often ruthless game that occupied most of his colleagues in Ottawa. It quickly became apparent that as Opposition Leader he was no match for the new Prime Minister, John Diefenbaker.

John G. Diefenbaker. Diefenbaker stood in marked contrast to Pearson. In place of Pearson's informal and personal approach, Diefenbaker possessed a crackling oratorical style capable of arousing large audiences. His years as a defence lawyer and a member of the House of Commons provided him with an abundance of political knowledge and technique. At the height of his career, following the election of 1957, Diefenbaker dominated Canadian affairs, overwhelming all those who surrounded him.

During the first months as leader of the minority Conservative government, Diefenbaker outlined a visionary programme that promised to develop the country more rapidly than ever before and to bring it more firmly under Canadian control. The people responded to his "vision" with enthusiasm. In 1958, feeling that he had gained the confidence of the electorate and that he deserved a majority in the Commons, Diefenbaker called another general election. On this occasion the Conservatives gained an unprecedented 208 seats. The Liberals elected only 49 members and the C.C.F. 8. The Social Credit failed to elect a single member. Even Quebec returned a majority of members for the Conservatives— the first time since the Macdonald era.

The Diefenbaker legislative programme was ambitious. A National Productivity Council was created to promote co-operation between management and labour; the South Saskatchewan River power and irrigation project was begun; an independent broadcasting authority, the Board of Broadcast Governors, was established to supervise both private and public television and radio; old age pensions were increased; a Canadian Bill of Rights was enacted as a federal statute; steps were taken to encourage Canadian periodicals; federal grants were allocated for technical and vocational training; new federal-provincial tax agreements were adopted; and plans were laid for the development of the North by the building of "roads to resources."

The Fall of Diefenbaker.   By 1962, in spite of these achievements, Diefenbaker was losing popular support. The "vision" on which he had campaigned so effectively, remained largely unrealized; the Prime Minister was unable to understand Quebec or to find a strong lieutenant in that province, and failed to retain its support; the Cabinet appeared to lack leadership and showed signs of internal dissension between the business-oriented members from central Canada and Diefenbaker's followers from the prairies. An economic recession and a high rate of unemployment particularly concerned the people. The government seemed unable to deal with these problems. The Conservatives had obviously lost the momentum of their early years in power. In the general election of 1962, the government suffered a severe setback: they retained only 116 seats in the Commons—once again a minority government. The Liberals increased to 99 and the C.C.F., now reorganized and renamed the New Democratic Party (N.D.P.), rose to 19. The Social Credit took 30 seats, mainly in Quebec where they showed amazing strength. Significantly, the Conservatives lost Quebec. Following the election, Diefenbaker clung grimly to power, although his government rapidly disintegrated around him. Harassed by the opposition parties (particularly a Liberal party that was showing signs of renewed strength) and racked by internal quarrels, the Conservatives avoided making major decisions involving economic and defence matters. During these months three ministers resigned over the question of defence policy. In February 1963, the opposition, united in their disgust at the shambles into which the administration had fallen, defeated the government in the House of Commons. Diefenbaker entered the ensuing election campaign faced with a divided party and the open hostility of many of his former supporters.

The Elections of 1963 and 1965.   Pearson, while still no match for Diefenbaker at his best, showed new confidence and more enthusiasm for campaigning. He had used the years as Opposition Leader to gain political experience and to introduce new, attractive figures into the upper echelons of the party. Taking advantage of the public discord within the Conservative ranks, he promised a return to an orderly administration of affairs, coupled with an aggressive and imaginative programme to promote high employment, further social welfare measures, regional development, and an increased pace of economic activity. In a special attempt to regain the Liberals' former stronghold in Quebec, Pearson promised a royal commission on bilingualism and biculturalism.

The defeat of the Conservatives came as no surprise; indeed it was perhaps a surprise that they retained as many seats as they did. The Liberals, holding 129 seats, now formed a minority government, dependent on the minor parties for survival. The election brought satisfaction neither to the Liberal party nor to the country. Pearson was at all times in a precarious position which was made miserable by the continuous heckling and filibustering of the opposition led by an exasperating Diefenbaker. A series of scandals, seized upon by the opposition, along with the ineffectiveness of the House of Commons led to a feeling of apathy among Canadians. Never had confidence in parliament been at a lower ebb. In 1965, frustrated by these problems and influenced by his advisors, Pearson decided to call an election in order to obtain a clear majority. His political judgment proved faulty, however. The Liberals won 131 seats, still short of a majority. Pearson led another minority government, the fourth in eight years.

The Pearson Government. Whether from bad luck or bad management, the Pearson administration failed to live up to expectation. The first budget was unmercifully criticized and had to be substantially altered before the Commons passed it. The much vaunted Liberal portable pension scheme met strong provincial opposition and was altered several times before passage in 1965. Similar delays and changes in policy affected Liberal plans for a medicare programme. But in spite of the government's constant stumbling, there were a number of solid achievements; a portable pension plan; a new Canadian flag, approved after a furious parliamentary battle; the establishment of a Canadian Development Corporation to assist new business ventures, particularly in underdeveloped areas; a much needed reform in parliamentary procedure; a new non-political procedure for the redistribution of Commons' seats; the first steps towards the establishment of a new basis of co-operation between the English- and the French-speaking Canadians; a new bank act; a Canada Assistance Act to guarantee a minimum income for old age pensioners; youth allowances; a liberalization of the divorce laws; provisions for the extension of technical and vocational education; a doubling of Canada's external aid programme; the abolition of capital punishment for a trial period of five years; the unification of the armed forces; a new immigration act; and provisions for collective bargaining by the civil service. New agencies established included the

Economic Council of Canada and the Company of Young Canadians. There were two agreements of major economic importance with the United States. An important trade agreement removed tariffs on automobile parts between the countries. The governments of Canada, British Columbia and the United States reached final agreement on the Columbia River Development Treaty in 1964.

The New Democratic Party. During the years of minority government, attention focused on the minor parties in the House of Commons. Of these the ⌐.C.F. was the most important. After reaching a high-water mark in 1945, when the party took 28 seats in the general election, the C.C.F. declined in subsequent elections. In 1958, their numbers in the Commons dropped to 8. (In provincial politics the C.C.F. was somewhat more successful. In Saskatchewan they formed the government for twenty years until 1965. In British Columbia they have been the official opposition since 1933. In Manitoba, as N.D.P., they took office in 1969.)

Although the party was highly regarded for the quality of its members and generally recognized as a significant "ginger group," particularly in federal politics, it failed to secure sufficient support to form a government. Increasing disappointment with this failure among the party's followers generated new interest in the idea of reorganizing the socialist forces into a new party with a wider base. In 1961, a convention sponsored by the C.C.F. and the Canadian Labour Congress met in Ottawa to found a new party. Adopting the name New Democratic Party (N.D.P.) the founders hoped that it would gain wide support from farmers, the educated middle class and labour (the latter having been conspicuous in its failure to support the C.C.F.). Chosen as leader was T. C. (Tommy) Douglas, the energetic and witty Premier of Saskatchewan, who was widely known for having led Canada's first socialist government. Almost from the beginning the N.D.P. showed signs of greater strength than the old C.C.F. In 1962, no doubt partly due to the disarray of the major parties, the N.D.P. won 19 seats in the Commons, in 1963, 17, and in 1965, 21. Less noticeable, but possibly of greater importance for the future, was the more professional appearance of the new party's organization and style of campaigning. It was also significant that by 1965 the N.D.P. was making a strong bid for support in Quebec as part of an attempt to become a truly national party, something the old C.C.F. had never been. The Quebec bid was unsuccessful, however, for the N.D.P. failed to win a single seat in that province in either the 1965 or 1968 elections. It still remained to be seen whether the N.D.P.'s enthusiasm would result in wider popular support or whether the party would remain little more than a splinter group like its predecessor.

The Social Credit Party. Though less important than the C.C.F.-N.D.P., the Social Credit party of Canada also drew more attention during the years of minority government. The party was never strong federally, for its support generally was confined to Alberta and British Columbia. (Alberta's Social Credit government had been in power since 1935 and Social Credit had captured British Columbia in 1952.) In the general election of 1958, Social Credit was wiped out federally in the wake of the Conservative sweep of that year. But, to the great surprise of most observers, Social Credit came into new prominence in 1962 when it elected 26 members to the Commons from Quebec as well as 4 from Western Canada. The Quebec wing of the party, led by a fiery car-dealer from Rouyn, Réal Caouette, capitalized on rural economic unrest in Quebec and a general mood of disenchantment with the "old-line" parties. The platform combined elements of Social Credit doctrine with a strong dose of Quebec nationalism and was presented with evangelistic vigour. The Quebec wing almost immediately over-shadowed its weaker and more conservative colleagues from the West in both strength of leadership and in the number of M.P.'s. Rivalry between the federal leader, Robert Thompson, and the Quebec leader, Caouette, quickly deteriorated into a public quarrel. Following the 1963 election in which Social Credit dropped to 24 members (in Quebec to 20), Caouette and most of the Quebec wing broke from the federal party to form *Le Ralliement des Créditistes* (Social Credit Rally). Social Credit lost its pretensions to being a national party and the House of Commons now had as a third "splinter" party, one that was based solely in Quebec. The 1965 elections saw the Social Credit party reduced to 5 seats and the *Créditistes* to 9. Two years later Robert Thompson practically eliminated Social Credit as a federal party when he resigned his leadership and joined the Progressive Conservatives. Réal Caouette and his aggressive handful of followers continued to press for Quebec's rights and monetary reform at every opportunity, however, and improved their position in the 1968 election by winning 14 seats. The traditional problem of regionalism continued to be a factor in federal politics.

New Leaders.   Between the fall of 1967 and the spring of 1968 both the Progressive Conservative and the Liberal parties changed their leaders. The conventions which brought this about were different from the earlier staid, routine meetings and were comparable to the American political conventions with banners, pep bands, cheer-leaders and organized exuberant demonstrations. With nation-wide television coverage, all Canadians shared in the excitement of politics. The first of these spectacles occurred in September 1967, with the Progressive Conservative convention in Toronto. The internal divisions and disillusion which had marked Diefenbaker's last years in office had reached a climax with the defeats of the Progressive Conservatives in 1963 and 1965. Party rebels forced a leadership convention. A fighting Diefenbaker lagged far behind the leading contenders from the first ballot and was eventually eliminated from the race. As his successor, the party elected Robert L. Stanfield, Premier of Nova Scotia.

Three months later, in December 1967, Prime Minister Pearson announced his intention to resign as leader of the Liberal party. Competition immediately developed among many capable and outstanding Liberals for the succession. A small group of Liberals in Quebec believed that one of the candidates must be from that province and persuaded the Minister of Justice, Pierre Elliott Trudeau, to run. In the boisterous Liberal convention of April 1968, the nation for the first time was exposed to the Trudeau charisma. He led from the first ballot to become the new leader. Immediately afterwards he assumed office as Prime Minister.

Robert L. Stanfield.   The new leader of the Progressive Conservative party was the third generation of Stanfields to participate in politics. As Premier of Nova Scotia, he had established a reputation of honesty, sincerity and stability. Born in Truro, in 1914, he graduated in economics and political science from Dalhousie Law School, did postgraduate work at Harvard, and was admitted to the bar in 1940. Eight years later he became provincial leader of the Nova Scotia Progressive Conservative party. At that time the Progressive Conservatives had not held power in Nova Scotia for twenty-three years and did not hold a single seat in the legislature. In 1956, Stanfield led his party into power and was successful in the three following elections, ultimately reducing the opposition to a mere 6 seats. He resigned as premier in 1967 to become leader of the federal Progressive Conservative party, was elected to the federal house in a by-election and became the Leader of the

Opposition. A proven vote-catcher, Mr. Stanfield was expected to unify the badly disorganized and divided Conservatives, to heal the wounds resulting from the bitter leadership contest, and to lead his party to victory in the next federal election.

Pierre Elliott Trudeau. The new leader of the Liberal party came from a wealthy Montreal family where both English and French were spoken fluently. He graduated from the University of Montreal and took postgraduate courses at Harvard, the University of Paris, and the London School of Economics. During 1948-49 he hitch-hiked around the world and was an eyewitness to many critical events of those two years, such as the German partition, the Arab-Israeli War, the Pakistan-India strife, the French-Indochina War, and the Communist revolution in China. Returning to Canada he served with the Privy Council of the Federal government, practised law in Montreal and then became Associate Professor of Law at the University of Montreal. He was a consistent opponent of Duplessis, the Premier of Quebec, supported strikers against police intervention at Asbestos, and published *Cité Libre*, a small journal which harshly criticized the Duplessis regime. In 1965, he ran successfully as a Liberal candidate in Quebec province. Within two years he was appointed Minister of Justice. In this office he was highly commended for the skill with which he introduced major changes in the Criminal Code relating to gambling, divorce, abortion and homosexuality. The federal-provincial conference of 1968 first brought him, through television, into national prominence. Here he ably supported his strong beliefs in federalism against the opposing views of Quebec's Premier Johnson. In April 1968, he was chosen leader of the Liberal party at the national convention in Ottawa. Later that same month he was sworn in as Prime Minister of Canada.

The Election of 1968. Within three days of being sworn in as Prime Minister, Trudeau asked for dissolution and called an election. The Liberals campaigned with Trudeau's slogan of a "Just Society," but greater than any slogan was the wave of "Trudeaumania" which swept the country. Unprecedented throngs gathered to see and hear the new leader. In contrast, the Conservative campaign was dull and uninspiring. The sincere approach of Stanfield was no match for the charisma of Trudeau. The Conservative approach seemed to be a repetition of the old style of politics. The party itself still suffered from the wounds of the convention and lacked a co-ordinated strategy. Furthermore, Stanfield was

unable to obtain a strong Quebec collaborator. In spite of the
hopes of the opposition parties that the Trudeau phenomenon was
only on the surface, the results of the election were definite. The
Liberals won 155 seats, largely at the expense of the Progressive
Conservatives who dropped to 72. The minor parties remained
almost constant: the N.D.P. 22 and *Le Railliement des Créditistes*
14. The election wiped out many former Progressive Conservative
leaders as well as the N.D.P. leader T. C. Douglas. (Douglas later
returned in a by-election.) For the first time since 1962 Canada
had a majority government.

The Trudeau Government. As Prime Minister, Trudeau soon
asserted his leadership. He demanded secrecy and solidarity from
his cabinet and modified House procedures in an attempt to make
Parliament more productive. Cabinet ministers no longer had to
be present at every question period and time limits were set for
debates. The federal government was reorganized by creating new
departments, by merging some of the old ones, and by changing the
scope of others. Drastic measures were taken to reduce the costs
of government departments in an attempt to balance the budget.
Military bases were closed at home and abroad. One of the most
significant of the early pieces of legislation was the Official
Languages Act, following the recommendations of the first report
of the Royal Commission on Bilingualism and Biculturalism. This
Act established English and French as co-equal languages for the
civil service, crown agencies, and federal courts in bilingual districts where the minority group consisted of at least 10 per cent
of the population. The Act received almost unanimous support
being opposed only by John Diefenbaker and 17 other Conservatives. Trudeau also encouraged the study of constitutional reform
by consultations between the federal and provincial governments.
He continued, however, to insist on his policy of a strong federal
government.

NATIONAL UNITY

Regional Disparity.   Historically Quebec and Ontario have developed as two cultural regions. Quebec has traditionally been the
homeland of an agricultural, Catholic, French-speaking people with
a minority English merchant class. Ontario, with its Loyalist and
British background, has been the heart of English-speaking Canada,
the centre of trade and finance. Today the southern parts of these

two provinces dominate Canada. Over 60 per cent of the total population, represented by over 60 per cent of the membership of the House of Commons, are in this region. Here are located almost all of the major secondary industries, the financial headquarters, and most of the major publishing and communications firms. The concerns of this area are primarily the problems of urbanization and protective tariff legislation. This rapidly-growing, concentrated, wealthy complex, with Ottawa in its centre, controls the economic, political and cultural attitudes of the nation.

In contrast the Atlantic provinces have had little population growth, either by natural increase or immigration. The economy is based almost entirely on primary resources. Comparatively few of these resources bring large-scale employment, industry or urbanization. The region is isolated from the markets of central Canada by distance and from those of the United States and Europe by international barriers. The Atlantic provinces continue to have the lowest standards of living in the country with little hope of improvement without considerable outside assistance.

The problems of scattered population and isolation are common to the three prairie provinces, the northern regions of Ontario and Quebec, and the northern territories. The prairie provinces, in particular, have an economy based on grain, petroleum and (increasingly) minerals. Their major problems are transportation and the marketing of goods on foreign markets. The scattered population, the dependence on outside financing, and the export of primary goods to pay for machinery are in strong contrast to the urban Toronto-Montreal complex.

British Columbia, separated from the rest of Canada by the Rocky Mountains, faces an emerging Asia. Both its economy and outlook differ from those of the prairies. Long distances have handicapped British Columbia's sales to central Canada and lack of nearby markets has discouraged secondary industry from developing on a large scale. As a result the province depends upon eastern manufactured goods. Nevertheless, with its great variety of primary resources and primary industries, it is the third province in area, size of population, and industrial output. Its standard of living and wage scales are among the highest in the country. Geographic and economic ties exist with the United States, but the foundations established by the early British traders and settlers have withstood this "pull" in favour of maintaining strong bonds with Canada.

Federal-Provincial Rivalry. The great emphasis in the 1960's on providing extended welfare benefits caused friction between the provinces and the federal government. Since many of the new schemes fell within the areas of responsibility given to the provinces by the BNA Act, or in which the responsibility overlapped, the provincial governments, were suspicious and resentful of federal encroachment. Moreover, to finance their own schemes, the provinces needed increased tax revenues. In 1941, the provincial governments agreed to suspend the imposition of income and corporation taxes; in return they would be reimbursed by the federal government. This "tax rental" system was discontinued in 1962. By a new agreement the federal government continued to collect all personal income taxes, but reduced its own rates so that the provinces could impose an amount equal to the reduction. If they wished, the provinces could increase this amount. All provinces completed agreements on this basis except Quebec, which collected its own income tax. Similar agreements were reached on corporation taxes (Quebec and Ontario collecting their own) and succession duties (Quebec, Ontario and British Columbia collecting their own).

Although this agreement was modified in later years to the advantage of the provinces, it has not been completely satisfactory. The provinces, with a fixed direct-tax base, find their sources of revenue limited while their responsibilities have greatly increased. This is especially true in the fields of welfare, health, education, public works and the development of natural resources. The federal government has attempted to alleviate this problem by grants of various kinds, by financial assistance to public work projects, and by shared-cost programmes. So-called "equalization grants" gave added assistance to the poorer provinces and regions. However, these concessions have not satisfied the provinces who realize that these grants, given by the federal government, can be withdrawn at any time. A new approach is needed on the problem of the tax structure and the responsibilities not only of both the federal and provincial governments but also of the municipalities. Several cities now have populations larger than those of the smaller provinces.

The Quiet Revolution. The traditional Canadian problem of maintaining a harmonious relation between the two founding races, English and French, became obscured during the war years. The Liberal administration in Quebec City was much more willing than its *Union Nationale* predecessor to cooperate with the Ottawa

Liberals in advancing the war effort; the only major source of friction was the conscription issue. But with the end of war the emphasis switched from international problems (the natural concern of the federal government) to domestic matters which were of direct concern to the provinces. In Quebec the return to power of Maurice Duplessis and the *Union Nationale* party in 1944 symbolized the predominance of these issues.

Le Chef proved to be an even more intractable foe of the federal government after the war than he had been before. With a strong appeal to French-Canadian nationalism he maintained a rigidly conservative control over Quebec affairs and refused to co-operate in such matters as federal grants to universities and the new proposals for a formula to amend the British North America Act. Despite criticism and mounting evidence of corruption within his government, Duplessis remained in power until his sudden death in September 1959.

Duplessis' death signalled the release of an astounding rush of ideas and plans within Quebec society. Later dubbed the "quiet revolution," the new atmosphere seemed at first to focus on Duplessis' successor as leader of the *Union Nationale,* Paul Sauvé, whose enthusiasm and energy in launching a reform of both party and province attracted national attention. But Sauvé died suddenly after only 100 days in office. He was succeeded by Antonio Barrette, a likeable but much less dynamic personality, who unfortunately had to face a rejuvenated Quebec Liberal party in the 1960 provincial election.

The Liberal party, led by a former federal cabinet minister, Jean Lesage, campaigned on the slogan, *Maitre chez nous.* Promising a broad programme of social reform to bring Quebec society into the twentieth century, a purge of corruption from government and more control of Quebec's resources and industry in French-Canadian hands, the Liberals appeared to embody the "quiet revolution." Their victory at the polls indicated the widespread demand in Quebec for a greater share in the benefits of modern society. The Lesage government quickly set out to makes these hopes a reality: the provincial power companies were brought under public ownership; a programme of educational reform was begun; a provincially supported steel industry was established; an aggressive campaign was launched to attract new industry; pension and medical insurance schemes were started; and large public subsidies were contributed to the arts.

Separatism. In contrast to these welcome signs of rejuvenation, there arose a new separatist movement in Quebec. Although seriously fragmented in terms of leadership and policies, the various separatist groups were united in claiming that French Canadians were a distinct national group. It was their belief that the Confederation experiment had been, for French Canadians, an irredeemable failure, and that their homeland, Quebec, should become an autonomous state. Separatist feelings became clear to the rest of Canada when some extremist groups undertook terrorist campaigns—bombing monuments and buildings that symbolized English-Canadian domination. By the end of the 1960's, the separatist movement was a significant political force in Quebec led by René Levesque's *parti Québecois* which had united several former splinter groups. Other French-Canadian voices, although more moderate than the overt separatists, called for the establishment of a *deux nations* policy which specifically recognized Quebec's unique position as the centre of French-Canadian culture in North America. In practice this policy meant greater participation of French Canadians in government, politics, and the control of industry. It also meant that Quebec's unique status would have to be recognized in legal and constitutional terms as well.

Under Jean Lesage, Quebec opted out of twenty-nine federal-provincial cost-sharing programmes and obtained a much greater percentage of income taxes, corporation taxes and succession duties. But in spite of these tax measures, the cost of his reform programme created a budgetary crisis. Also, Lesage's Liberals failed to understand the desires and problems of the basically conservative, non-urban population. These weaknesses resulted in the Lesage government losing the election of 1966 to the reorganized *Union Nationale* under Daniel Johnson which obtained 55 out of 108 seats in the National Assembly. (Lesage resigned in 1969 as leader of the provincial Liberal party.) A brilliant man, with a strong personality, Johnson maintained pressures on Ottawa for a revision of the constitution and special status for Quebec under veiled suggestions of "separatism." When Johnson died suddenly in the fall of 1968, he was succeeded by Quebec's Justice Minister, Jean-Jacques Bertrand, a man with similar policies.

The effect on the rest of Canada of the ferment within Quebec was immense. Public concern over the dangerous possibilities of extremist opinion spread across the country. All of Canada's political parties, to a greater or lesser extent, experienced internal quarrels over the extent to which French-Canadian demands were

to be met. The conclusions of the Royal Commission on Biculturalism and Bilingualism emphasized how serious the problem was.
The over-all concern was that French-English relations should not
be allowed to deteriorate to the point where the very existence of
Confederation might be endangered.

Federal-Provincial Co-operation. Although the Quebec extremists
received much publicity it became increasingly obvious during the
late 1960's that every region of Canada was dissatisfied with some
aspects of the BNA Act. This situation had two possible solutions.
A completely new constitution could be constructed or, as an alternative, harmony could be achieved by mutual agreements. The
latter method seemed to be the more practical and efficient for the
immediate future although continued study leading to a new
constitution was recognized as a necessary long-term project.
Towards this end, a series of annual conferences of provincial
premiers began in 1960. The federal prime minister also attended
the most significant of these conferences. The main topics of
discussion were constitutional changes, regional disparities, and
language rights. Some of the conferences were open and televised,
and enabled all Canadians to become aware of national problems
and to see their leaders in action. The open conferences of 1968
and 1969 showed the provinces to be willing to accept Canada as
a bilingual country, but also showed differences of opinion as to the
need for revision of the BNA Act. While Quebec, with some
support from Ontario, urgently advocated drastic changes, some
provinces were lukewarm to any but minor alterations. The general
attitude was that the most efficient method of settling federal-
provincial problems was to appoint small committees in special
fields when needed.

CANADA IN WORLD AFFAIRS

Following the war Canada's attitude toward foreign affairs
changed. In place of the former reluctance to take an active part in
international relations that had little direct bearing on domestic
affairs, there was an eagerness to participate in events on the world
scene. In place of the former narrow attitude that saw international
affairs as little more than a means of widening and strengthening
national autonomy, there was a new willingness to assume genuine
responsibility. Although the new attitude was partly a response to
new world conditions dominated by "big power" rivalries and the
appalling threat of nuclear war, it was also a result of greater

national confidence growing out of the successful war effort and the nation's enhanced industrial and economic strength.

During the immediate post-war years Canada's five major concerns in foreign policy were: (1) support of the United Nations as the best way to promote world peace; (2) support of the North Atlantic Treaty Organization as an important force for defence; (3) co-operation with the United States in continental defence; (4) co-operation within a strong Commonwealth; and (5) the relief of world tensions by assisting poorer and undeveloped nations.

Following the election of 1968, Prime Minister Trudeau began a review of Canada's foreign policy. Although the international scene was still dominated by two great nuclear powers, nevertheless there had been world changes of significance to Canada. Nations which had formerly been colonies were now independent nations; economically and politically insecure, they desperately needed assistance. China developed an established political regime and Canada moved towards closer economic and political relations with that country. The resurgence of Japan as an industrial power brought trade and capital to Canada. The voyage of the American tanker *Manhattan* in 1969 alerted Canada to the possibility of a challenge to her claim of sovereignty over the Arctic waterways. Canada became increasingly aware that her interests now extended in every direction. This viewpoint demanded that a new approach be taken to foreign affairs with a new evaluation of priorities.

The United Nations. Although Canada had not played a large role in the founding of the United Nations, she was an original signatory of the Charter. In the ensuing years, she became increasingly involved in the activities of the organization. Canada is a member of the 13 Specialized Agencies of the U.N. and the International Atomic Energy Agency. Her total contribution to the U.N. and related bodies totalled approximately $439 million during the period March 31, 1945–March 31, 1969. In 1969, Canada was the eighth largest contributor to the regular budget. Canada actively supported the United Nations by contributing to the U.N. force in the Korean War (1950-54). In 1956 Canada played a leading role in the Suez crisis. It was her Minister of External Affairs, L. B. Pearson, who advanced the idea of a "United Nations Emergency Force" (UNEF), which would restore peace to the troubled Middle East area and remain there as a stabilizing force. Canada contributed troops to the force until it was disbanded in 1967. (Canada's General E. L. M. Burns had been the first commander of UNEF.)

In the Congo crisis of 1960-1964 a similar peace force was dispatched by the United Nations. On this occasion Canada contributed a corps of 352 signallers as well as a small number of administrators. In 1963 Canada contributed to the U.N. peace force in Cyprus. In 1965, Major-General Bruce Macdonald of Edmonton led a U.N. observer group to supervise the truce between India and Pakistan in the disputed Kashmir area. Canada also participated in U.N. Observation forces to Lebanon (1958/59), West New Guinea (1962/63) and Yemen (1963/64). Since 1954 Canada has been one of the supervising members (with India and Poland) of the International Commission for Supervision in Indochina and has maintained military and civilian personnel there.

Canada was a non-permanent member of the Security Council of the United Nations on three occasions, 1947, 1957 and 1967. Many Canadians held important posts in U.N. administration. Among these were General Burns, Dr. Brock Chisholm, first Director of the World Health Organization, Dr. Hugh Keenleyside, first Director-General of the U.N. Technical Assistance Administration, Mrs. Adelaide Sinclair, Deputy-Director of UNICEF, Escott Reid of the World Bank, Dr. George Davidson of the Economic and Social Council and later High Commissioner for Refugees, and Lester B. Pearson, President of the General Assembly in 1952/53. The Food and Agricultural Organization was established in 1945, and the International Civil Aviation Organization (ICAO) was established in 1946, with its permanent headquarters located in Montreal.

NATO. The division of the world into two great rival blocks soon after 1945 involved Canada in the demands of Western defence. Prime Minister St. Laurent was an early supporter of the idea of a defence alliance embracing the North Atlantic nations. In 1949, the North Atlantic Treaty Organization (NATO) was formed, composed of Canada, her two Atlantic partners Britain and the United States, and 12 other Western countries. In addition to contributing military equipment and training air crews for other member countries, Canadian forces were stationed in Europe. Canada's attempt to encourage NATO to expand its activities into such fields as economic co-operation, however, were blocked by the disinterest of other members. For twenty years Canada's main defence commitments were in support of NATO, but with the foreign policy review of the Trudeau government, Canada began to question the value of its own contributions to international and national security.

In 1970, as a first step in reorganization, Canada began a phased withdrawal of its NATO personnel in Europe.

Canadian-American Relations. History and geography have made Canada and the United States neighbours with many common interests, both economic and cultural. Movement of individuals across the border is relatively free. Both participate actively in important organizations such as NATO, GATT and the U.N. There are numerous joint bodies such as the International Joint Commission and bilateral agreements such as those which made possible the St. Lawrence Seaway and the Columbia River project.

Close co-operation in defence between Canada and the United States continued after the war. Lying directly between the Soviet Union and the United States, Canada was of great strategic importance to her powerful neighbour. The Permanent Joint Board on Defence was reorganized and a continental defence system was begun that included joint manoeuvres, and a network of weather and radar stations in northern Canada. This co-operation increased in 1958 with the creation of the North American Air Defence Command (NORAD) which brought about a wide measure of air defence integration.

The Commonwealth. The development of the Commonwealth interested many Canadians. Canada watched with sympathy the move to independence of many of Britain's former colonies and tried to promote the possibilities for international co-operation provided by an enlarged and more diverse Commonwealth. In 1965, when a Commonwealth Secretariat was established to be a central clearing-house for information and activity, a Canadian, Arnold Smith, was appointed the first Secretary General. Through the Commonwealth, Canada was able to increase her contacts with emerging nations. These contacts won a degree of respect for Canada that allowed her to take a more effective role as a participant in international affairs, particularly at the U.N.

Canadian External Aid. Mainly through bilateral agreements, Canada participates in a number of educational, economic and technical assistance programmes abroad. This assistance may be divided into three categories: capital project, commodity and technical assistance. Capital project assistance means the construction of power stations, the supplying of machinery and the carrying out of studies in certain specified regions. This type of aid accounts for nearly one-half of Canada's total external aid expenditures. Commodity assistance constitutes supplying raw materials or foodstuffs. Technical assistance provides for teachers and specialists to go abroad and for students to come to Canada. Canadian external aid is divided into several programmes which illustrate its wide-spread application. These programmes include: the Colombo Plan for South-east Asia, the Commonwealth Caribbean Programme, the Special Commonwealth Africa Assistance Plan (SCAAP), the Commonwealth Scholarship and Fellowship Plan, the Assistance to French-speaking States in Africa and the Latin-American Programme. In addition, Canada contributes to the many assistance programmes of the U.N. and its specialized agencies. Canada has committed herself to transfer 1 per cent of her gross national income to less-developed countries. The $360 million spent on foreign aid in 1968 was about one-half of this amount.

Canada and Latin America. Canada's relationships with Latin America have been of comparatively minor importance. Geographically Canada is separated from Latin America by the United States. Historically Canada's cultural ties have been with Britain and France while those of most Latin American countries have been with Spain and Portugal. Politically, the governments which have developed in Latin America have differed in outlook from that of Canada. There are few Commonwealth countries in Central or South America. Latin America has no interest in NATO. Economically, although trade between the two regions has a long history, it has never been of major importance to either.

Nevertheless, developments in transportation and communication have increased the ties between Canada and these countries in the last twenty-five years. During this period commercial exchanges have increased eleven times in value, although they still represent only 3.8 per cent of Canada's total. The number of university and scientific exchanges are increasing annually. Many Canadians are beginning to take holidays in Latin America. Common association in the United Nations has increased understanding. However, Canada does not belong to the Organization of American States (OAS) which includes the United States and most of the countries south of it. Discussions for and against membership in the OAS continue, but whatever the results of the deliberations Canada's present policy is to improve relations with the Latin American countries.

Canada and the Pacific Rim. The first maritime fur traders on the west coast of North America found their markets in China and

Japan. A century later the Canadian Pacific Railway was called "the all red route" since one of its main objectives was to link Britain with its colonies in Asia and the South Pacific. Its completion increased trans-Pacific travel and opened up new areas of contact with the East. One of Canada's first diplomatic missions abroad was established in Tokyo in 1929. Until World War II, however, Canada's Pacific interests were subordinate to those with Europe and the United States.

Since 1945, developments in the Pacific have brought a growing recognition that Canada is a Pacific nation. The crises in Korea and Viet Nam focused world attention on East Asia. Canada is a member of the International Control Commission in Viet Nam, Laos and Cambodia. The Colombo Plan, established in 1950 to assist the poorer nations of South-east Asia, receives a sizeable portion of Canadian foreign aid. Canada hosted Colombo Plan conferences twice, in Ottawa (1954) and Victoria (1969). The People's Republic of China (mainland China) is a major market for Canadian wheat exports and, with one-quarter of the world's population, is a potential market for many other products. By late 1969 Canada was negotiating to open diplomatic relations with mainland China. But among the Pacific countries which have ties with Canada, the foremost is Japan. It is at present Canada's third largest trading partner and numerous trade agreements and understandings have been completed between the two countries. The substantial increase of Japanese investment in Canada is of major importance. This new source of capital has created significant developments in natural resources, transportation and manufacturing. The investment has been especially important to the economic expansion of Alberta and British Columbia. Japan was a major exhibitor at Expo '67 in Montreal, and Canada and three provinces had pavilions at Expo '70 in Osaka. It seems inevitable that in the coming decade the importance of Canada's relations with the Pacific countries will assume an ever-increasing importance.

CANADA'S SECOND CENTURY

It is sometimes said that Canadians have less national identity and spend more time searching for one than any other people in the world. With the passing of the Centennial Year in 1967, this exercise in national soul-searching became, if anything, even more pronounced. Canadians could not help but realize that they had much for which to be grateful, and that their history was one in

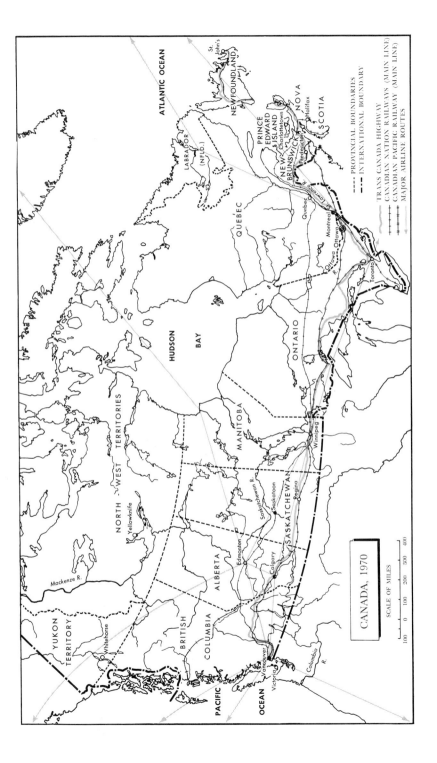

ATLANTIC OCEAN

St. John's

NEWFOUNDLAND

LABRADOR (NFLD.)

PRINCE EDWARD ISLAND
Charlottetown

NEW BRUNSWICK
Fredericton

NOVA SCOTIA
Halifax

QUEBEC

Quebec

Montreal

Ottawa
Ottawa R.

Toronto

HUDSON BAY

ONTARIO

NORTH WEST TERRITORIES

Yellowknife

MANITOBA

Winnipeg

SASKATCHEWAN

Saskatchewan R.

Saskatoon

Regina

ALBERTA

Edmonton

Calgary

Mackenze R.

YUKON TERRITORY

Whitehorse

BRITISH COLUMBIA

PACIFIC OCEAN

Vancouver

Victoria

Columbia R.

- - - PROVINCIAL BOUNDARIES
— · · — INTERNATIONAL BOUNDARY
— · — TRANS CANADA HIGHWAY
—+—+— CANADIAN NATION RAILWAYS (MAIN LINE)
—+—+— CANADIAN PACIFIC RAILWAY (MAIN LINE)
———— MAJOR AIRLINE ROUTES

CANADA, 1970

SCALE OF MILES

100   0   100   200   300   400

which they could take pride. From a collection of diverse colonies scattered across a vast and often forbidding land they had created a unified and highly developed nation-state in the space of one short century. Indeed, in any other period of history such an accomplishment would have been considered a monumental feat of empire building.

And yet, it is inescapably obvious that many of the fundamental problems that had existed in 1867, and which the creation of the Dominion had been intended to solve, still plague the modern leaders of Canada. The original problem of maintaining an independent identity in the face of strong cultural, economic and political influences from the United States is a recurring source of anxiety and controversy. Similarly, the problem of regionalization remains a serious barrier to the development of a single Canadian cultural expression. Yet another problem is found in the disparity of the influence and economic development of the various regions of Canada. Even the question of relations between the English- and French-speaking peoples continues to elude lasting solution and at times apparently threatens the very existence of Canada.

Despite this, Canadians had reason to feel encouraged as they entered their second century. The experience of over one hundred years had given them confidence that the problems of geography, economics and culture could be solved. They faced the future determined to overcome their problems at home and to fulfil their obligations as members of the global community.

BIBLIOGRAPHY

BEALE, J. C. *The Pearson Phenomenon.* Longmans, 1964.

GWYN, R. *Smallwood—Unlikely Revolutionary.* McClelland and Stewart, 1968.

NEWMAN, PETER C. *The Distemper of Our Times.* McClelland and Stewart, 1968.

NEWMAN, PETER C. *Renegade in Power: The Diefenbaker Years.* McClelland and Stewart, 1964.

NICHOLSON, P. *Visions and Indecisions.* Longmans, 1968.

PEACOCK, D. *Journey to Power.* Ryerson, 1968.

REGENSTRIEF, PETER. *The Diefenbaker Interlude.* Longmans, 1965.

RICHARDSON, B. T. *Canada and Mr. Diefenbaker.* McClelland and Stewart, 1962.

ROLLAND, S. C. *My Country, Canada or Quebec*. Macmillan, 1964.

SMILEY, DONALD V. *Canadian Political Nationality*. Methuen, 1967.

STEUBING, D. (ed.). *Trudeau, A Man for Tomorrow*. Clarke, Irwin, 1968.

TALLANT, CLIVE. *Canadian Problems*. Gage, 1968.

TRUDEAU, P. E. *Federalism and the French Canadians*. Macmillan, 1968.

TUPPER, S. R. and BAILEY, D. L. *One Continent, Two Voices*. Clarke, Irwin, 1968.

VAN DUSEN, T. *The Chief*. McGraw-Hill, 1968.

WAINWRIGHT, A. *Notes for a Native Land*. Oberon Press, 1967.

Appendix

KINGS AND QUEENS SOVEREIGN OVER CANADA

FRENCH, 1534-1763

FRANCIS I	(1515)–1547
HENRY II	1547–1559
FRANCIS II	1559–1560
CHARLES IX	1560–1574
HENRY III	1574–1589
HENRY IV	1589–1610
LOUIS XIII	1610–1643
LOUIS XIV	1643–1715
LOUIS XV	1715–(1774)

BRITISH, 1763-

GEORGE III	(1760)–1820
GEORGE IV	1820–1830
WILLIAM IV	1830–1837
VICTORIA	1837–1901
EDWARD VII	1901–1910
GEORGE V	1910–1936
EDWARD VIII	1936
GEORGE VI	1936–1952
ELIZABETH II	1952 ...

GOVERNORS OF CANADA SINCE CHAMPLAIN

Oct. 15, 1612 Champlain, Samuel de
(to July 20, 1629)

May 23, 1633 Champlain

June 11, 1636 Montmagny, Charles Jacques Huault de

Aug. 20, 1648 Ailleboust de Coulonge, Louis d'

Oct. 14, 1651 Lauzon, Jean de

July 11, 1658 Argenson, Pierre de Voyer, Vicomte d'

Aug. 31, 1661 Avaugour, Pierre Dubois, Baron d'

Sept. 15, 1663 Mézy, Augustin de Saffray, Sieur de

Sept. 12, 1665 Courcelles, Daniel Rémy, Sieur de

Sept. 12, 1672 Frontenac, Louis de Buade, Comte de Palluau et de

Oct. 9, 1682 La Barre, Joseph Antoine Lefebvre de

Aug. 1, 1685 Denonville, Jacques René de Brisay, Marquis de

Oct. 12, 1689 Frontenac, Louis de Buade, Comte de Palluau et de

Sept. 14, 1699 Callières, Louis Hector de

Sept. 17, 1705 Vaudreuil, Philippe de Rigaud, Marquis de

Sept. 2, 1726 Beauharnois, Charles, Marquis de

Aug. 15, 1749 La Jonquière, Jacques Pierre de Taffanel, Marquis de

July, 1752 Duquesne de Menneville, Marquis

July 10, 1755 Vaudreuil-Cavagnal, Pierre de Rigaud, Marquis de
(to Sept. 8, 1760)

Aug. 13, 1764 Murray, James

Oct. 26, 1768 Carleton, Guy

June 27, 1778 Haldimand, Frederick

Oct. 23, 1786 Dorchester, Baron (Guy Carleton)

Apr. 27, 1797 Prescott, Robert

Oct. 24, 1807 Craig, Sir James Henry

July 15, 1812 Prevost, Sir George

July 12, 1816 Sherbrooke, Sir John C.

July 30, 1818 Richmond, Duke of

June 19, 1820 Dalhousie, Earl of

Governors (*Cont'd*)

Feb. 4, 1831   Aylmer, Baron
Apr. 2, 1835   Amherst, Earl
Aug. 24, 1835   Gosford, Earl of
May 29, 1838   Durham, Earl of
Jan. 17, 1839   Colborne, Sir John
Oct. 19, 1839   Thomson, Charles Poulett
Fel. 10, 1841   Sydenham, Baron (C. P. *Thomson*)
Jan. 12, 1842   Bagot, Sir Charles
Mar.30, 1843   Metcalfe, Sir Charles T.
Apr. 24, 1846   Cathcart, Earl
Jan. 30, 1847   Elgin, Earl of
Dec. 19, 1854   Head, Sir Edmund W.
Nov. 28, 1861   Monck, Viscount
Feb. 2, 1869   Young, Sir John (Lord Lisgar)
June 25, 1872   Dufferin, Earl of
Nov. 25, 1878   Lorne, Marquis of
Oct. 23, 1883   Lansdowne, Marquis of
June 11, 1888   Stanley of Preston, Baron
Sept. 18, 1893   Aberdeen, Earl of
Nov. 12, 1898   Minto, Earl of
Dec. 10, 1904   Grey, Earl
Oct. 13, 1911   Connaught, H.R.H. Duke of
Nov. 11, 1916   Devonshire, Duke of
Aug. 11, 1921   Byng of Vimy, Lord
Oct. 2, 1926   Willingdon of Ratton, Viscount
Apr. 4, 1931   Bessborough, Earl of
Nov. 2, 1935   Tweedsmuir of Elsfield, Lord
June 21, 1940   Athlone, Earl of
Apr. 12, 1946   Alexander of Tunis, Viscount
Feb. 28, 1952   Massey, Vincent
Sept. 15, 1959   Vanier, Georges
Apr. 17, 1967   Michener, Roland

PRIME MINISTERS OF CANADA SINCE CONFEDERATION

Rt. Hon. Sir John Alexander Macdonald	*July 1, 1867–* *Nov. 5, 1873*
Hon. Alexander Mackenzie	*Nov. 7, 1873–* *Oct. 16, 1878*
Rt. Hon. Sir John Alexander Macdonald	*Oct. 17, 1878–* *June 6, 1891*
Hon. Sir John Joseph Caldwell Abbott	*June 16, 1891–* *Nov. 24, 1892*
Rt. Hon. Sir John S. D. Thompson	*Dec. 5, 1892–* *Dec. 12, 1894*
Hon. Sir Mackenzie Bowell	*Dec. 21, 1894–* *April 27, 1896*
Hon. Sir Charles Tupper	*May 1, 1896–* *July 8, 1896*
Rt. Hon. Sir Wilfrid Laurier	*July 11, 1896–* *Oct. 6, 1911*
Rt. Hon. Sir Robert Laird Borden	*Oct. 10, 1911–* *July 10, 1920*
Rt. Hon. Arthur Meighen	*July 10, 1920–* *Dec. 29, 1921*
Rt. Hon. William Lyon Mackenzie King	*Dec. 29, 1921–* *June 28, 1926*
Rt. Hon. Arthur Meighen	*June 29, 1926–* *Sept. 25, 1926*

Rt. Hon. William Lyon Mackenzie King	*Sept. 25, 1926–Aug. 6, 1930*
Rt. Hon. Richard Bedford Bennett	*Aug. 7, 1930–Oct. 23, 1935*
Rt. Hon. William Lyon Mackenzie King	*Oct. 23, 1935–Nov. 15, 1948*
Rt. Hon. Louis St. Laurent	*Nov. 15, 1948–June 21, 1957*
Rt. Hon. John George Diefenbaker	*June 21, 1957–April 22, 1963*
Rt. Hon. Lester Bowles Pearson	*April 22, 1963–April 20, 1968*
Rt. Hon. Pierre Elliott Trudeau	*April 20, 1968–*

CANADIAN ELECTION RESULTS SINCE CONFEDERATION

Election Year	Conservatives	Liberals	Unionists	Liberal Conservatives	Progressives	Liberal Progressives	United Farmers	Co-operative Commonwealth Federation	New Democratic	Social Credit	Le Railliement des Creditistes	Communists Independents and Others	Total Number of Seats
1867	101	80											181
1872	103	97											200
1874	73	133											206
1878	137	69											206
1882	139	71											210
1887	123	92											215
1891	123	92											215
1896	89	117										7	213
1900	78	128										8	214
1904	75	139											214
1908	85	133										3	221
1911	133	86										2	221
1917		82	153										235
1921		117		50	65							4	235
1925	116	101			24							4	245
1926	91	116			13	9	11					5	245
1930	137	88			2	3	10					5	245
1935	39	171						7		17		11	245
1940	39	178						8		10		10	245
1945	67	125						28		13		12	245
1949	41	190						13		10		8	262
1953	51	170						23		15		6	265
1957	112	105						25		19		4	265
1958	208	48						8				1	265
1962	116	99							19	30		1	265
1963	95	129							17	24			265
1965	97	131							21	5	9	2	265
1968	71	154							23		15	1	264

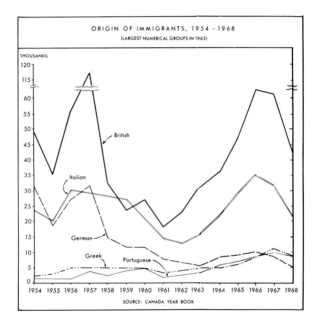

ORIGIN OF IMMIGRANTS, 1954 - 1968
(LARGEST NUMERICAL GROUPS IN 1963)

SOURCE: CANADA YEAR BOOK

CANADIAN POPULATION BY ETHNIC ORIGIN,
1961 CENSUS

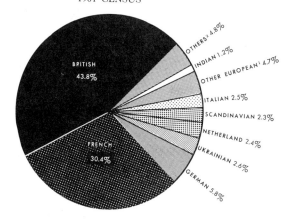

1. Polish, Hungarian, Czech & Slovak, Austrian, Belgian, Yugoslavian, Rumanian, Lithuanian
2. Japanese, Chinese, Greek, Syrian and unspecified

Information on ethnic groups was not collected in the 1966 census.

CANADIAN POPULATION BY PROVINCE,
1969 ESTIMATE

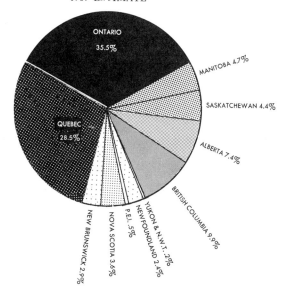

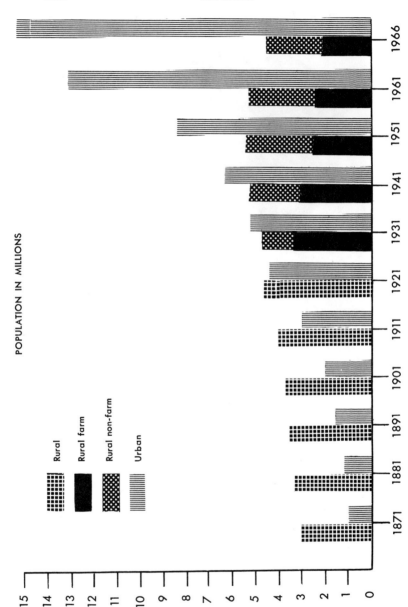

POPULATION IN MILLIONS

Rural

Rural farm

Rural non-farm

Urban

Urbanization in Canada 1871–1966

A farm is defined for the census as an agricultural holding of one or more acres with sales of agricultural products worth $50 or

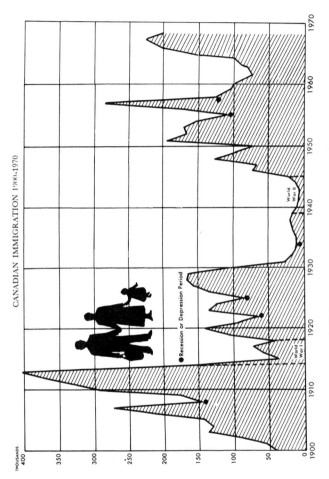

CANADIAN IMMIGRATION 1900-1970

Figures available only up to 1968 at time of publication

Canada's Economic Growth: Some Typical Indicators

MINERAL PRODUCTION

Year	Value
1901	66,000,000
1911	103,000,000
1921	172,000,000
1931	230,000,000
1941	560,000,000
1951	1,245,000,000
1956	2,085,000,000
1961	2,582,000,000
1966	3,972,000,000

VALUE OF WHEAT PRODUCTION

Year	Value
1911	148,000,000
1921	243,000,000
1931	124,000,000
1941	193,000,000
1951	857,000,000
1956	614,818,000
1961	486,000,000
1966	1,457,123,000

GROSS VALUE OF MANUFACTURES

Year	Value
1900	481,000,000
1910	1,166,000,000
1921	2,489,000,000
1931	2,555,000,000
1941	6,076,000,000
1951	16,392,000,000
1956	21,637,000,000
1961	23,438,000,000
1966	36,709,000,000

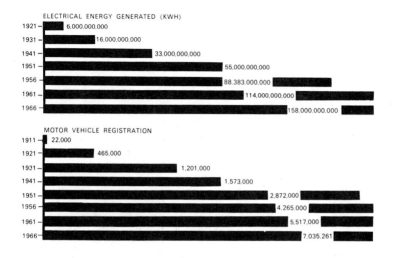

ELECTRICAL ENERGY GENERATED (KWH)

1921 — 6,000,000,000
1931 — 16,000,000,000
1941 — 33,000,000,000
1951 — 55,000,000,000
1956 — 88.383.000.000
1961 — 114,000,000,000
1966 — 158.000.000.000

MOTOR VEHICLE REGISTRATION

1911 — 22,000
1921 — 465,000
1931 — 1,201,000
1941 — 1.573,000
1951 — 2,872,000
1956 — 4.265.000
1961 — 5,517,000
1966 — 7.035.261

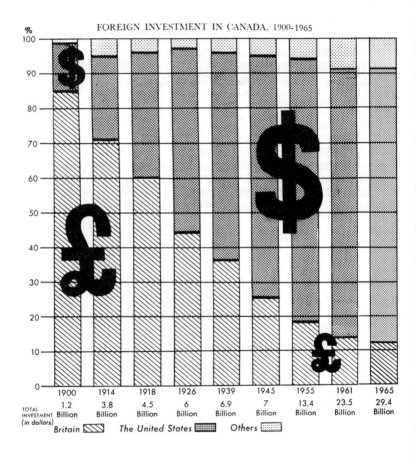

FOREIGN INVESTMENT IN CANADA, 1900-1965

Britain [////]   The United States [▦]   Others [▒]

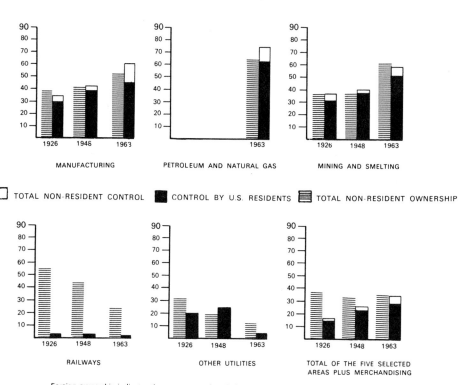

Foreign ownership indicates the percentage of capital owned by non-residents in each selected industry. Foreign control indicates the percentage of capital invested by everyone (that is, by residents and non-residents) in companies whose voting stock is controlled by non-residents.

Foreign Ownership and Foreign Control in Selected Areas of Canadian Industry

THE EQUALIZATION PAYMENTS TO THE PROVINCES (in thousands of dollars)

Fiscal Year	1957-58	1958-59	1959-60	1960-61	1961-62	1962-63	1963-64	1964-65	1965-66	1966-67	1967-68	1968-69	Estimate 1969-70
Nfld.	$ 11,579	12,155	14,292	15,391	11,194	13,517	14,985	18,373	22,163	29,007	65,169	72,745	85,920
P.E.I.	$ 2,955	3,074	3,005	3,454	2,811	3,073	3,821	5,464	6,033	7,243	13,602	14,247	16,734
N.S.	$ 17,375	15,575	20,665	21,019	18,172	19,529	19,051	26,200	35,519	41,561	70,562	83,577	91,279
N.B.	$ 8,645	8,651	16,864	17,416	16,002	15,514	16,479	22,925	35,696	35,141	62,188	74,904	83,347
Que.	$ 43,060	55,004	68,631	70,365	62,632	77,755	70,216	103,142	125,192	155,529	229,411	284,004	361,469
Ont.	$ —	—	—	—	—	—	—	—	—	—	—	—	—
Man.	$ 13,932	12,889	12,981	14,104	11,933	15,212	13,625	21,578	25,342	32,648	41,040	40,413	41,922
Sask.	$ 19,197	19,862	20,180	23,723	21,222	27,646	22,404	24,055	26,676	34,289	21,885	18,829	10,495
Alta.	$ 14,744	7,991	15,109	17,511	14,862	8,107	6,837	4,818	492	293	1,551	—	184
B.C.	$ 4,491	8,237	11,258	5,926	5,902	−3,710	—	—	−2,102	−196	—	—	—
Total	$135,978	143,438	182,985	188,969	164,734	176,643	167,418	226,555	275,011	335,515	505,408	588,719	691,350

Figures are from Commons Debates in *Hansard*, February 18, 1970.

ENERGY SOURCES IN CANADA, 1945—1963

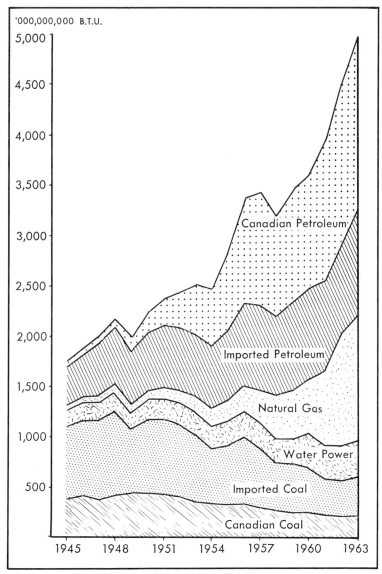

'000,000,000 B.T.U.

Canadian Petroleum

Imported Petroleum

Natural Gas

Water Power

Imported Coal

Canadian Coal

SOURCE: CANADA YEAR BOOK, 1965

This chart was discontinued in the 1968 *Canada Year Book* so that current figures are unavailable.

General Bibliography

BASIC SOURCES

Encyclopedia Canadiana. Grolier Society, 1966.

BROWN, G. W., TRUDEL, M. and VACHON, A. *Dictionary of Canadian Biography.* University of Toronto Press, 1966.

Canada in World Affairs. Canadian Institute of International Affairs Series. I. SOWARD, F. H., *et al. The Pre-War Years* (1941); II. DAWSON, R. M. *Two Years of War, 1939-1941* (1943); III. LINGARD, C. C. and TROTTER, R. G. *September, 1941 – May, 1944* (1950); IV. SOWARD, F. H. *From Normandy to Paris, 1944-1946* (1950); V. SPENCER, R. A. *From U.N. to N.A.T.O., 1946-1949* (1959); VI. HARRISON, W. E. C. *1949-1950* (1957); VII. KEIRSTEAD, B. S. *September, 1951 to October 1953* (1956); VIII. MASTERS, D. C. *1953-1955* (1959); IX. EAYRS, JAMES. *October, 1955 to June, 1957* (1959); X. LLOYD, TREVOR. *1957-1959* (1968); XI. PRESTON, R. A. *1959-1961* (1965); XII. LYON, P. V. *1961-1963* (1968). Oxford University Press.

KERR, D. G. G. (ed.). *An Historical Atlas of Canada.* Nelson, 1966.

KERR, D. G. G. and DAVIDSON, R. I. K. (eds.). *Canada: A Visual History.* Nelson, 1966.

REID, J. H. S. MCNAUGHT, K. and CROWE, H. S. *A Source Book of Canadian History.* Longmans, 1967.

WALLACE, W. S. (ed.). *The Macmillan Dictionary of Canadian Biography.* Macmillan, 1963.

GOVERNMENT OF CANADA PUBLICATIONS

Consult the *Canada Year Book* which has a comprehensive listing of official government sources of information arranged by subject (for example, Agriculture, Constitution, History, Mining, Vital Statistics, etc.). The *Year Book* also has an extensive bibliography of books on Canada.

The following is a list of sources which provide many publications of special interest for history:

CBC Publications, Box 500, Terminal A, Toronto 116.

Department of Consumer and Corporate Affairs, Ottawa.

Department of External Affairs, Information Division, Ottawa.

Department of Trade and Commerce, Trade Publicity Branch, Ottawa.

Dominion Bureau of Statistics, Information Division, Ottawa.

Hansard, Queen's Printer, Ottawa. Contains the House of Commons Debates.

Public Archives, Ottawa. Available here are booklets of the Canadian Historical Association covering a wide variety of subjects.

PERIODICALS

Boreal Express, Clarke, Irwin.

Canadian Affairs, Box 1097 Terminal A, Toronto.

Canadian Geographical Journal, The Royal Canadian Geographical Society, Ottawa.

Commentator, 228 Bloor St. W., Toronto 5.

Saturday Night, 55 York St., Toronto 1.

GENERAL REFERENCE

APPLETON, THOMAS E. *Usque ad Mare.* Federal Department of Transport, 1968.

BREBNER, J. B. *North Atlantic Triangle.* McClelland and Stewart, 1968.

BROWN, J. J. *Ideas in Exile.* McClelland and Stewart, 1967.

CARELESS, J. M. S. *Canada, the Story of Challenge.* Macmillan, 1963.

GRAHAM, G. S. *A Concise History of Canada.* Nelson, 1968.

KIRWIN, L. P. *A History of Polar Exploration.* George J. McLeod, 1960.

LANCTOT, GUSTAVE. *A History of Canada*. 3 vols. Clarke, Irwin, 1963-5.

LIPTON, CHARLES. *Trade Union Movement in Canada 1827-1959*. Copp Clark, 1966.

MACKIRDAY, K. A. *et al. Changing Perspectives in Canadian History*. Dent, 1967.

MORCHAIN, J. and WADE M. *Search for a Nation*. Dent, 1967.

MORTON, W. L. *The Kingdom of Canada*. McClelland and Stewart, 1963.

MORTON, W. L. *Manitoba*. University of Toronto, 1957.

MORTON, W. L. and CREIGHTON, D. G. (eds.). *Canadian Centenary Series*. 18 vols. (when complete). I. OLESON, TRYGGVI J. *Early Voyages and Northern Approaches* (1963); III. ECCLES, W. J. *Canada Under Louis XIV, 1663-1701* (1964); V. STANLEY, G. F. G. *New France: The Last Phase, 1744-1760* (1968); VI. NEATBY, HILDA. *Quebec, 1760-1791* (1966); VII. CRAIG, GERALD M. *Upper Canada, 1784-1841* (1964); IX. MACNUTT, W. S. *The Atlantic Provinces, 1712-1857* (1965); X. CARELESS, J. M. S. *The Union of the Canadas, 1841-1857* (1967); XI. RICH, E. E. *The Fur Trade and The Northwest to 1857* (1967); XII. MORTON, W. L. *The Critical Years, 1857-1873* (1964). McClelland and Stewart.

ORMSBY, M. *British Columbia, A History*. Macmillan, 1958.

SCOTT, F. R. (ed.). *The Blasted Pine*. Macmillan, 1967.

STANLEY, G. F. G. *A Short History of the Canadian Constitution*. Ryerson, 1969.

WADE, MASON. *The French Canadians, 1760-1967*. 2 vols. Macmillan. 1968.

GENERAL REFERENCE SINCE 1867

BRAULT, L. (ed.). *A Century of Reporting*. Clarke, Irwin, 1967.

CARELESS, J. M. S. and BROWN, R. C. *The Canadians, (1867-1967)*. Macmillan, 1967.

CARRIGAN, D. OWEN. *Canadian Party Platforms*. Copp Clark, 1968.

HUTCHISON, B. *Macdonald to Pearson*. Longmans, 1967.

HUTCHISON, B. *Mr. Prime Minister*. Longmans, 1964.

ONDAATJE, C. and SWAINSON, D. *Prime Ministers of Canada, (1867-1968)*. Pagurian, 1968.

PEART, H. W. and SCHAFFTER, J. *The Winds of Change*. Ryerson, 1961.

Index

A

Abbot, John, 141
Abercrombie, General, 43
Aberhart, William, 181-82
Acadia, 15-16, 17, 19, 37, 40, 41-2; University, 87
Acts: British Navigation, 90; British North America (1867), 116, 139, 140, 171; Canadian Pacific Railway (1881), 134; Colonial Laws Validity (1865), 171; Constitutional (1791), 1, 60-61, 86, Dominion Lands (1872), 129; Indemnification (1849), 98; Industrial Disputes Investigation, 199; Jesuit Estates (Quebec), 140; Manitoba (1870), 126, 140; Military Service (1917), 161; Military Votes (1917), 161; National Resources Mobilization (1940), 196; National Selective Service (1942), 199; National Transcontinental Railway (1903), 147; Naval Service (1910), 153, 154; Non Intercourse (1809), 76; Quebec (1774), 51-3, 54, 59; Reform (British, 1832), 92; Rivers and Streams (1884), 139; Stamp (1765), 54; Sugar (1764), 54; Tea (1772), 54; Townshend (1767), 54; Trade Unions, 129; Union (1707), 86; Union (1841), 97; War Measures (1914), 157; Wartime Elections (1917), 161

Agriculture, 4, 5, 8, 23-4; Canadian Council of, 166; development in West, 129, 172, 173, 176, 177; in Depression, 176, 177; Lower Canada, 72, 85; Upper Canada, 85
Aix-la-Chapelle, Treaty (1748), 41
Alabama Claims, 128
Alaska, 63, 106, 127; boundary dispute, 149; Highway, 200
Albanel, Father, 32
Alberta, 8, 27, 145, 182, 185, 204, 207, 225
Alexander, Sir William, 17
Algoma Steel Co., 176
Algonquins (see Indians)
Allan, Sir Hugh, 129, 130
Alverstone, Lord (Richard Everard Webster), 149
American Revolution (see Revolution)
Amherst, Jeffrey, Lord, 47
Amiens, Battle (1918), 158
Anglican (see Church of England)
Anglo-Canadian Relations: British North America Act, 120; Balfour Report, 171; Chanak Crisis, 169-70; Colonial Laws Validity Act, 171; Halibut Fisheries Treaty, 170-71; Imperial War Cabinet, 162; League of Nations, 162, 169, 188; Naval Aid Bill, 156; Naval Service Bills, 153; Washington Conference (1921), 169; Washington Treaty (1871), 128; World War

265

J

James I (England), 17
James Bay, 5, 27, 32
Japan-China War, 188
Jay, John, 62
Jay Treaty (1794), 62-3, 69
Jesuit: Estates Act (Quebec), 140; Order, 19-22, 140; *Relations*, 20
Johnson, Daniel, 227, 232
Joliet, Louis, 33

K

Kaministiquia, 41
Kashmir dispute (1965), 235
Keenleyside, Dr. Hugh, 235
Kennedy Round negotiations, 213
King's College: New Brunswick, 87; Nova Scotia, 87; Toronto, 87
King, William Lyon Mackenzie, 164-65, 167-78, 183-200, 202-3
Kingston, 30, 87, 89
Kirke, David and Thomas, 19
Kootenay River, 67
Korean War, 205, 234

L

La Barre, Joseph A. L., Sieur de, 32
Labour Party, British, 181
Labrador, 10, 11, 81, 209
Lachine, 32
Lachine Canal, 89
La Chine (*see* La Salle)
Lafontaine, Sir Louis Hippolyte, 97, 98
Lake of the Woods, 36, 56, 68
Lambton, John George (*see* Durham, Earl of)
Lapointe, Ernest, 171, 194, 195, 196
La Salle, René Robert Cavalier, 33, 35

Latin America-Canadian relations, 237
Latin-American Programme, 237
Laurier, Sir Wilfrid, 141, 143-54, 156, 162, 164
Laval, Bishop, 31
Laval University, 87
La Vérendrye, Pierre Gaultier de Varennes, 36, 50
Law: British North America Act, 120; English Common, 50, 59, 60; French, 50-51, 59
Lawrence, Governor Charles, 42
League of Nations, 162, 169, 188
Le Caron, Joseph, 19
Lemoyne, Jean-Baptiste Bienville, 35
Lemoyne, Pierre, 35
"Lend lease," 198
Lesage, Jean, 231, 232
Levesque, René, 232
Lexington, 54
Liberal-Conservative party, 112, 113
Liberal party, 130, 131-33, 140, 141, 143-54, 161-62, 167, 168, 178, 180, 183, 195, 202, 204-5, 221-23, 226-28, 231 (*see also* Reform party)
Lincoln, Abraham, 107
Little, P. F., 99
Lods et ventes, 24
Long Sault Rapids, 89
Louis XIV (France), 21, 22, 32, 35, 36
Louisburg, 40-41, 43
Louisiana, 35, 45
Lower Canada, 1, 60, 61, 72; commerce, 90; education, 87; government, 91, 93-4; immigration, 84-5; settlement, 84-5
Loyalists (*see* United Empire Loyalists)
Lumber, 4, 85-6, 89
Lundy's Lane, Battle, 78